Reclaiming Value in International Development

Reclaiming Value in International Development

THE MORAL DIMENSIONS OF
DEVELOPMENT POLICY AND
PRACTICE IN POOR COUNTRIES

Chloe Schwenke

PRAEGER

Westport, Connecticut
London

Library of Congress Cataloging-in-Publication Data

Schwenke, Chloe.
  Reclaiming value in international development : the moral dimensions
of development policy and practice in poor countries / Chloe Schwenke.
    p. cm.
  Includes bibliographical references and index.
  ISBN 978–0–313–36332–0 (alk. paper) —
  ISBN 978–0–313–36334–4 (pbk. : alk. paper)
  1. Developing countries—Economic policy.   2. Economic development—
Developing countries—Moral and ethical aspects.   3. Social justice—
Developing countries.   I. Title.
  HC59.7.S356   2009
  174—dc22   2008038703

British Library Cataloguing in Publication Data is available.

Library of Congress Catalog Card Number: 2008038703
ISBN: 978–0–313–36332–0
ISBN: 978–0–313–36334–4 (pbk.)

First published in 2009

Praeger Publishers, 88 Post Road West, Westport, CT 06881
An imprint of Greenwood Publishing Group, Inc.
www.praeger.com

Printed in the United States of America

The paper used in this book complies with the
Permanent Paper Standard issued by the National
Information Standards Organization (Z39.48–1984).

10   9   8   7   6   5   4   3   2   1

For my father, Colonel C. Ray Schwenke, USMC, Ret.

Contents

Preface

Human survival, well-being, and flourishing—the field of international development tackles these fundamentals. The practitioners, scholars, policymakers, and specialists active in international development are, by and large, mission-driven people who have chosen this vocation because they really believe that they can make the world a better place. They care about the plight of the billions of persons in poverty or suffering under repressive rule, and they strive to do something meaningful about it. Yet despite their caring, their sense of mission, and their dedication and persistence, these people rarely engage with each other or with outsiders about their moral values. International development—an area of human endeavor rich in moral content—seems to lack a common moral vocabulary.

This book is intended to begin to plug that gap by offering a view of international development through the moral lens of development ethics, in language that is understandable and relevant to practitioners, policymakers, bureaucrats, and interested persons—anyone immersed in or perplexed by international development. Readers will broaden their own understanding and effectiveness by seeing development framed in the language and concepts of applied ethics, without requiring recourse to a doctoral degree in philosophy or ethics.

Many of the book's anecdotes and observations are situated in Uganda, where from 2005 to 2006 I taught ethics and carried out my research as a Fulbright professor with the Ethics and Public Management Programme at the Faculty of Arts, Makerere University. After over 25 years of prior service, mostly based abroad (Kenya, South Africa, Philippines, and England) as an architect and planner, and later as a specialist in local governance, the year in Uganda was a unique personal opportunity to take stock. This book is the product of that stocktaking, and while its chapters are nearly all based in Uganda, the situations that each chapter describes are relevant throughout the developing world.

Ethics, to be effectively applied in a cross-cultural setting, requires reflection and evaluation sensitive to local realities and local values, while still being authentic and responsive to the moral values that inform the observer. I have included personal anecdotes and short case studies both to ground my own moral perspective and to connect the reader with a sense of the realities that development practitioners frequently face. My 14 years of living and working in Africa, and my many additional years working elsewhere in the developing world, taught me that while abstract moral principles and theories have an essential role to play in structuring ethical systems, nothing takes the place of being there. International development is about people, and I have chosen to share some of my experiences with people in developing countries to connect the reader with their lives, hopes, and struggles.

The field of development ethics has come of age, and as will be seen in these chapters, offers many robust approaches and insights to diagnose, understand, and respond to the urgent demands of development across many sectors. While covering all development topics and sectors is beyond the scope of any single volume, this book does apply both moral intuition and several of the most prominent moral theories to offer insights, guidance, and perhaps some observations new to readers on education, ethical leadership, deliberative participation, integrity and corruption, hunger, conflict, urbanization, the treatment of minorities, and the measurement of ethical performance. Each of these sectors, as well as the many aspects of international development that I have been unable to include, has its own rich literature of theory, lessons learned, case studies, methodologies, and technical reviews. Few have been viewed though the moral lens. This book has been written therefore as a small effort to redress that curious imbalance and to enrich and empower a dialogue among practitioners, inviting them to embrace the language and concepts of development ethics.

Acknowledgments

This book evolved as did I, over many years of professional practice and teaching, and through profound changes in my life. The contributions to this evolution are legion, and I will barely do them all justice.

More than anyone, I owe an enormous debt of gratitude to my spouse, Christine Anne Lucas, and my children, Ian Schwenke and Audrey Schwenke, whose patience at times was sorely tested as I allocated seemingly endless hours of family time to this endeavor. Through these transitioning times, where my authoring a book was but one of her life's smaller challenges, Christine's love, loyalty, and understanding have been beyond measure.

I am also thankful for the financial support offered by Marina Fanning and Larry Cooley of Management Systems International (MSI) in Washington, D.C., without which my year in Uganda—which provided the crucible for the formulation of this book—would have been impossible.

Ann Beltran deserves special praise for her tireless editorial efforts, her insightful suggestions, and her honest and constructive criticism at key points in the writing of this book.

Understanding Uganda was critical to my thinking, and I would especially like to thank Sarah Kihika for her thoughtful advice and unwavering support as I grew to understand development issues in that country and to understand my own identity. Other helpful advice and contributions came from Kevin Doris Ejon, Julius Kaggwa, Nikki Salongo, and my dear friend Byaruhanga Rukooko. My colleagues at the Department of Philosophy at Makerere University in Kampala were also instrumental in shaping my views, and in particular, I thank Edward Wamala and Gervase Tusabe. Other Ugandans who also deeply influenced my thinking include Edgar Agaba, Ashaba-Aheebwa,

Angela Bafokuzara, Lillian Keene Mugerwa, Damon Kitabire, Sam Mukasa-Kintu, Peter John Opio, and Hannington Sengendo. The support of Alyson Grunder at the American Embassy and Bharat Gupta at Landplan in Uganda was also most appreciated.

Finally, I offer deep appreciation to my loving sister, Barbara Cartmell, who has supported me in so many ways throughout this creative endeavor and during these times of change.

CHAPTER 1

Introduction

Makerere University is Uganda's oldest, and many would say its best, institution of higher education. The campus sits atop one of Kampala's many plentiful hills, and it's a landmark in this nation's capital. From 2005 to 2006, it was my pleasure to serve as a Fulbright professor at Makerere, but getting to and from the campus by car each day meant navigating through the inevitable traffic jams at the chaotic Wandegeya intersection. As I would sit in my car, often lost in some random thought, I not infrequently encountered a tap on my window. A woman, dressed in simple and worn clothes, holding a very young and rather dirty looking baby, was seeking a handout. Hers was a regular presence there, enduring the high pollution and dangerous driving tactics of taxis and other vehicles and subjecting her small baby to this extremely unhealthy environment as she sought a handout. My question to myself was always the same: should I give her some money?

The arguments about how best to handle such solicitations are well rehearsed. Giving her the requested handout of small change might have provided her with the means to achieve a modicum of relief in an otherwise austere, harsh existence. It might also have encouraged her dependency and could have been an inducement for her to remain in that unsavory environment, subjecting both her and her innocent, vulnerable baby to the many dangers there. Any handouts given may also have discouraged her from seeking a more sustainable and wholesome lifestyle somewhere else, perhaps back in a rural district among her extended family. Also, there was my own sense of identity and connection with those around me to consider; I pondered the mildly discomforting thought that by providing such handouts, she and others like her would stop seeing me as a person, but only as another rich so-called "*mzungu*—a wealthy white foreigner and a source of easy money.

And should I have decided to give her a handout, then where would I stop? Would I give her something every single time I saw her (and if not, why not)? Ought I to have invested in her welfare more substantially, finding a way to learn more about her and her history, and helping her to find a way out of poverty—assuming that she was motivated to pursue such a course? What if she had some deeper psychological problems, which rendered her unable to hold a job and threatened her competence as a parent? And, of course, what of the many, many more persons like her—why this one woman and her baby, and not them? Were all the poor people living near me in Kampala to adopt her tactics, there would be innumerable taps at my window each day.

As an American living in Uganda, I frequently encountered such daily reminders from many beleaguered victims of poverty. Before and following my year in Uganda, while living and working in Washington, DC, coming face to face with poverty was and is a less frequent—and usually less extreme— experience. Yet despite Africa feeling like a second home after 14 years of work based there, still the majority of my working and teaching career associated with international development was conceived of, and managed from, Washington. Many others who are practitioners of international development, teachers or theorists of international development, or policymakers in international relations, live relatively insulated lives divorced from the daily Wandegeya intersection, face-to-face encounters with poverty. While these colleagues in international development are almost certainly well intentioned, sensitive, and caring persons, the problems of development that they wrestle with may necessarily appear abstract and remote to them. Those living in Uganda haven't the excuse of distance to explain their moral detachment from the plight of those in poverty around them, yet in my experience, wealthier Ugandans and foreigners (expatriates, or expats) also often treated poverty as an abstract phenomenon. They avoided looking the problem in the face.

The abstraction of poverty isn't in itself wrong, but consciously choosing to ignore poverty raises many moral concerns. Abstraction can be a powerfully objective tool; using empirical data to focus objectively and impersonally on poverty and the plight of the victims of poverty is an essential and responsible part of the process of seeking to analyze, understand, and find solutions to this complex phenomenon. Through our research and observations, we regularly encounter the statistical footprint of global poverty and injustice, poor governance and corruption, international crime and terrorism, brutally violent conflict, and the many incarnations of globalization. In both the more economically advanced countries (the North) and the less developed and poorer countries (the South), many persons struggle to understand why poverty, poor governance, and conflict are such intractable problems to remedy, but the moral weight of the dilemmas has been less clearly articulated. Is the reminder of the Wandegeya intersection beggars and the likely prognosis for the life of that mother and her infant just too painful to ponder in too bright and personal a light? Perhaps surrendering one's objectivity to confront poverty at a personal level is even counterproductive to our ability to find sustainable solutions. The statistical lens is more tractable, less prone to emotionally clouded or sentimental reactions, and more relevant in our economics-based worldview.

Economism, however, provides but one perspective on extreme poverty and the consequences of conflict and injustice.[1] I would argue that we lose something important when we convert the faces and the voices of the poor into statistical data, and—for those of us involved in international development, peace building, and good governance—that through such abstraction we become less sensitive to the urgency and the moral dimension of development. While the moral burden of those afflicted by poverty, poor governance, or conflict may be more acute than we as individuals can cope with, or effectively respond to, I am certain that ignoring or abstracting away the personal tragedies of poverty does nothing to diminish the moral burden. The mother and infant at Wandegeya will be there today and tomorrow. Whenever I return, I will have to look her in the eye again (or, if feeling cowardly or perplexed, close my window and pretend not to see her). Yet even if I choose not to look, the moral dilemma is inescapable and all around us. We live in societies defined by interdependencies and by a complex web of obligations, many of which are moral and ethical.

If this is true (and intuitively each of us knows that it is so), then why is it that in development dialogue, research, policy, and practice, we seldom deal directly—*in moral terms*—with the moral issues and moral language of development, governance, and conflict? Where is the moral lens through which to see, evaluate, understand, and respond to these important challenges?

As I will argue, the moral lens is both available and a potentially powerful component in the development toolkit. First, however, we must see what other lenses we have grown accustomed to, and reliant upon, and why.

ECONOMISM: THE ECONOMICS PARADIGM

As individuals, we are drawn to live in relationship to others, and we structure our social institutions and governance arrangements to make this possible and, ideally, even pleasurable and rewarding. To a considerable extent, our own personal development and the meaning that we derive out of our lives are products of interactions with other persons. We have defined our particular social order to set the terms of our daily social interactions, which in turn—along with the influence of our individual character and virtues—establishes the safety and freedoms that we enjoy, the obligations that we bear, the justice that we perceive, and the opportunities that we are able to pursue. Society shapes us, and we shape society.

It is no surprise then that we are so preoccupied with understanding and improving our social world. In this endeavor, those of us involved in development have been trained to view our social world and our constituent social institutions primarily through the neoclassical economics lens. The discipline of neoclassical economics is a potent tool for perceiving important parameters and components of society, but, like any lens, it shows only part of the spectrum. We frequently limit our area of interest to that spectrum; when we speak about development, we often add the adjective *economic*—economic development. Sometimes we equate development with economic growth, as if growth alone were the goal, instead of economic growth as a means to achieve human flourishing. Yet the spectrum of human development is wider and more than economics can explain; society also embraces important political, psychological, spiritual, and moral dimensions. It is curious, then, that the institutions that we establish (or that evolve) to govern society are generally described primarily in economic and political terms. The spiritual aspects of our being are compartmentalized away into separate domains, often under formal religious institutions, while psychology and personal morality are relegated to the contemplation of the murky inner workings of each individual or to an evaluation of conceptual behavior, cognitive processes, genetic epistemology, or the behavioral aspects of personal moral development.[2]

Similarly, for those of us engaged in the general and policy dialogue of development, the morality and ethics of society and the existence of an intricate web of moral obligations and moral community are topics that are seldom discussed in any comprehensive way (other than by philosophers and ethicists). Our relative silence in this sphere may be due to the apparent lack of a robust common language of values, morality, and ethics, particularly in comparison to the authoritative and largely unified language of economics and political science. The literature of development portrays this perceptual bias, being dominated by economists and to a lesser extent by political and social scientists, with well-known thinkers from these disciplines featuring prominently.[3]

The economism that I am describing, based on neoclassical economics, reigns supreme—and for a good reason. Even with the complexities of regression analyses and economic theory, the economics lens is relatively easy to apply, and the empirical dimensions of development, governance, and conflict that economics illuminates for us are essential to our effectiveness and understanding. The statistics themselves are amoral and value free, but the message that they convey can range from heartening to sobering to alarming, when placed in the context of the misery and suffering of underdevelopment. Heartening, as the numbers tell us that people do in fact care about those less fortunate; in response to the devastation wrought by the Asian tsunami of December 26, 2004, the world responded with an unprecedented contribution of over US$12 billion (Efron, 2005). Yet despite this demonstrated ability of the more developed world to rush to the aid of the less developed world, the numbers also describe a more sobering reality: rich countries currently spend less than this sum—or about US$11 billion annually—for *all* development assistance targeted at basic social services. Over 60 percent of this comes from individuals in rich countries through contributions to international NGOs; the other 40 percent comes from their governments (United Nations Development Programme [UNDP], 2003,

p. 290). Estimates place this combined sum at just 3.6 percent of the amount that would actually be needed to eradicate severe poverty,[4] or US$300 billion annually, a figure that would lessen significantly over time (Pogge, 2002). This sum may sound like a lot, but the surprising reality is that were we to raise annual development expenditures to this level, those living in the wealthiest countries (who only represent 15 percent of the world's population) would experience an almost imperceptible diminution in their quality of life.[5] Yet current global annual funding levels at US$11 billion are less than the financial response to the tsunami alone (World Bank, 2004, p. 253). Why the discrepancy between the response to one dramatic natural tragedy and the response to a long-standing global crisis?

Through the economics lens, we can see that many of the poor clearly are not living quality lives. Around the world, the view through the economics lens is alarming. There are 2.4 billion (mostly female) persons who lack access to basic sanitation, and more than 1 billion (mostly female) persons who now exist on unsafe water (UNDP, 2003, pp. 6, 9, 87). Stepping down from the billions plateau, nearly 800 million persons are undernourished (UNDP, 1998, p. 49). Perhaps even more profoundly disturbing, 34,000 children younger than five years old die each day from hunger and preventable disease—that's almost 24 children each and every minute of every month of every year (U.S. Dept of Agriculture, 1999). If awesome numbers start to sound fuzzy, think in fractions. About one-third of all human deaths are linked to poverty, deaths that are in most cases preventable (Food and Agriculture Organization of the United Nations, 1999).

Compared to these deaths due to poverty, perhaps the mother and infant begging at the Wandegeya intersection in Kampala are among the fortunate ones? But is the mere fact of continued survival the appropriate measure of fortunate, of what a human life ought to be? Where ought we to draw the threshold of basic services, basic nutrition, even basic human rights and freedoms? How do we value a human life, and on what basis do we allocate the available—but woefully inadequate—resources to those in need? What more ought we to do to assist others in need, and why? What responsibility do those in need have to be the agents for their own solutions to their poverty and their own development? Are we obliged only to facilitate their development, leaving the ultimate responsibility to the poor? When we draw the boundaries of our moral community, who ought to be included, and who left out? Beyond the obvious implications of political unrest and insecurity, and the threats that the disgruntled poor pose to our self-interested goals, why ought we to care about—and act to alleviate—the plight of those less fortunate, particularly if they live so far away?

When we move to the questions of *ought*, the economics lens grows dark, or at best, blurry. Even utilitarianism, which is the moral theory that underpins neoclassical economism and that advocates maximizing utility for all, fails to provide answers to critically important questions of how development *ought* to be distributed equitably, while at the same time protecting important individual rights and freedoms from being eroded for the sake of the greater good. Using *ought* conjures up a moral vocabulary and simultaneously challenges us to reflect upon what morality means for each individual, for our society, and for our choice of priorities and actions. As soon as we move more directly into this moral landscape, however, some yawning chasms confront us. Morality is about values, but whose values? What is *morality* anyway?

Bernard Gert provides perhaps one of the best definitions of morality: "Morality is an informal public system applying to all rational persons, governing behavior that affects others, and includes what are commonly known as moral rules, ideals, and virtues and has the lessening of evil or harm as its goal" (Gert, 1998, p. 13).

With the concept of morality being so relative, and so imprecise, what is any person contemplating international development to gain from a view through the moral lens, other than confusion and discord? The moral perspective—the moral point of view—must be ordered if it is to be of value as a tool for improving human development. Ethics is the ordering of moral value systems, and through ethics, moral concepts can be systematically considered, evaluated, and applied.

THE MORAL MORASS: WHOSE VALUES?

The moral vocabulary often is confusing to many, particularly as it is not yet commonplace in the dialogue on development, governance, and conflict. As indicated above, morality encompasses a variety of value systems, which sometimes overlap and often compete. Cultural values, religious values, secular values, and idiosyncratic personal values all contribute to the shaping of a society's sense of identity and purpose—a society's set of shared values—but that identity is forged as much by the conflict of values as by their harmony. When society takes on the deliberative task of resolving conflicting values and articulating a set of shared values, this in turn helps to clarify the moral obligations of all members of that society and sheds light on the relationship of a society to other communities, nations, or groups.

Ethics is the discipline that a society uses to reconcile and reach a consensus of values that otherwise conflict.[6] Ethics brings order and structure to moral values and creates rational and persuasive moral systems by considering fundamental principles that define values and that specify and assign moral obligations, and by examining the characteristics of virtue and vice. By deliberating about what is *good* or *right* (and *bad* and *wrong*), in terms of actions or human character, a society brings some order to its moral values.[7]

CONTEMPORARY INTERNATIONAL DEVELOPMENT PRACTICE

International development and related areas of research, policy, and practice that include governance and peace building are pursued in a formal process that can be called the *development industry*. Economism, as I have defined it here, has framed the development pursuit into a business—an industry—and the international, national, and bilateral institutions that fund and drive the majority of development activities organize their operations in this format. Even civil-society organizations active in international development, governance, and peace building operate in a business environment, by the rules of business, claiming the virtues of efficiency, effectiveness, and accountability to those who provide the funding (taxpayers or contributors) as their standard. Each of these development role players, to a greater or lesser extent, seeks to identify their own unique mission and strategic objectives, their own intervention methodologies, and their own relationship to the intended beneficiaries.

These many different development role players formulate and implement their activities though their own permanent staff of experts, support staff, consultants, advisers, and in some cases, volunteers, and each of these persons brings different values and motivations to her or his participation. Probably few of these individuals stop to reflect on these values, some ascribe their motivation to a pursuit of professionalism or religious conviction, while others simply adopt the ideological or political framework of their employers. All of them share some sense of bringing aid and assistance to the needy, of helping *them*, but there is very little conscious agreement in the development industry about how priorities should be set and by whom. The fundamentally moral relationship of accountability between *them* and *us* remains muddy.

The fact that such a varied and complex development industry operates directly in and on the context of the us–them, rich–poor, North–South dichotomous character of global moral relationships without significantly better articulated ethical guidance is puzzling. Given the pluralist character of value systems that globalization inexorably brings in its wake, the dominant liberalist[8] tolerant paradigm of academia, and the contrasting realist school of foreign policy by which nations use a superficial veneer of morality to mask their self-interested quests for achieving and maintaining global power, the development industry surely stands in great need of a moral compass. The ethical bearings, however, are few and often of little guidance to those involved in international development. It is little surprise then that at a Society for International Development event—a group whose members would probably define themselves at least to some extent as being motivated by altruism—the self-assured comment during questions and answers period by then administrator of the U.S. Agency for International Development, Andrew Natsios, that in the context of American foreign aid policy "altruism is dead," met with so little reaction. Instead, Natsios argued that international development must now be seen as America acting in national self-interest.[9]

DEVELOPMENT ETHICS

Is altruism dead? Were those practitioners, researchers, and students of international development gathered in Washington, D.C., ready to accept

Mr. Natsios's cynical assessment without challenge? Or were they intellectually unprepared for such a morally problematic assertion, having little regular practice in the contemplation of their own moral orientation or on the larger task of ethical reflection on the ends and means of socioeconomic change in poor countries and regions?

Ethical reflection of this nature is the objective of development ethics. Development ethicists argue that the moral dimension of development theory and practice is just as important as the scientific and policy components. What is often called *development*—economic growth, for instance—may be bad for people, communities, and the environment. Hence, the process of *development* should be reconceived as *beneficial change*, usually specified as alleviating human misery and environmental degradation in poor countries (Craig, 1999; Crocker, 2001, pp. 5–6).

In describing what development ethics is about, the philosopher David Crocker asks the philosopher's question, "In what direction and by what means should a society 'develop'?" (Crocker, 2001, p. 1). His succinct description of development ethics encompasses a complex endeavor by philosophers, ethicists, development practitioners, policymakers, and others to create and apply a rigorous intellectual discipline and philosophical grounding to the challenges of development, governance, and peace building, and to the many moral questions to which these topics give rise.

Development ethics offers a so-called ethics toolkit in the form of a comprehensive set of persuasively articulated moral approaches that facilitate reflection and dialogue upon—and consideration of appropriate responses to—the many urgent moral concerns, motivations, obligations, and competing priorities associated with development, governance, and peace building. Norms such as human dignity, essential freedoms, social justice, peace, civic virtue, human flourishing, the common good, gender equality, safety and security, care and compassion, participation and inclusion are among the many that are routinely encountered in development theory and practice. These topics illustrate the subject matter of development ethics.

Development ethics is a relative newcomer in applied ethics, having only begun to take explicit and self-conscious form in the 1980s (Crocker, 2001, pp. 2–3). Since that time, however, there have been robust additions to the body of thought framed by development ethics, and the literature within the new discipline now is becoming substantial. The primary contributions principally have come from philosophers and ethicists, both in the North and the South,[10] but when practiced by Africans, Latin Americans, Asians, and non-Anglo Europeans, development ethics also draws on philosophical and moral traditions distinctive of their cultural contexts.[11]

Development ethics, by intention, seeks to extend beyond academia and involve development practitioners, policymakers, and others.[12] Many universities are also now offering courses or entire programs of study in development ethics,[13] and new civil-society organizations have been formed to focus on development ethics.[14]

The ethical focus on development, governance, and peace building also extends beyond the domain of development ethics, whose boundaries in any event are loosely defined. Closely related to the concerns of development ethics, significant work is being advanced in research and dialogue on social and human capital, environmental ethics, social ethics, business and professional ethics (including corporate social responsibility), political theory of development, urban and regional planning theory, development economics, deliberative democracy, and geography. The many-faceted attention now placed on the moral dimensions of development does call into question whether there is a need to establish some territorial boundaries for development ethics. For example, should development ethics extend into trade relations, military affairs and the global arms trade, human migration and trafficking, international organized crime networks, and terrorism? Should development ethics consider issues of development, conflict, integrity and corruption in developed countries? These issues remain unresolved and continue to elicit spirited debate.

Engaging in ethical reflection on critical development, governance, and peace building issues is not merely an intellectually stimulating academic pastime. Many of the choices that individuals, institutions, groups, and governments make affect others, for good or for ill. We are also often called upon to make decisions as to what others *ought* to do or have done. In either case, we ought to carefully evaluate such choices factually, conceptually, and ethically. Political and cultural leaders, policymakers, development practitioners, civil-society activists, and many others confront weighty ethical issues on a daily basis, and the choices they must make may be harmful or even tragic for some—or many—persons. When human greed is unconstrained, resources scarce, human needs great, civic virtue in short supply, and existing economic distributive mechanisms ineffective or skewed, the moral weight of decisions can be particularly acute. As noted by Guido Calabresi and Philip Bobbitt, such decisions on resource allocations ought to be made in "ways that preserve the moral foundations of social collaboration" (Calabresi & Bobbitt, 1978, p. 18). Failing this, violence and civil unrest may ensue or poverty may worsen, with the associated increase in human suffering. Such choices also ought to be made with the full knowledge that we are living in a world of human imperfections—greed, hunger for power, ignorance and shortsightedness, and prejudice and ethnocentrism—and that social, cultural, political, and economic institutions often reflect these imperfections (Chadwick, 1998, p. 759).

In summary, development ethics raises the profile and accessibility of the moral dialogue in the theory, policy, and practice of development, governance, and peace building. Development ethics directly addresses the most fundamental—and the most controversial—topics in these areas, generally considered to be the following: the dignity and worth of each human being, the moral equality of all human beings, the moral dimensions that motivate and sustain development actions, peace building, and what values and virtues constitute the *good* of good governance. Development ethics also considers who ought to make development decisions and the meaning of both *peace* and *development*. Development ethics similarly provides a valuable and insightful perspective on the meaning and role of such important concepts as the extent and nature of our moral obligations to and claims on others, the moral demands of social justice, the moral bases of legitimacy of government, and the moral justifications for broad-based stakeholder participation in analysis, deliberations, and decision making on development and governance.

This is a long list of so-called hot topics. Make no mistake—the door that development ethics opens can allow in both the fresh air of clarity as well as the turbulent winds of dramatic change. The comfortable status quo enjoyed by the few is being questioned by more people, and with more intensity, than ever before. The pretense that national boundaries also determine the limitations of our moral obligations is now being challenged.

The structured normative reflection and critical thinking fostered by development ethics strengthens our understanding of our common humanity. Development ethics turns the tables, as it places the burden of proof on any who would deny the validity of the claims of those seeking common standards of international justice; those who argue for serious consideration of the implications of an ethic of care; and those who argue that the constructive, transformative leadership and influence of persons of demonstrated civic virtue is essential to the health and responsiveness of our social, economic, political, and cultural institutions. Development ethics exposes the indecency and moral impermissibility of poverty, violent conflict, and bad governance to all human beings everywhere and to the natural environment in which we are placed. Ultimately, development ethics challenges each of us to reflect upon—and possibly amend—his or her own values and priorities. Such a process, carried out by an ever-increasing number of thoughtful persons, can be profoundly transformative to our selves, our communities, our nations, and our world.

The following chapters in this book are intentional looks through the moral lens at a range of the development challenges of our time, as they affect Uganda, East Africa, and to a large extent all developing countries: education, leadership, deliberative participation, corruption in public procurement of goods and services, security, conflict, urbanization, the plight of sexual minorities, and how to measure ethical performance. Many other important development topics—health, decentralization, and humanitarian relief, to name but a few—I have not addressed in this volume. The moral lens, however, remains an appropriate means by which to consider them and all aspects of international development, both individually and in the totality of human flourishing.

CHAPTER 2

Education

With nearly all my adult life as a development practitioner, I considered myself well qualified to come to work in Uganda as an educator, where a foundation in practical experience and international best practice examples are valued by students. Yet even as a practitioner/educator, I was aware that the role of education is to pass along values, frame a sense of identity and individual worth, and constantly improve knowledge. Values however differ; my Washington, D.C., values would surely not align perfectly with those of my Ugandan students. Yet in development ethics, the moral sensibilities of each culture are considered alongside those moral sensibilities that arguably all humans share. In Uganda, as in most of Africa, I have found this moral resource is perhaps most easily accessed through recourse to the rich tradition of folk stories.

Once upon a time there was a village known as Singino. Many different animals—such as the elephant, giraffe, antelope, buffalo, hare, lion, tortoise, hyena, and the wolf—lived in Singino. The giraffe was their king.

One day there was a shortage of water in the village. There were no natural springs and not enough rain. This was a big problem. King Giraffe called a meeting of all animals in the village to discuss how to solve the problem of water. They all agreed to dig a well that, they believed, would provide enough water for all. But Mr. Hare was against the idea. He didn't want to dig.

Almost all of the animals gathered together and dug the well. Mr. Hare did not help; instead he laughed at the animals as they were digging.

Within a short time, the animals had good, clean water. King Giraffe, however, prohibited Mr. Hare from using the well water.

Since Mr. Hare could not get water, he decided to trick the animals. He went to the elephant who was on duty to guard the well and said, "I have some honey, which is very sweet. Would you like to taste it?" The elephant tried some and, liking it very much, asked for more. Mr. Hare said, "I will give you more honey, but first I have to tie your hands and legs. You will enjoy it even more this way." Mr. Hare then tied up the elephant and jumped into the well. He drank some water, swam, and ran away laughing and laughing.

African folktales like this are commonplace in Uganda and feature human beings and animals, either separately or together. The hare appears prominently as a trickster in many such tales, often portraying cunning, lying, manipulative, and cheating ways to protect itself against much larger and more powerful animals. Stories such as these are used not only for entertainment, but also for social commentary, instruction, and as an effective way to pass along group values to children. The animals and birds take on human characteristics of greed, jealousy, honesty, loneliness, and so forth, and through their behavior or misbehavior, many valuable lessons can be learned.

Of course, this particular story is incomplete. The hare, so far, has succeeded in getting the rewards (water) without the hard work (digging), and has even made a fool of the largest land animal of all (elephant). If one were to stop there, as some such stories do, the person hearing this story would have to wonder what moral values were being advocated and whether Ugandans were teaching their children to tell tall tales from a very tender age!

In reality, this story finishes with the hare being tricked in turn by the tortoise, and the hare is punished for his laziness and mischief. The values are obvious; this is, after all, a folktale intentionally about values. Ugandans, like Americans to a lesser extent, rely on their separate traditions of moral stories and folktales to convey important common moral values to the young. Yet parents and adults in all cultures also transmit other less intentional stories to the young—the examples from their own lives, the telling of their personal stories, and exposure to stories from popular entertainment and news media. What values do our lives and our respective societies now teach the young, and should all be left to chance? These were the questions raised by Ugandans at a workshop that I participated in on the role of ethics in the national educational curriculum.

Few of the Ugandan participants in that workshop, and arguably few of us anywhere, have paused to consider such questions carefully. People in many places in the world commonly despair about the messages of greed, superficial social status, selfishness, and materialism that modern advertising conveys, and they grumble about loss of values and the pernicious influences of globalization. These common musings about values are generalized, fleeting, and anything but rigorous; yet the Ugandan participants at the workshop sensed some urgency. They believed that the time to think consciously and carefully about values in education in their country had arrived. To them, shaping the values and attitudes of Uganda's future generations was among the most important of priorities, neglected at their peril.

What those workshop participants referred to as *values education*, together with the cultivation of what was once called *civic virtue*, arguably are not what government ought to be about. In most of the more developed democracies of Europe and North America, there is outspoken public resistance to the use of taxpayers' funds to support moral or values education in publicly funded schools, although the moral thinking that underpins this position—liberalism—is itself strongly values based. Liberalism is a doctrine that places greatest emphasis on individual freedoms and the right of each person to pursue his or her own private vision of the good up to the point of interfering with the pursuit of another (Berkowitz, 1999). This thinking long ago caused public schools in countries under this intellectual influence to pull away from any programmed, government-sponsored civic education, particularly when the proposed curricula advocated specific moral values or tacit interpretations of the common good, lest such values be seen as an impingement on the freedom of someone else's moral values and beliefs. Only the most clearly universal and secular of moral values would remain on the tax-funded curriculum: integrity, tolerance of diversity, honesty, hard work and diligence, and—to varying extents—patriotism. Parents who wanted their children educated in a more intentionally values-focused environment had to seek private education at their own expense.

As I sat among the room full of Ugandans, I pondered whether Uganda ought to follow the hands-off example of the more economically developed countries and, on principle, dedicate few if any resources to publicly funded moral education. What would be the arguments in support of including even *any* formal ethics-based education in Uganda? If Uganda were to choose to include values education in their national curriculum, then who ought to bear the primary responsibility to define and then provide this grounding? If Ugandans decided to teach values, then what values should they teach, and why? How should Ugandans teach moral values? And at what age should such values education begin?

This chapter considers these questions, with particular emphasis on Uganda's ongoing initiative to shape a values education program, reflecting a larger debate in education policy affecting many developing countries.[1]

THE DEBATE ABOUT "CIVICS"

A democratic and free society depends for its existence on its citizens' understanding of and commitment to democratic values and freedoms. It is now common wisdom that power corrupts and erodes democratic freedoms unless citizens are vigilant and outspoken in defense of democracy. Such values as respect for moral equality; for a universal right to participate in the shaping of the decisions that affect all citizens' lives; and for the recognition of the exercise of compassion for the suffering of those worst affected by poverty, violence, and minority status are the foundations of a democratic future for any country seeking the democratic path of development. Citizens of such countries who claim that democratic values are important share a common bond in advocacy for and protection of certain freedoms—although the definition and priority given to these various freedoms does vary from one society to another. Still, the traditional democratic values share more commonalities than differences, embracing the freedom to peacefully express views and have some influence in political decisions that affect one, to worship as one chooses, to associate with whomever one wishes, to travel without constraint, to enjoy due and proper processes of justice, to enjoy security (social, political, economic) and peace, and—more controversially—to express one's authentic sexual orientation and gender identity.

This package of democratic values, framed to emphasize a particular society's own traditions, was once called *civics* in many countries of the North. There, citizenship education was intended to provide young people with the knowledge, skills, and understanding they needed to play their part in society, helping them to become informed, thoughtful, and responsible citizens. According to this thinking, teachers were held to have a special opportunity and a unique obligation to focus on the ideals of citizenship in ways that were age appropriate, helping to instill these values during a child's first years at school, but often continuing throughout their years of public education. While the debate about the appropriateness of using public funds to teach civics rages on in the North, in many developing countries there is no similar concern. Instead, the focus is on how democratic values ought to be taught and what specific values and sources for values—secular, ideological, or religious—should be included.

Teaching civics is a process of educating young people in how to identify and reflect on often complex public or social issues so that they are able critically to make reasonable choices. In turn, they ought to be able to show persuasively how their choices align with the democratic values articulated as common and important within their society. For such values education to be effective, teachers historically needed new teaching skills beyond rote education. Teaching civics is a process in deliberation, a topic addressed in detail later in chapter 4; yet for young people, deliberation needs to be nurtured, often facilitated, and framed within that set of democratic values made explicit by the teacher. Teachers should provide an educational environment where democratic values of good citizenship can be as much *caught* as taught. Where do teachers learn these skills? Are they even motivated to initiate age-appropriate activities that promote this special pedagogical environment characterized by a participatory (and therefore engaging) approach to learning? In short, how ought teachers to help their pupils develop the moral values intrinsic to good citizenship?

While my thoughts were directed at these challenging practical questions, it soon became clear to me from the deliberations at the workshop that the majority of Ugandans were concentrating on the underlying need for civics education. They were vexed by the apparent erosion of moral values in their country and the rise of such immoral activities as corruption, electoral fraud, obsessive materialism, and the persistent and obscenely brutal conflict in the north with the Lords Resistance Army (a conflict described in more detail in chapter 7). The common sentiment was that *the rot must be stopped*, but it was also generally felt that it was now too late to generate such a profound reorientation of expectations and attitudes for most Ugandan adults. Attention—and hope—turned mostly toward the young. The civics agenda was large, and ambitious, for my Ugandan colleagues gathered at this workshop.

While there may be academic interest in the debate about the public role of moral education in a free society, the more compelling demand in Uganda was to create the foundation for a more ethical society. As is the case in most countries, basic principles of moral behavior, moral accountability, virtue, and essential skills in ethical discernment were rarely discussed in Uganda outside of the churches or mosques. All of the workshop participants considered it to be an enormous challenge to introduce effective, practical, and affordable means to teach democratic values—*civics*—to young people, but they were also concerned by the ethical environment itself. How best should civics education foster an ongoing, sustainable dialogue between very different ethnic groups, and between young and old, women and men, rich and poor, urban and rural, given the many moral and ethical concerns that face Ugandans in their daily lives and work? It is a question that perplexes thoughtful people around the world, as they consider their own societies.

TAUGHT, OR CAUGHT?

Anyone who thinks that children—even very young children—cannot detect hypocrisy is either an exceptionally unobservant person, or not a parent. "Do as I say, not as I do" doesn't fool young people. Young people learn most from the example of their elders, and parents' actions speak much louder and more persuasively than their words. As American author Robert Fulghum cautioned us, "Don't worry that children never listen to you. Worry that they are always watching you" (Gruwell & McCourt, 2007, p. 200).

If we consider ethics and moral values as a subject only to be taught alongside mathematics, science, and languages, we are already misdirected. Ethics is much more likely to stick when it is *caught* and not just taught, although a formal introduction to ethics remains important, if handled in an age-appropriate way. The best classroom for ethics, however, is life; an ethical environment and the example of ethical leadership (inside and outside school) are significantly more important in shaping the development of an ethical society than any formal education in ethics, particularly for younger students.

A child's life is affected by the values he or she is taught at home, in the mosque, or in church, and so too is the child influenced by the many moral values inherent in all subjects currently taught in the existing curriculum. Most Ugandan teachers and students were unaware of how values-rich much of the traditional material on their current curriculum is, yet these values quickly emerged as the participants at the workshop took the opportunity to engage in dialogue about values and ethics. It quickly became apparent that the educational process or rote learning—widespread in Uganda—was remarkably ineffectual in training young minds to think ethically. Discussion and dialogue are much more effective in assisting young people to feel their way through ethical issues; to draw on the moral resources and insights of their peers and elders; and to build and internalize a sense of the right, the good, and the virtuous.

I can hardly emphasize the role of dialogue enough. My years of experience in Africa and elsewhere as an urban and regional planner facilitating a large number of what planners refer to as visioning workshops led me to an important observation. In such workshops, stakeholders were urged to visualize the desired future quality of their communities, and I consistently found that people were able and eager to talk about values if given the chance (and a bit of encouragement to get over their shyness!). Similarly, education must provide structured opportunities for discussing the moral concerns of young people—and they have many such concerns. Children, just like adults, would benefit from a forum where they feel that they are respected and supported, where everyone has an opportunity to speak, and where all are committed *to listen*. In its more polished form, this is known as *deliberative democracy*, and there are excellent examples from around the world about how to organize and nurture such processes—even starting with the young. This topic is dealt with in some detail in chapter 4.

Bringing ethics into the consciousness and dialogue of young people won't happen without leadership or the strategic input of educators. There is no mystery here—getting teachers to be more aware of the ethical environment all around them and to mainstream ethics into all that they teach is the best way to strengthen ethics education in schools. Specific efforts must be made by leaders within educational ministries and institutions to strengthen the ethical awareness and ethical discernment skills of teachers, so that they are able to draw upon the almost limitless opportunities within the educational process to accentuate moral issues and foster ethical thinking and behavior.

As I spoke with my Ugandan colleagues, I wasn't without my doubts and concerns. After all, I thought, aren't primary school children too young to engage in formal moral education? Indeed, the efficacy of formal classroom-based ethics training for young children is open to considerable doubt. In the well-known work of Dr. Lawrence Kohlberg, he argued that the psychological and developmental growth of children occurs in stages that are directly relevant to their stages of moral awareness and their internal sense of moral discernment (Kohlberg, 1971). Are such young children sufficiently morally aware to master rudimentary ethical discernment skills?

In my opinion, *formal* ethics training of primary-school-aged children may not be a wise investment of scarce educational resources. At that workshop in Entebbe, I argued that it would be better to use resources to concentrate less on formal ethics training and more on raising moral consciousness among young people, strengthening their own sense of moral worth. In their interactions with each other and with their teachers, young people model social behavior and learn social skills that are fundamentally moral. If we can draw children's attention to this quality and engage them on how they treat each other, how they deal with the inevitable conflicts that arise, and how they can express their feelings in healthy ways, then don't we have the essential elements in place for ethics training of younger children? While the Ugandans gathered at the workshop agreed with this as far as it went, they still held out for something more and challenged me to reflect carefully on my own position.

My position was, after all, that of an outsider. My approach to teaching ethics and values to the young was grounded on having a more conducive ethical environment—far removed from the harsh realities of day-to-day survival that many Ugandans and others throughout the developing world face—for the important moral lessons to be *caught* by example. Was I being called to evaluate Uganda's morality? When I argued the importance of character education and ethical performance of teachers, and the need for a related outreach to parents, was I passing judgment on whether Ugandan parents and teachers provided the right type of model? Everyone at the workshop accepted the obvious truth that very young children are most impressed and influenced by example, particularly the example of those whom they most look up to (teachers, parents and older family members, and perhaps religious leaders). The virtues and vices of such role models are remarkably apparent to children, even if children don't often articulate this in words. But was the problem in the perceived moral decline in Uganda to be blamed on offering Uganda's children bad examples? If so, where would that finger of blame point, and who would be doing the pointing? That wasn't my role or intention; in fact, it was quite the contrary. Uganda—like any country—is well supplied with moral heroes, and it was of them that I spoke. In any society, the examples of people of virtue have a powerful but often ignored impact—yet it is a positive and valuable impact that could be greatly magnified with some careful thinking about the role of virtue in each society.

Virtue for many people brings up images of a long-lost and perhaps entirely mythical Golden Era, when a gentleman's word was honored far more than any contract, and when an unresolved slight to one's reputation was the worst thing that could happen. While many philosophers and ethicists are returning to focus on the role of virtue, and the field of virtue ethics is now once again vibrant, few people are comfortable with the language of virtues and vices. Instead, we are more likely to discuss *character* and to consider the best opportunities to provide *character education*. Character education is how ethics training for young people is most frequently referred to. Through a conscious process of thinking through their actions and interactions—often using examples that children dramatize and model—young people are exposed to how their thinking and actions affect others, and how others affect them. The messages are simple, but through this simplicity, they have significant potential to be internalized and incorporated within a child's character and identity. The most important message of all is that each child is important, valuable, and worthy of respect and love. The simplicity of this message of moral equality and worth is remarkable but often misunderstood. Teachers and adults sometimes impose their authority though diminishing the importance of each child, making children feel like second-class or inferior beings. Sometimes girls are treated with less respect than boys, and adults often feel disinclined to really hear a child out. In the typically large classes of the global South, overflowing with children, the challenge to treat each child equally as a valuable and loved human being is an awesome moral and practical challenge to teachers and isn't always possible. The effort, however, must still be made. Children who internalize within their own character a sense of being both valuable and valued are much better able to treat others in a similar respectful, caring fashion.

The Ugandans at the workshop didn't need to be told that character education among the younger children also ought to address the basic skills and moral values that knit societies together. These skills, however, had not been thought of in Uganda as an appropriate component of ethics education. I therefore shared with them the example of a small American Quaker elementary school in College Park, Maryland, which incorporates conflict resolution into its curriculum from kindergarten onward.[2] I explained how this includes learning to exercise restraint—cooling down—in the face of perceived abuse, insults, or inappropriate behavior. Conflict resolution for young children and adults alike begins with respecting the values of mutual respect and tolerance, which are conflict-prevention strategies that even children are able to master.

Perhaps not surprisingly, I was asked by the Ugandans why, if the young ones can be taught the basics of conflict resolution, can't we get them to master the concepts of virtues and vices? I responded that perhaps we should resist the temptation to expand character education to address a number of specific virtues and vices; children are after all children. Keep the expectations contained, and concentrate on cultivating the foundations of a virtuous, caring character. Mutual respect, conflict management, and possibly also learning how to intentionally validate, affirm, and support one's peers is a sufficient agenda for children under 12 years old.

WHO SHOULD INCULCATE VALUES IN CHILDREN?

The Ugandans at the workshop united in the view that teachers generally are not motivated to teach ethics. Like teachers in any developing country, they have too many demands on their very limited time, and most have little if any training in ethics. Several issues immediately surface when we consider the role of teachers in this context. Are they qualified to teach ethics, and if not, what would be needed to make them so? Do they really have insufficient time? Why aren't they properly motivated, if this is in fact the case? Most importantly, are they the most appropriate persons to take on this role?

Teachers have the power to influence children's lives more than anyone else other than their parents. As Bruno Bettelheim, the child psychologist and author, said, "The question for the child is not 'Do I want to be good?' but 'Whom do I want to be like?'" (Bettelheim, 1991).[3] Other than parents and close family, teachers are who children most want to emulate. For this reason alone, a strong argument exists that government should train teachers in ethics and character education and assign them to lead in this capacity. While I share in this conviction as far as involving teachers, I have a somewhat different view regarding leadership.

Teachers should be trained to understand the enormous power and responsibility that they possess to shape the moral character of young people. In addition, this so-called shaping process ought to be pursued only in collaboration and partnership with parents, who share in this obligation and bear the primary moral burden of bringing up their children. No government has a mandate (or resources) to train parents, but governments (ideally at a local level) can sponsor programs that include and actively seek parental participation, and that help raise parents' awareness of their critical role in transmitting moral values and forming the character of their children.

Some participants at the workshop were openly cynical about a larger role in values education for Uganda's teachers. After all, they argued, haven't Ugandan teachers' moral values degenerated to such an extent that they are neither capable nor credible as teachers of ethics? I have heard this said so many times that I am sure there is more than a grain of truth to this concern. However, I told the Ugandan workshop participants that in my view there are also some—and possibly many—teachers of exceptional integrity in Uganda. My response to these cynical and discouraged outpourings was to advocate that we should recognize and celebrate those teachers who are exemplars of integrity and use their example and conduct as the benchmark upon which to measure the performance of other teachers. Holding teachers accountable to some abstract external code of ethics or set of principles is difficult, in that often these codes, principles, or rules seem abstract or only establish a baseline of unacceptable behavior instead of providing practical guidance for ethical performance. While codes have their place, far better results are likely to be achieved when teachers are able to compare their own and their colleagues' moral and ethical behavior to the ethical performance of exemplars—fellow teachers of recognized and celebrated integrity.

Are teachers willing to help? Many people at the workshop argued that teachers must be pushed into this expanded ethics training role; more specifically, they felt that only by incorporating formal testing on moral values would teachers be motivated (or coerced) to teach about ethics. I was not in a position to evaluate that claim, but I did express a concern about the source and direction of such motivation. Teachers who are motivated primarily to see as many children as possible pass exams are very different from teachers who are invested in the moral development of young people. My question to them was simple: who would you rather have teach your children?

WHICH VALUES, WHOSE VALUES?

There are many Ugandans and people everywhere who contend that the use of a religious studies curriculum is an effective and appropriate method to

teach moral values in public education. I strongly disagree. I knew that taking such a stand might be contentious, and I accepted that my position was in
part a reflection of my own national values as an American (and my religious
convictions as a Quaker). Still, it was important for me to point out that religious values are based on religious beliefs, which are amenable to only limited
challenges based on reasoned deliberations. Relying primarily on religious
beliefs instead of reason to justify and explain one's moral values, I argued,
would mean that one must quickly fall back on the belief structure and creed
of that particular religion. When one person in the dialogue defends her position with a statement such as "Well, that's just what I believe," that's where
deliberative dialogue ends. Challenging someone to justify (or change) her
beliefs simply isn't appropriate or productive.

In comparison, national and secular values (as commonly included in a constitution) are based on a social and political consensus—they are values that
we *all* agree on in a rational process of deliberation. The Ugandan Constitution stipulates that there shall be no state religion, and in Uganda, as in
many countries, there are many religions and denominations. Trying to base
ethics education (and character education) therefore on religious justification
is, in my view, an invitation to a process that accentuates our differences, not
our similarities.[4] In Uganda, the tension between religious and secular values
remains intense, however, particularly as many traditional and cultural values
are now framed in religious terms. For example, every well-known church
leader in Uganda joins with every leading politician to attack the so-called
"evil of homosexuality and to support the draconian punishments that exist in
Ugandan law to punish homosexuals. Seeking to engage in a rational, deliberative debate on the human rights of homosexuals—even when it is argued
that human rights are underpinned by secular and universal values—will fail
to trump the conflated religious and cultural values held by the majority of
Ugandans. This situation may explain why my arguments in favor of public
education in ethics being based on secular values may ultimately fail to find
the necessary support among Ugandans.

If not religion, then where are educators to find moral resources to ground
the values that they propose to inculcate in their youth? Many will argue
that African traditional culture was once very successful in moral and ethical
training and development, but the prevailing view at the workshop was that
this capacity has been lost. I wasn't ready then and remain unprepared to
accept that assertion without empirical evidence and further consideration,
as I am guessing that the moral example and influence that parents bring to
shape their children's values is still strongly influenced by traditional culture
in Uganda and throughout the South. The values of traditional culture suffer
many of the same problems as religious values in that there is no objective,
rational basis to question the merits of such values. Yet many of these traditional moral values define the identity of Ugandans, as they do people in similar cultural environments. Arguing that a value has merit simply because it is

"our tradition" at least leaves the door slightly ajar to anyone questioning the relevance of traditions to current realities; unlike religious values, most people accept that traditional values evolve and can be discussed. While important universal moral principles such as diversity, gender equality, and freedom of expression often fall victim to traditional values, the potential positive influence of traditional values may offer moral resources far greater than many people would expect.

EACH SOCIETY'S TASK

We all have a stake in achieving immediate and tangible results in the fight against corruption and in support of integrity in every society. Similarly, we have a strong vested interest in inculcating positive, virtuous values and disciplines in our young people. Parents are the natural and appropriate partners in this endeavor, and perhaps the biggest challenge now facing educators is how best to bring parents into such a collaboration.

We also know that schools can only do so much, as schooling is just one part of a child's life experience. The effectiveness of schools in strengthening ethical awareness and fostering ethical behavior in young people is entirely limited by the demonstration of a larger national commitment to strengthen the ethical environment in each country. Each society must undertake this large task and begin it simply—through offering structured opportunities in jobs, homes, institutions, and faith communities—to share views about moral issues and to strengthen abilities and courage to confront and resolve ethical challenges.

How ought the Ugandan government to begin this undertaking? I suggested that strategic, measurable results would be achieved by adopting a strategy that would apply equally well to any developing country. Such a strategy would do the following:

1. Identify a variety of accessible moral resources for integrity (so-called moral champions, such as teachers of integrity)
2. Use the values articulated in the Constitution (and not religious education) as the principal vehicle for training on national values
3. Focus on both training teachers in ethics and holding them accountable for ethical performance
4. Involve parents in a central—perhaps even primary—role in moral character development

As I left the workshop that evening, I thought of a reference from my own culture's moral resources—a quotation from an American president long ago, Theodore Roosevelt: "To educate a person in mind and not in morals is to educate a menace to society."[5] Surely, Uganda and all societies face sufficient development challenges already without cultivating a population that falls into President Roosevelt's latter category!

CHAPTER 3

Leadership

I was astounded!

It was March 2006, and Mr. Nasser Ntege (Seya) Sebbagala had just been elected mayor of Kampala. Surely, I reasoned, most people would not consider the new mayor of Kampala to be the personification of transformational leadership. After all, he was a man of dubious character, who had cut short his undistinguished earlier term as Kampala's mayor in a vain attempt to defend himself against bank fraud and money-laundering charges in Boston. Now, back from 15 months in an American prison, he stood triumphant; the convicted former criminal had returned to Uganda, rehabilitated by his electoral victory. The voters obviously saw in Sebbagala a man of charm, charisma, and political aptitude, but it would be very difficult indeed for anyone to argue that his qualities or his proposed policies for this city of nearly a million persons could be called inspirational or visionary. Sebbagala isn't known for his intellectual prowess either, or for fluency in the business language of the Ugandan capital—English. While he did fashion himself as a champion of the common man, in my view Sebbagala meets few of the criteria generally construed to constitute a transformational leader. As an unenfranchised foreigner, I had to come to terms with the ineluctable fact that he was now the popularly elected mayor of Kampala. As a resident of his city, I awaited the fruits of his leadership with more than a few misgivings.

One municipal election is hardly an adequate indicator of electoral behavior and governance aspirations in Kampala, much less in Uganda, but it did raise for me an interesting question. Is there room in the political culture of East Africa for transformational leaders? Is there demand for such leadership? Given the very slow progress to date in tackling extreme poverty and the multitude of social and ethical problems confronting the region,

I certainly felt that the need for such leadership was obvious, even urgent. If Ugandans shared my assessment, why had they elected this man? Was there nothing they could do to find or foster leadership of a transformational character?

Using the experience of local and national leadership in Uganda, this chapter explores the concept of the transformational leader in the broader context of East Africa, but with relevance to developing countries worldwide. I begin with an overview of the current thinking about the moral dimensions of leadership, and I briefly examine the recent history of national leadership in Uganda, as well as in neighboring Kenya and Tanzania, from the perspective of a moral ideal—the transformational leader as the virtuous leader. I also give some consideration about where Ugandans ought to be looking for better leadership. As will be seen, in my view, those who assign greatest priority to fostering transformational leadership beginning at the apex of national leadership are unlikely to succeed in recrafting well-entrenched senior leadership patterns, or even in achieving the political will needed to tackle the major development problems that confront East Africa.

Few if any should be able to surpass the citizens of Uganda in their knowledge of poor leadership and its dire impacts. Idi Amin and Milton Obote are gone and seldom talked about, but not forgotten by those over 30. Even under the current leadership in Uganda, with a president who seems determined to remain in power indefinitely, many thoughtful people argue that a thorough, dramatic, and rapid transformation is needed throughout the country if the ravages of poverty, conflict, and underdevelopment are to be addressed in a manner morally responsive to the urgency of such issues. For the foreseeable future, however, such a leadership transformation is more likely to be driven—if at all—by the Ugandan people than by their political leadership, and only then incrementally and relatively slowly.

Fostering an achievable, credible ideal of virtuous leadership may be essential for Ugandan governance to become an exemplar or beneficiary of good governance, but hoping to cultivate virtue at the top in the belief that such an example will trickle down to all subsidiary leadership levels is an exercise in futility. Yet I am not entirely cynical; even if we don't *begin* at the president's office, I am convinced that proselytizing for ethical, competent leadership and for good governance generally remains essential. The targets of this crusade are the top leadership and the middle classes on which top leadership typically depends, if only to begin to sow the seed that senior leaders everywhere ought to lead in setting the standards of quality in governance and be held accountable on that basis. Expecting such a seed to blossom amid the current top leadership—the product of a political system that counts success in terms that seldom include ethics—is unreasonable, but establishing in the public consciousness the ideal of transformational leadership as a goal is an important start.

TRANSFORMATIONAL AND
TRANSACTIONAL LEADERSHIP

Accurate terminology is important when addressing a concept as widely interpreted as *leadership*, as is evident in any scan of the extensive literature on this topic. Joseph C. Rost, who is among the most respected scholars on leadership today, described in detail the significant evolution in the definition of leadership, allocating much of his 1991 book *Leadership for the Twenty-first Century* to this task. Rost offered his own definition: "Leadership is an influence relationship among leaders and followers who intend real changes that reflect their mutual purposes" (Rost, 1991, p. 102). This definition has the merit of being parsimonious, but to me seems to leave out relevant moral content. Another leading scholar in leadership studies, Joanne Ciulla, offers to my mind a richer definition when she describes leadership as follows: "Leadership is not a person or a position. It is a complex moral relationship between people, based on trust, obligation, commitment, emotion, and a shared vision of the good" (Ciulla, 2004, p. xv).

Defining leadership is only the starting point. All forms of leadership are not the same, so I begin by describing the generally accepted attributes of an authentic *transformational* leader, comparing this form of leadership with *transactional* leadership and examining the role of morality in both of these leadership forms. The moral character of leadership has been written about extensively, so a brief overview of this literature is helpful.

Bernard M. Bass and Paul Steidlmeier, and others before them, argued in their writings that the ethics of effective and authentic moral leadership depend on three key normative attributes: (1) the moral character of the leader, (2) the ethical values that characterize the leader's vision and program (as accepted or rejected by the electorate), and (3) the moral qualities of the processes of social ethical choice and action in which leaders and followers collectively engage. In short, authentic transformational leadership is characterized by its high moral and ethical standards (Bass & Steidlmeier, 1998). Bass and Steidlmeier have claimed that transformational leaders are known by four key personal attributes—charisma, inspirational motivation, intellectual stimulation, and individualized consideration.

If the leadership is transformational, its charisma or idealized influence is envisioning, confident, and sets high standards for emulation. Its inspirational motivation provides followers with challenges and meaning for engaging in shared goals and undertakings. Its intellectual stimulation helps followers to question assumptions and to generate more creative solutions to problems. Its individualized consideration treats each follower as an individual and provides coaching, mentoring and growth opportunities. (Bass & Steidlmeier 1998)

Rost offers a variation on his earlier quoted basic definition of leadership to capture his sense of *transformation* within transformational leadership: "Real transformation involves active people, engaging in influence relationships based on persuasion, intending real changes to happen, and insisting that those changes reflect their mutual purposes" (Rost, 1991, p. 123).

Transformational leadership is commonly compared to the more common model of the transactional leader. The latter typically uses promises, praise, rewards—as well as threats, negative criticism, fear, and disciplinary actions— to achieve the desired actions and behavior from his followers. Another prominent voice in this topic, David Boje, refers to these as *modal values*, or values of the means, contrasted to transformational leadership's focus on the end-values such as liberty, equality, justice, compassion, and human flourishing (Boje, 2000).

In practical terms, leadership is usually both transactional and transformational, and the character and legitimacy of both aspects of leadership have deep roots in moral theory and ethics. Transactional leadership is more closely associated with the leader's pursuit of self-interest, as transactional leaders typically view followers and constituents as means to their own ends. The legitimacy of this form of leadership, however, still depends on honesty, respecting promises, providing genuine incentives, exercising fairness in the distribution of rewards and benefits, and affording to others the same degree of opportunities and freedoms that one grants to oneself (Bass & Steidlmeier, 1998). Transformational leadership, by comparison, is morally grounded in the leader respecting each follower or constituent as an end in himself or herself, and not as a means to the leader's ends. While the transformational leader has a strong sense of self and a vision that he or she wishes to pursue, I contend that the sense of self in this leader is situated in the context of community, family, and friends—so that the welfare of others or of the whole community is generally more important than just the welfare of the leader. The transformational leader appeals to choice and not to coercion; followers are invited and inspired to embrace ideals with commitment, to pursue creative solutions, and to exercise moral discretion. Transformational leadership seeks to generate change within the hearts and minds of followers, while transactional leadership concentrates on managing results, with much less concern as to how those results are achieved.

Virtues must contend with vices. Bass and Steidlmeier, together with Carey, Solomon, and Hollander, warn against the possibility of the *pseudotransformational* leader, and they differentiate between moral and immoral transactional leadership.

To bring about change, authentic transformational leadership fosters the modal values of honesty, loyalty and fairness, and the end values of justice, equality, and human rights. But pseudotransformational leadership endorses perverse modal values such as favoritism, victimization, and special interests and end values such as racial superiority, submission, and Social Darwinism. It can invent fictitious obstacles, imaginary enemies and visions that are chimeras. Likewise, transactional leadership is moral when truth is told, promises are kept, negotiations are fair and choices are free. It is immoral when information harmful to them is deliberately concealed from associates, when bribes are proffered, when nepotism is practiced, and when authority is abused. (Bass & Steidlmeier, 1998)

THE VIRTUOUS LEADER IDEAL

I am hardly alone in suggesting that the best known recent example of the ideal, virtuous national leader in Africa is Nelson Mandela. Other prominent national leaders are known for their ideals and virtues, but in many cases, they were doomed to failure for their vices or weaknesses. Think no further than Patrice Lumumba, Léopold Sédar Senghor, or Amilcar Cabral. East Africa, too, has its own history of remarkable leaders, the best known of whom—Julius Nyerere—was clearly transformational and arguably virtuous. Outside of Africa and into the larger sweep of human history, the model of the transformational leader as a moral ideal is well established, from Plato's philosopher king to the virtuous minister of state under Confucian thought. It is a common and appealing theme: the moral sage, the self-effacing exemplar of virtue who is raised to leadership not by his own raw ambition but by popular demand, the wise and benevolent ruler, and the honest small-town lawyer pressed by the citizenry into public service are all common archetypes from literature and history.

In the spring of 2006, Radio One, the largest broadcaster in Uganda, invited me to be their guest on the evening radio talk show *Spectrum*. Given that President Museveni, recently reelected under a process rife with overt manipulation, was about to nominate his new cabinet, the host of the talk show wanted me as an ethicist to address the appropriate qualifications for high office: what ought the president to be considering as he pondered his choices? My answer was neither complicated nor original; I read aloud to the radio audience the phrase that appears no less than 10 times in the Ugandan Constitution to describe essential qualifications for public office: "being of high moral character and proven integrity." Clearly this must mean something to appear so often in the foundational document of Ugandan law and governance, yet not once in my prolonged association with many Ugandans over more than 20 years had I ever heard anyone express an expectation that their ministers would be of high moral character and proven integrity. If anything, their expectations were just the opposite, and when I shared this observation, the phone lines became very active indeed.

Despite some heartening responses from those who called in, an underlying question lingered in my mind then, as it does now. Why *should* any leader be moral? For that matter, why should anyone be moral?

From the perspective of virtue ethics, the question itself is avoided by the premise that it is human nature to want to seek a meaningful life, and that a central method of pursuing this goal is to develop one's character through acquiring an elevated level of moral awareness. Such an ethical sensibility incorporates such virtues as caring about the kind of person we are and facilitating (or at least not impeding) the efforts of other persons to become the kind of persons that they wish to become. A leading thinker in virtue ethics, Christine McKinnon, asserts that the motivation to act in ways that are taken to be ethically admirable arises naturally out of the internalization and expression of moral sensibility (McKinnon, 1999).

A leader, of course, need be neither a self-aware moral agent, nor a virtuous person. Yet my interest is the transformative leader—itself a concept that entails moral agency—elevated to the status of a moral ideal. What constitutes such a leader's character? What attributes must he or she have to be regarded as an effective *moral agent*—a person who is morally aware, cares about moral values, exercises critical evaluation in selecting which values and principles to be guided by, chooses moral ends, and selects the means by which to pursue such ends?

Bass and Steidlmeier are unequivocal about the moral attributes of the transformative leader as a morally autonomous person. They argue that such a person is notable by his or her inner moral compass and is committed both to the individual moral development and growth of each follower as well as to the larger moral good of society. This leader sees and fosters the best in people—not only their good works, but also their character virtues. As Bass and Steidlmeier state, "The heart of the moral enterprise is the development of good character, which is defined by commitment to virtue in all circumstances" (Bass & Steidlmeier, 1998). Other prominent thinkers agree: a transformational leader is emotionally mature, committed to accountability, and concerned about the consequences of his or her decisions and actions (Cooper, 2004).

If the ideal of the transformative leader is framed in the language of virtue, arguably the best approach to explore this ideal further would be to employ virtue ethics. In the past decade, there has been a resurgence of interest in virtue ethics, with important contributions from scholars such as G.E.M. Anscombe, Christine McKinnon, Alasdair C. MacIntyre, Ian Maitland, and Michael Slote, among others. Virtue ethics, with its roots in the ethics of Aristotle, Plato, and the Stoics (and later religiously situated by Thomas Aquinas), once dominated moral philosophy. Up until the time of Thomas Hobbes and Machiavelli, when moral pessimism replaced moral optimism, the concept of the virtuous person was the primary focus of ethical discourse. Under this ideal, the virtuous person attended to self-interest, but through the exercise of such cardinal virtues as temperance, justice, prudence, and courage, he placed the interests of others and of society as a whole as greater moral obligations.

Machiavelli did not dispute the existence or influence of virtue, but instead questioned its relevance to the demands of survival in a violent, conflict-ridden world—a context not dissimilar to the north of Uganda recently and many parts of sub-Saharan Africa today. Hobbes considered virtues, as well as such moral judgments as to what is good or bad, as matters of preference, and he placed them at the service of self-interest, while arguing that the effacement of self-interest was unnatural (Pellegrino, 1989).

Many other moral thinkers, from Friedrich Nietzsche, Bernard Mandeville, John Locke, David Hume, Lord Shaftesbury, Francis Hutcheson, and

Ayn Rand, either dismissed or significantly reinterpreted the role and usefulness of virtues. In some cases, virtues were even presented as vices, new weight was given to the moral legitimacy of the pursuit of self-interest over all other interests, and it was suggested that virtue should be subordinated into something that brought pleasure or happiness to the moral agent but served little other purpose. Through such criticism, virtue ethics fell out of the mainstream of modern Western rationalism; yet it remained very much alive in the domain of religious studies (MacIntyre, 1984).

Some moral thinkers did come to the aid of virtue ethics, with Ralph Cudworth, Henry More, Joseph Butler, and Richard Cumberland arguing that virtuous acts were both reasonable and valuable. In the more recent resurgence of interest in virtue ethics, thinking about virtues goes in new directions, often trying to link virtuous character and altruism to psychological or even genetic factors more than to philosophical ones.[1]

Virtue ethics continues to suffer, however, from its inability to define the concept of virtue itself. While giving significantly less weight to the rational application of moral rules, principles, codes, or values, virtue ethics does not explain the *mechanism* by which virtue helps us to resolve moral dilemmas. There is the problem of circularity inherent in the major premise of virtue ethics: "the right and the good is that which the virtuous person would do, and the virtuous person is one who would do the right and the good" (Pellegrino, 1989). To break this circularity, either *right* and *good* must be defined, or we must define what constitutes the virtuous person.

Pellegrino raises yet other concerns with virtue ethics:

Further difficulties include the relations of intent to outward behavior. Is good intention a criterion of a virtuous person? How do we determine intention? Can a good intention absolve the agent of responsibility for an act which ends in harm—a physician telling a patient the truth out of the virtue of honesty, and thereby precipitating a serious depression or even suicide? Few are virtuous all the time. How many lapses move us from the virtuous to the continent, incontinent, or vicious category? How does virtue ethics connect with duty and principle based ethics which give the objectivity virtue ethics seems to lack? (Pellegrino, 1989)

These criticisms are persuasive to an extent, and current virtue ethicists are devoting considerable effort to addressing them. I won't try in this chapter to pursue the merits of these arguments further, yet I remain convinced that the quality of the actions of morally autonomous persons—which includes transformative leaders—is determined in large measure by the character of the person choosing the action. Character also shapes how people perceive and define a moral problem and how they decide which moral values and principles, as well as amoral facts, are relevant to the prevention or resolution of such problems. Whether a leader is motivated by self-interest or altruism may not affect the value of the outcome of his or her decision, yet I think it remains an important determinant in the assessment of leadership quality over time.

From the perspective of virtue ethics, and in my own view, character matters. Becoming a virtuous person is more than an exercise of selecting certain values and principles and rejecting others. Good character is a product of excellent moral and intellectual attributes, but there are also many other traits and qualities that lead to the development of virtuous character. Successful moral leadership results from a conscious and disciplined process of building a character of integrity and virtue, occurring within and for a community. At the end of the day, that character matters to all of us; we want our leaders—as persons of virtue—consistently and dependably to know what is right and good and to be able to explain and model this to their followers in language and actions that are persuasive and inspirational. We want to be assured that our leaders are doing the right thing for the right reason, that they are timely in their handling of moral problem solving, and that they are accountable to us for what they do.

EVALUATING THE VIRTUES OF UGANDAN POLITICAL LEADERSHIP

I began this chapter with Kampala's Mayor Sebbagala, and his example calls me back from the theories of virtuous or transformational leadership to the realities of leadership as actually experienced by Ugandans, and throughout the developing world generally. Since independence, Uganda's political leaders have varied from inspired (Museveni in his early years) to tragically bizarre (Idi Amin). As early as 1966, Milton Apollo Obote elevated the role of president from a largely ceremonial function to the most powerful position in the land. A prominent Kenyan political historian and scholar of leadership, Eric Masinde Aseka, judged the late president Obote as a "skilled transactional operator," while at the same time noting that his few efforts at transformational leadership were very short-lived (Aseka, 2005). Under Obote's rule, the principles of the Westminster ideal of democracy that were assumed at independence—meritocracy, honesty, integrity, incorruptibility, and dedication to duty—were very quickly eroded, leaving the Westminster model largely hollow. In the ensuing vacuum, Ugandan politics deteriorated into a zero-sum system of winner take all. Transactionally, Obote's regime was also characterized by incompetence, as basic planning was ignored, taxation was raised to unsustainably high levels, the administration of the military became highly unprofessional, and the scheduling of elections became erratic. Of particular concern for Uganda's future, the armed forces were intentionally co-opted by Obote to become a personal army, dominated by members of his own Lango tribe.

When Idi Amin replaced Milton Obote in a coup in 1971, the fabric of civility deteriorated precipitously. Amin presided over the militarization of Ugandan politics—including the executive branch and the judiciary—creating a tradition of governance that I found still very much in evidence in Uganda. Amin's military comrades were granted positions of power as rewards, and such men used these positions to accumulate wealth through blatant exploitation, corruption, smuggling, theft, extortion, and worse. Amin also favored Islamic interests (while clearly not adhering to Islamic moral principles), ignored and then formally subordinated the constitution to presidential decrees, made a tragic mockery of the ideal of rule of law, and used terror and fear as tools to reinforce his power and control. Amin is most clearly remembered for bloodshed and brutality; approximately 300,000 Ugandans died under his despotic and brutal rule.

After the Tanzanian invasion of Uganda that toppled Amin, and a period of turbulence and short-lived presidencies, Yoweri Kaguta Museveni assumed power in 1986 through a bush war that overthrew the brief and largely dictatorial return to power of Milton Obote. Not until 1996 did Museveni turn to the electorate to legitimize his rule, standing again for reelection in 2001 and in 2006.

From 1979 through 1989, while a resident in neighboring Kenya, I watched Museveni's rise to power and his early performance at the helm. It was clear to me and to my many Ugandan colleagues that Museveni had a very tall mountain to climb—the reconstruction of the social, political, economic, physical, and moral infrastructure of the entire country. After years of misrule and chaos, war and brutality, Uganda had reached the bottom rung of the long ladder to civility and development. To his credit, Museveni approached this challenge with charisma, vision, energy, and a military standard of personal discipline. His political agenda was far-reaching and unlike anything ever seen in Uganda before. He presided over extensive decentralization of governance, vastly increasing public participation in decision making and raising the political awareness of the country. He provided security and peace, reigned in the military's abuses of power, and demanded accountability from his officials. To many others and me, Uganda's development progress was nothing short of spectacular. Nearly the entire country benefited from his leadership—with the prominent exception of the northern parts of the country, which until very recently were mired in a violent two-decade conflict with a ruthlessly brutal armed cult known as the Lords Resistance Army.

How do I now judge this president? Museveni's presidency certainly began with high hopes, and through his first decade in power, his policies and accomplishments did much to impress me and, more importantly, to earn his country's and the world's respect. His approach to leadership, however, was transactional at best. He has done very little to cultivate leadership in others, and over his many years in power, he has come to represent a one-man-show approach to governance. Museveni's political commitment to decentralization has weakened considerably in recent years, many of his former key supporters have defected to other parties, and he has become more isolated from Ugandan citizens. Many Ugandans argue that he is excessively arrogant, blind to his own failings, and hesitant to take advice.

I'm now joined by many Ugandans who think that Museveni is fixated on retaining power, by whatever means necessary, and of using this power to hold himself unaccountable and beyond serious reproach from political opponents. When the constitution's limitation of two terms became inconvenient to his ambitions, Museveni manipulated Uganda's parliament to remove term limits from the constitution, and he duly stood for and won a third term in March of 2006. Given that the 2001 election was fraught with electoral irregularities—including as many as 1.3 million so-called ghost voters among the 7.5 million votes actually cast,[2] it is not surprising that the 2006 election was similarly troubled. Human Rights Watch announced its conviction that the 2006 election was neither free nor fair, due to the lack of a level playing field and widespread government harassment of opposition candidates.[3] After so many years in power, President Museveni and his National Resistance Movement (NRM) party are clearly intent on not losing the privileges, influence, and patronage networks that come with such well-entrenched power. Museveni joins such dubious company as Robert Mugabe of Zimbabwe and Mwai Kibaki of Kenya in deforming the entire electoral process to serve the solitary aim of retaining power. It is hardly a legacy to admire.

THE EXPERIENCE OF SENIOR LEADERSHIP IN EAST AFRICA

The Ugandan experience of political leadership that I describe above should be placed in a context. To many, including some of Africa's most notable political leaders, the continent is in decline, both developmentally and morally. Former President Olusegun Obansanjo of Nigeria placed the blame for this decline squarely on poor leadership (Obansanjo 2000). Indeed, leadership in Africa has never been under more scrutiny, and so far, the results are far from heartening—yet the wringing of hands is hardly the place for me to leave such an examination. As Salim Ahmed Salim, the former Organization of African Unity (OAU) secretary-general stated:

As we move into the new century and Africa faces up to its challenges, it is important that the leadership factor is given due attention. The role of leadership needs to be clearly understood, appropriate modalities of nurturing and appointing dynamic leadership have to be developed, and also critical is the need to foster accountability and transparency in the exercise of the leadership function. (Obansanjo 2000).

Salim's emphatic call for dynamic leadership makes only a passing reference to the moral attributes of accountability and transparency. This is a far cry from advocacy for the moral ideal of a transformational leader of virtue. Where is the African demand for virtuous, moral leadership?

Perhaps Ugandans and all Africans cannot demand what they have little or no experience of—models of virtuous senior-level transformative leadership in Africa are rare. The recent political history of East Africa demonstrates to me and even more directly to Africans the tangible realities and adverse impacts of poor—and often immoral—leadership in stark terms. In my 11 years living and working in Kenya and Uganda, my own hopes and expectations for the coming to power of an East African Mandela figure were—at best—guarded.

In his scholarly analysis, Aseka asserts that East Africa's leaders are alienated from their followers by an embedded system of economic plunder of national resources starting at the top, and by a record of electoral processes often resulting in the selection of what he terms "devious political characters" who have frustrated the development of the essential institutions that East Africa needs to achieve progress. He summarizes his views as follows:

East African leadership, with the exception of Nyerere to some extent, has failed to weave the fabric of civility in its organizational quests. It allowed its ethnicised leadership ambitions, goals and demands of ethnic entitlement and its coercive subjection of other communities to lead to political malpractices. (Aseka, 2005, p. 19)

In Aseka's words, leadership in East Africa is about "power over" instead of "power to," with little or nothing to do with his "fabric of civility" (Aseka, 2005, p. 73). In Kenya and Uganda, rigging of electoral processes has become the norm. Throughout the region there are numerous examples of multiparty democracy being more about the distribution of small bribes in exchange for votes[4] and the manipulation of tribal sentiments, and less about offering true choices of differing political and social visions for the future. Despite the presence of charismatic leaders such as Jomo Kenyatta or Julius Nyerere, transactional leadership is the norm in East Africa. Unlike transactional leadership in more developed countries, however, which is linked more closely to the exercise of bureaucratic power, the transactional leadership of East Africa maps more closely to Max Weber's traditional authority framework—the domain of the feudal prince (Boje, 2000). The feudal model of governance is hardly an environment conducive to, or indicative of, the cultivation and flowering of transformative and virtuous leadership, particularly at the top of the political power structures.

I'll now turn to look at Kenya in more detail—a country whose drive to independence clearly benefited from the flamboyant and charismatic leadership of its first president, Jomo Kenyatta. However, unfortunately for Kenya, the political framework under which Kenyatta came to power elevated him above the law. This elevation left him with little obligation for accountability and a huge advantage in outmaneuvering his political opponents. Not surprisingly then, Kenyatta presided over a process of ever-expanding executive power, and the conversion of the state to a personalized, patrimonial fiefdom. Women fared particularly badly in the political world of Kenyatta's Kenya, with far lower parliamentary representation than in Tanzania or Uganda.[5]

In the 1960s and 1970s under Kenyatta, Kenya began a rapid process of institutional decay, rendering the public service largely ineffectual in the management of public affairs. Many scholars attribute this institutional decline to the systematic political undermining of the integrity of these institutions, leading to an institutional ethos of patrimonial capitalism, in which civil servants informally privatize public institutions.

Jomo Kenyatta, as a transactional leader, was not disposed toward visionary societal change. Kenyatta did not seriously advocate any particular social philosophy and instead proffered a very indistinct political philosophy—*Harambee*. Kenyatta placed highest priority on the establishment and maintenance of law and order through the exercise of punishments and rewards, not through fostering integrity. Public morality—arguably essential for creating and sustaining the demand for transformational leadership—languished under his leadership, as a growing list of unethical practices became the order of the day.

Following Kenyatta's death in 1978, Kenya's vice president, Daniel arap Moi, assumed the presidency. The former beneficiaries of Kenyatta's favoritism made a concerted effort to displace him, but Moi proved to be a formidable political force and quickly moved to raise his public profile and secure his position. He promised continuity with Kenyatta's *Harambee* vision, gradually forming his own version, which he termed his *Nyayo* philosophy.[6] Neither *Harambee* nor *Nyayo* compare to the intellectual rigor of Nyerere's *Ujamaa* philosophy of African Socialism. While all three claimed the lineage of African Socialism, only Nyerere seriously pursued his political beliefs as an authentic vision of governance. *Harambee* and *Nyayo* were simply affectations and rhetorical devices used for political advantage, not robust visions intellectually persuasive or morally grounded.

Moi was almost certainly underestimated by his political opponents, as time proved that he was a consummate political strategist, keenly aware of opportunities to bargain, persuade, or reciprocate. This transactional style of leadership allowed him to navigate through a period of considerable insecurity and gradually to consolidate his power, often employing severe measures. For example, one of Moi's earliest moves, just three years after assuming power, was to reinstate the colonial era detention laws, allowing the president to override the constitution in denying individual human and legal rights, as and when it suited him. In short order, parliamentary supremacy also was subordinated to the executive branch and to the ruling party. By 1986, Moi had even successfully moved to limit the judiciary's authority over presidential discretion—and over presidential excesses.

Throughout this expansion of his power, Moi pursued a strongly ethnic agenda, in which he de-Kikuyunized the civil service (Jomo Kenyatta was of the Kikuyu tribe), replacing powerful Kikuyus with people of his own ethnic group, the Kalenjins, while largely maintaining the Kenyatta tradition of leaving the development claims of the large Luo tribe to languish (Adar, 2001). Moi demonstrated the continuity of political power and control linked to ethnicity and strong, personal rule from the executive, as he approximated the manner and style of a paramount tribal chief. His rule undermined the importance of institutions to governance, which weakened under the weight of rampant corruption and growing ineffectiveness. Parastatal organizations and even many private banks collapsed due to corruption, and the important linkages between society's aspirations and needs, cultural traditions and values, and leadership unraveled under Moi. As Aseka argues, Kenya under Moi was

building a primitive culture of glorifying the dishonest and corrupt 'big man' (*bwana mkubwa*) syndrome that is strongly engrained in the community perception of status and social function in society. This is encouraging the further development of deviant leadership that has no transformative agenda. (Aseka, 2005, pp. 416–17)

Moi's successor, President Mwai Kibaki, initially impressed many Kenyans—as well as many international investors—as a highly competent steward of Kenya's economy. Under his leadership, Kenya's economic growth accelerated dramatically, but almost from the beginning, his time in power was characterized by serious political insecurity, allegations of flagrant corruption among his cabinet ministers and even his vice president, and his failure during a referendum approval process to push through the new constitution that he supported, which placed even greater powers in the executive branch. Kibaki was no visionary leader, other than nurturing a vision of maximizing political power within the executive. He embarked on no ambitious leadership initiatives that could be called transformational and espoused no new vision for Kenya's future.[7] Instead, he is now largely considered to have usurped power by not admitting that his political rival, Raila Odinga, won the December 2007 national elections. Kibaki's power grab created a three-month stalemate that made Kenya the victim of vicious ethnic fighting, inflicted monumental economic damage, and left its national reputation as a peaceful and maturing democracy in tatters. More than 800 Kenyans died, including many women and children, and over 700,000 Kenyans were displaced during these troubled months due to ethnic violence fanned by the political rivalries of Kibaki (of the Kikuyu tribe) and Odinga (of the Luo tribe) and their supporters.[8] When I visited Nairobi in May 2008, the sentiment most often shared by Kenyans with me was that both leaders were callously self-interested and unconcerned about the damage their political standoff had caused. By the time that former United Nations Secretary General Kofi Annan facilitated a political compromise that ended the bloody standoff, many Kenyans had lost respect for both of these Kenyan leaders as suitable persons to hold the public trust of the nation at the highest positions of power.

Tanzania followed a different path in terms of leadership. One of my earliest memories of Tanzania was watching President Nyerere driving through the residential streets of the capital, Dar es Salaam, not in an ostentatious presidential motorcade with motorcycle escorts, but only with his driver. Even his car was old and unpretentious, and I marveled as I watched him stop at the red light—perhaps the only African president ever to stop for red lights! Within East Africa, Tanzania is distinctive due to the somewhat enigmatic but clearly charismatic leadership and personality of its founding father, Julius Nyerere. Many would join me in characterizing Nyerere's leadership style as a combination of *leadership by example* and *leadership by command*, but it is clear to me that Nyerere was deeply influenced by moral exemplars.[9] Nyerere applied his intellectual prowess, formidable debating and rhetorical skills, and visionary spirit throughout most of his long political career to articulate a distinctive development path for Africa in general and Tanzania in particular. The result was his doctrine of African Socialism, or *Ujamaa*, with its central project being the establishment of a modern interpretation of long-established African traditions by creating a public morality in Tanzania in which the individual was subject to the interests of the collective.

Nyerere incorporated many radical moral ideas into his ideology, such as the premise that leaders should build a relationship of equality with their followers. He spoke out strongly about leadership character, emphatically rejecting leadership that was arrogant, oppressive, or ostentatious, calling instead for leadership that embodied the virtues of courage, justice, and equal treatment for all. Nyerere and his leadership cadres failed, however, to offer practical means to translate these ideals into reality or sufficiently practical solutions to the very real human problems of tribalism, greed, gender discrimination, and religious intolerance.

As Nyerere came to recognize his inability to transform the attitudes and moral behavior of his followers through his ideology of African Socialism, he became much more focused on his own power and authority and became increasingly intolerant of dissent. His party became the locus of centralized power and the supreme institution in the country. Large numbers of people considered as political threats were placed under detention, suffering significant human-rights abuses. By 1977, Tanzania had more of its citizens under detention than did South Africa under apartheid at the same time (Aseka, 2005). Nyerere placed restrictions on civil society, discriminated against Muslims (he was a devout Roman Catholic), and linked the issuance of business licenses and even permission to attend university to membership in the ruling party. As a de jure one-party state, political expression outside the auspices of the ruling party was severely constrained. This culture of political monolithism became implanted, creating a powerful disincentive for independent thinking in leaders and managers, and strengthened the growing culture of patrimonial rule.

Nyerere's retirement from the presidency did not entail a retirement from the political stage, and his successor as president—Ali Hassan Mwinyi, from Zanzibar—had to rule in Nyerere's shadow. Nyerere remained chairman of the ruling party, and Mwinyi therefore attended more to management than leadership, with his interest primarily in Tanzania's institutions of governance. Even though Nyerere continued to dominate the policy agenda for the country, Mwinyi's presidency is remembered as a time of improving civil rights and greater political freedoms for the populace. With Nyerere's blessing, Mwinyi was able to guide Tanzania into more liberal economic and political policies, which in turn resulted in a significant boost to development.

In 1995, Benjamin William Mkapa was elected to the presidency, and his 10 years in power were characterized as an extension of Mwinyi's move toward liberalization. The scholarly Mkapa consolidated his position within the ruling party, replacing many of the old guard with more liberal-minded party officials. Mkapa has his critics, however, who have accused him of having a low regard for the rule of law, little commitment to ending high-level corruption, an inability to constrain or stop government abuses of power (such a widespread police brutality), and a disregard for freedom of expression. His initiatives to fight high-level corruption were high profile, such as the much publicized special presidential commission under the chairmanship of former Prime Minister Joseph Warioba, but little action was ever taken by Mkapa to bring the most corrupt senior officials to justice. Mkapa had more success improving the governance of Tanzania' largest city, Dar es Salaam, following his dissolution of the highly corrupt and inefficient city council.

With Nyerere's death in 1999, Mkapa was free to set Tanzania's policy direction, and he did make some strides in measures against midlevel corruption. He achieved his most notable success however not as a transformational leader championing the cause of government integrity, but as a transactional manager addressing economic reforms. Mkapa's presidency resulted in improved fiscal performance, placing Tanzania among the fastest-growing economies in the Africa. However, his larger political goal, as stated in the National Development Vision, of achieving a middle-income status by 2025 was the stuff of vague dreams and wishful thinking, not inspirational vision.

The model of Tanzania's political leadership may be distinguished among East African countries by its smooth succession from one administration to the next. President Mwinyi's peaceful transfer of power to Mkapa was replayed again, as Mwinyi gracefully transferred power to Tanzania's new president, Jakaya Mrisho Kikwete, in late December 2005. Kikwete is an accomplished bureaucrat, having served as Mkapa's foreign minister since 1995. His performance to date combines the attributes of both a transactional and a transformative leader, and he unashamedly reflects his previous close bond with Julius Nyerere in his policies and views. As his biography makes clear, Kikwete is a natural leader. While a young man, he served as president of student government at the University of Dar es Salaam, and later in life, he reached senior officer rank in the Tanzanian army. His political climb elevated him to membership in the national executive committee of the ruling party, Chama Cha Mapinduzi (CCM). He subsequently served as a member of parliament (Bagamoyo district), and, at age 44, he became the youngest finance minister in Tanzanian history. To date, Kikwete has already been more effective than any of his predecessors in fighting corruption and supporting a significant upgrading of education throughout the country—including a dramatic expansion of 1,500 new secondary schools. He is active in advocating for public service reform and demonstrated his commitment to the new national HIV/AIDS testing program by being the first person to be tested.

EVALUATING LEADERSHIP—VIRTUES OR VALUES?

Early in April of 2006, two Ugandan colleagues and I were invited to Oxford, England, to the unusual (for Oxford) brick campus of Keble College, to participate in an event with the immodest name of the World Ethics Forum. Sponsored by the International Institute for Public Ethics, the World Bank's then nascent (and, due to the lack of a political champion of stature within the Bank, now largely moribund) Global Integrity Alliance, the U.S. Agency for International Development, Australian Aid, and British aid (DFID), this well-attended and energized international convocation left me with the impression that the ethical leadership agenda was moving into center stage among development theorists, practitioners, and policy experts. Even though the institutional offspring of the conference—the Global Integrity Alliance—ultimately faltered long after the Forum, the vibrant dialogue of that conference and several similar initiatives[10] does signify to me that people are beginning to differentiate *leadership* from *management*. They are casting leadership in the context of the vision-driven development of the human spirit and the deepening of public morality. Managers do things right, while leaders do the right thing, to borrow from Safty's succinct classification (Safty, 2003).

As I previously described, one of the most notable features of authentic transformative leaders is that such leaders are self-aware, autonomous moral agents, cognizant of their moral choices and intentions, and of their accountability for the consequences of such choices. This moral core to transformative leadership raises in me an immediate concern, as I wonder what values and virtues are involved. To what extent are such values universal or relative? How does such leadership address the tension that exists between conflicting universal and relative values? And what role does virtue play in this mix?

To understand better the leader's motivation to do the right thing, his or her ability to resolve moral conflicts between competing values, and to unpack the many moral attributes of leadership, the analytical lens of virtue ethics may offer valuable insights. The theoretical challenge that virtue ethics confronts in this context is to create plausible linkages and integration within the concept of the virtuous character between moral values and moral behavior, between principles and character, between moral awareness and the motivation to behave in a morally admirable (or at least morally permissible) way, and between self-interest and altruism.

For me, the effectiveness of leadership is linked directly to these values and virtues questions. Leaders are challenged to find ways to bridge between competing interests, to craft a persuasive and credible common ground where competing interests find their greatest convergence and harmony. If leaders are to be judged by their virtuous character, an assessment is needed of their ability to provide consistent and reliable moral guidance, to inspire moral growth in followers, to uphold and internalize core moral values, and to shape public morality.

Perhaps the most significant role that virtue plays in the ethics of leadership is the concept that the virtuous person doesn't merely subscribe to ethical principles and moral values or apply such values to ethical decision making. Instead, the virtuous leader internalizes and embodies these values within his or her character. The life of virtue is a disciplined, reflective, and diligent life, molding one's character on the basis of carefully considered values, life experiences, and access to a wide variety of moral resources. Virtuous leadership springs from this internalized moral core, whereas simple moral leadership is less deeply grounded and perhaps more intellectually—even strategically—situated.

Virtuous character in leaders is subject to consistent public scrutiny, but there are no empirical measures appropriate to establish a so-called virtue quotient. Qualitatively, however, people tend to know (and respect) virtue when they see it. Moral leaders traditionally would sacrifice almost anything to protect their virtue; at the first sign of public doubt regarding their virtue, they would resign so that the challenge to this prerequisite qualification for any office of public trust could be examined without impediment and all doubt removed.

Virtuous leaders also project a simple but compelling message, which is an inspiration to many followers: *virtue is its own reward.* There is clarity as to what motivates a virtuous leader to assume a position of leadership; such a leader is not seeking external or material advantage but instead is answering an internal calling. This ethos may best be illustrated by an ancient source:

For Confucius, the moral sage (*shengren*) is the key person in bringing about personal righteousness and social justice. A superior person (*jyundz*) is a moral person, who walks the moral way and attempts to practice virtue through self-cultivation. Both the sage and the superior person live under the restraint of virtue and aim to transform society accordingly. (Bass & Steidlmeier, 1998)

From the Confucian point of view, transformative leadership is a matter of virtue more than value, of modeling an internalization of ethics and virtues. The consistency and pattern of behavior of such a leader over time speaks to his virtue more than his words, in stark comparison to the modern moral flip-flop style of leadership. While still distasteful to many, it is now commonplace for leaders to adopt politically strategic positions (or to rely on advisors to spin their positions to this end), offering expedient moral justifications or no moral justifications at all for their decisions.

The image of the virtuous leader as a source of inspiration and guidance is appealing, yet many people will criticize such a view as remarkably naive. The forces of self-interest, materialism, and the lust for power are all too evident. What chance does the model of a virtuous leader's life and guidance have to constrain capitalistic values that so persuasively promote greed and self-interest?

History answers this objection best. Authentic transformational leadership, founded upon leaders generally regarded as virtuous, can achieve radical results, overturn the status quo, and advance a new way of thinking—perhaps even a new sense of public morality. While the definition of what constitutes virtue has varied (often considerably) over historical time, leaders beginning as far back as Moses, Ramses II, Alexander the Great, and Martin Luther, as well as more modern examples such as Charles Grey, James

Madison, Franklin D. Roosevelt, Mahatma Gandhi, Martin Luther King Jr., Nelson Mandela, and arguably even Mao Tse-Tung, together provide solid evidence that "what is" doesn't necessarily preclude achieving "what ought to be." The key to the validity of the moral transformational leader's challenge to the immoral status quo is that the virtue must be authentic. The force needed for radical positive change sufficient to overcome vested interests in the status quo is the force of character, not intellectual argument. If the virtue of the character that drives this force is found to be wanting, superficial, or fraudulent, the force quickly dissipates as trust is shattered. As Bass noted, "The trust so necessary for authentic transformational leadership is lost when leaders are caught in lies, when the fantasies fail to materialize, or when hypocrisies and inconsistencies are exposed" (Bass & Avolio, 1990).

If we come to regard the virtuous character of leadership as a desirable social objective, worthy of nurture, what can be done to measure and promote virtuous leadership? Perhaps the cultivation of character may present a worthy avenue of investment of public resources. While Western liberal thought frowns on such notions as character education in public schools, fearing that to pursue such an agenda would threaten individual freedoms to define value preferences, I wonder if it may be time to revisit that objection (see also chapter 2). The state may have an overriding interest in articulating a range of virtues that are worthy of cultivation and in finding effective ways to accomplish this.

A PEOPLE-DRIVEN IDEAL OF VIRTUOUS LEADERSHIP

Adel Safty makes an important distinction, relevant not only to Uganda but universally, between a ruler and a leader. Leaders, after all, can be immoral yet still highly effective in pursuing a vision and motivating their followers—one need not think any farther than Idi Amin, Saddam Hussein, or Adolf Hitler. Safty's distinction is hardly without precedent, however. James MacGregor Burns in 1978 argued for a *Leadership* with a capital *L* by asserting that leadership that is amoral is not leadership at all, neither transformational nor transactional. Burns held that "naked power wielding coercive" dictators are rulers with no moral purpose, and should not be classified as leaders (Boje, 2000).

Safty, like Burns, believes that an authentic leader is distinguished as someone with a higher moral purpose, while a ruler lacks this quality. A ruler is someone who exerts his will through force, fear, intimidation, exploitation, or deceitful manipulation.

From the dawn of history, leadership of all humanity has been either the call of the prophets, or the exclusive purpose of empires. The former relied mainly on moral authority, the latter principally on sheer physical force. One is more evocative of norms and principles and thus is closer to our conception of leadership, while the other stresses control and subjugation, akin to our view of rule. (Safty, 2003)

My brief historical overview of leadership in East Africa would indicate far more of the *empire* than the *prophet*, the *ruler* instead of the *leader*. Moral authority and the ideal of the virtuous leader is not often associated with the presidents of Uganda and Kenya, and only partially with the presidents of Tanzania. With the exception of Tanzania, East Africa has had a serious deficit in moral leadership, and there appears very little to be done about it at the top, given the prevailing atmosphere of pessimism and loss of popular legitimacy in the institutions of governance in both Kenya and Uganda.

Is it really as bad as all this? Ask many Ugandans, who watched as their 2006 presidential election was stolen yet again, in which democracy again became the victim of widespread manipulation, harassment, and rigging. Ask the Kenyans—those still alive after the turbulence and violence of early 2008—as their election, too, was stolen by a president who placed his longevity in power over the lives and welfare of his people. His opponent, Raila Odinga, hardly comported himself with civic virtue or any superior traits of compassion for the victims of his protracted struggle with incumbent Mwai Kibaki. Even the peace settlement that stopped the violence largely patches over wide cracks instead of making the genuine repairs to Kenya's torn civic fabric. Kenyans or Ugandans who were among the losing opposition side (despite their almost certain actual majorities) are likely to be cynical and despondent.

Given these all too recent and profoundly disappointing outcomes, is there an alternative path to the flowering of public morality and moral—even virtuous—leadership? Perhaps there are several ways. Perhaps thinking from the top down is counterproductive and bound to lead to disillusionment. It may even be time to change the rules of the game, so that an alternative set of differently oriented, differently qualified (and almost certainly younger) persons stand a chance of assuming leadership.

Safty has mused about these alternative paths to leadership, which he terms "people driven moral leadership," (Safty, 2003) and he derives considerable satisfaction and moral comfort from the wave of pro-democracy movements, people-led, that swept through Central and Eastern Europe. He draws attention to the catalytic role of civil society in raising both moral awareness and moral expectations among the general populace. Safty's conviction is that

people are rising to the challenges of leadership, doing the right thing, consolidating common values, and promoting human development. Leadership is no longer the monopoly of corporate chiefs, army commanders, or politicians. Leadership has become a people's business. Leadership, in effect, is being democratised. (Safty, 2003)

How can people-driven moral leadership be organized? Civil society has a major role to play in this context, and already there are some organized initiatives that have begun, which may create a pattern for many similar initiatives to follow. The African Leadership Capacity Development Project (ALCD), for example, is a program intended to provide capacity development projects entailing education, training, information, and network-based support to young Africans from diverse backgrounds who demonstrate strong leadership potential. This program's mission is directly focused on enabling young people to grow into transformational leadership roles, addressing issues of leadership vision, ethics, knowledge, sophistication, resourcefulness, creativity, and access to global resources. The well-known advocacy institution Freedom House is also beginning a similar African Leadership Initiative in the continent, which I have been actively involved in.

A Global African Professionals/Experts/Scholars/Intellectuals Network has also recently been established, with one of its several objectives being to facilitate discussion and the dissemination of ideas about leadership and governance (among other topics). It is intended to nurture and provide intellectual support and mentoring to emerging leaders of Africa, to assist in the establishment of African Leadership Information Centres in African countries, and to hold annual international African Leadership and Progress Conferences.[11]

There is also the recently formed (but entirely virtual) African Leadership Institute (AfLI), under the patronage of Archbishop Tutu, which is focused on identifying Africa's future leaders and offering them a platform for leadership learning and application. AfLI's goal is to create and support a network of future leaders across Africa.[12]

African universities are also initiating courses on leadership, which—like Makerere University's master's degree program in leadership—include comprehensive exposure to the moral and transformational dimensions of leadership. Africa's professionals are also getting involved; the Association of Professional Societies of East Africa (APSEA) has made significant progress in training their professionals to be ethical leaders within their fields of expertise. It has been my pleasure and privilege to assist them in this initiative, which continues.

These are small beginnings to the solution of a monumental leadership challenge, but they are well-conceived, earnest small beginnings.

A QUEST FOR VIRTUOUS LEADERS?

The history of Uganda's political leadership is replete with moral failure and lack of moral virtue, and recent events in Kenya are anything but encouraging in this context. Nearly all of East Africa's prominent past or current political leaders are or have been authoritarian, with a questionable allegiance to the principles of democracy and a disdain for their follower's aspirations to be treated as dignified human beings. Authoritarian leaders in East Africa play transactional patrimonial politics, dispensing rewards and punishments to self-interested followers and placing longevity in power as the ultimate agenda. Evidence of leadership that is authentic in its social consciousness and committed to the cultivation of positive moral values is largely absent at the most senior echelons of power. Transformational leadership patterns are even more rare.

Transformative leadership, whether grounded in the virtuous leader concept or, perhaps less ambitiously, in the model of the leader attentive to moral
values, is not without its critics. As noted by Steidlmeier and others, there are
those who see transformative leadership as an exercise in the manipulation of
sentiment and emotions instead of an appeal to reason. Boje argues that transformational leadership promises to be emancipatory but does little to deliver
marginalized peoples from command-and-control governance. Other critics
worry that the force of personality of such leadership can distort democratic
deliberations and override necessary checks and balances. The response to
such criticisms, which I share, is that the power of inspirational and morally centered leaders to overcome narrow self-interest, greed, and exploitation rests with the identification and harnessing of the power of shared moral
values, a common purpose, and a clear commitment to the welfare of all. In
Bass and Steidlmeier's words:

Truly transformational leaders, who engage in the moral uplifting of their followers,
who move them to share in the mutually rewarding visions of success, who enable and
empower them to convert the visions into realities, should be applauded, not chastised.
(Bass & Steidlmeier, 1998)

The quest for morally centered leaders or—more ambitiously perhaps—for
virtuous leaders is unlikely to bear fruit in the current distorted democratic
processes in Uganda or Kenya, being systems that have evolved to create and
sustain transactional top leaders of questionable virtue and thin commitment
to the priority of welfare and development of the populace. If transformational leaders are to be identified, nurtured, and succeed in the rise to power
and influence throughout East Africa, both the demand and supply sides of
the equation require attention. Public morality, and the expectations that the
public holds for ethical leadership, must be freed from cynicism, pessimism,
and lethargy. Through expanded opportunities for structured dialogue on
the ethics of leadership, and through related measures to raise moral awareness, a new popular consensus on the need and urgency for ethical—even
virtuous—leadership may be stimulated. Simultaneously, the ethically oriented middle-level leadership, and East Africa's youth generally, should be
challenged by a well-articulated and widely disseminated ideal of the virtuous
transformational leader. Moral exemplars already exist in East Africa, but to
be influential to the shaping of public morality, they need to be identified,
publicized, and celebrated.

Finally, urgent attention must continue to be placed on Kenya and Uganda's
institutions of governance, so that moral awareness can be strengthened, ethics training made relevant, and integrity fostered.

Advocating for the return to the ancient ideal of the virtuous leader or
at least supporting aspirations for a new form of moral leadership in Kenya
or Uganda is intentionally bold. The status quo of immoral rule by self-
interested, callous leaders does not go away by thinking timidly. A culture

of leadership that allows poverty, violent conflict, underdevelopment, and bad governance to continue in these two countries for so long must be challenged and changed. New transformational leaders are called for who are able to craft inclusive visions for a different and better direction, motivated by genuine care for their fellow citizens and empowered with the ability to inspire, uplift, and lead their followers—not rule, but lead, perhaps even lead with virtue.

CHAPTER 4

Participation

There was tension in the room. More than 250 people had gathered in the hall at the South African coastal town of Umhlanga Rocks to participate in the discussions about the future development plans for what was then known as the North Local Council of Durban. Logie Naidoo, the chairman of the Council's Executive Committee, looked about nervously. The mayor looked directly at me, as if to question what might be causing the anticipation; the agenda certainly wasn't that contentious. All that my team of town and regional planners and I were there to do on behalf of the Council was to present and solicit feedback on the draft spatial development plans that we had formulated based on the input we received from the previous participatory gathering, which had proceeded without incident. Professor Dan Smit was now seated and ready to commence in his role as chairman of the workshop, but no sooner had he risen and completed his formal welcome in his deeply sonorous voice than all eyes turned to one participant who had also risen to his feet. The chairman called him to order, but he was determined to have his say. Naidoo whispered to me that this particular fellow was a known troublemaker with his own political agenda and a long list of grievances, and the journalists present were already scribbling down notes and observing the drama unfolding. Was the workshop about to be hijacked?

Participatory workshops of this kind often fall prey to grandstanding or hijacking; the public spotlight is simply too tempting for persons seeking a ready-made public forum. In this case, Smit firmly but politely asked the speaker to desist in his ad hoc oratory but thanked the speaker for his advocacy. Smit invited the speaker to submit in writing to him, the chairman, a full list of grievances within the course of the day, so that it could be taken into consideration by the members of the public assembled there and by the local

Council officials. The speaker was clearly unprepared for such a gracious and nonconfrontational invitation and quietly assented; the tension in the room immediately dissipated, and the workshop carried on.

Later in the morning, as provided for in the agenda for the day, a representative of the largest landowner in the area governed by the Council rose to make his presentation. Tongaat-Hulett is a major South African agri-processing business, active in sugar cane production and processing, land management, and property development. Their sugar cane fields and processing factories spread throughout the North Local Council and well beyond, but in recent years, they were converting many of their agricultural holdings in the North Local Council into lucrative housing developments. Tongaat-Hulett had its own in-house land-use planning department, and the head of that department now spoke. His maps, diagrams, schematics, and tables were colorful, impressive, and authoritative, and his persuasiveness as a public speaker was remarkable. For the average citizens gathered at this workshop, this polished presentation created a buzz. Of course, that is what it was intended to do. Tongaat-Hulett had its own agenda, and they had a strong interest in seeing that their land-use priorities became an integral part in the North Local Council's official plan.

In both cases, the public participatory process at this planning workshop was being subjected to deformation. In the first case, someone sought to use the forum to pursue a separate set of goals, hoping to rally public support, even though his objectives were quite distinct from what the workshop had convened to accomplish. In the second case, the presenter was working from the inside—on the agenda—but with such rhetorical panache that he overshadowed the other contributions from members of the general public, from the Council, and—if truth be known—even from us. We had been upstaged, and Tongaat-Hulett was now positioned to have a disproportionate influence in shaping a consensus on what was in the best interest of the North Local Council. That is, after all, what these participatory development planning events are intended to accomplish; through a deliberative process the participants are supposed to articulate what constitutes the common good.

THE COMMON GOOD

In its most general sense, the common good may be said to consist of the policies and actions that best serve to promote the essential components of human well-being or flourishing for all. Identifying the *common good*, or its equivalent phrase, the *public interest*, is a controversial issue because of differing conceptions of human well-being or flourishing. In utilitarian thinking, the common good is the best net score of aggregated individual interests in the community—a concept that obviously sacrifices some people's interests to that of others. Others contend that the common good can be articulated only roughly and is often subject to moral disagreements. According to this view, it is only through a more painstaking, time-consuming deliberative democratic process of reasoning together that the common good can be agreed upon and mutually acceptable decisions can be arrived at with legitimacy (Gutmann & Thompson, 1996). Amy Gutmann and Dennis Thompson describe a process in which people with conflicting views of what constitutes the common interest decide to reason reciprocally, intentionally recognizing the moral worth of the opposing person, even if they consider his or her position not to reflect the common good. It is an attractive ideal, but based on years of field experience in participation, it is very hard to imagine applying this outside a very small group in a noncontroversial context.

People do not naturally sacrifice their self-interest. In serving the public good, however, such a sacrifice is often called for. Richard Flathman observed that a moral demand is placed upon members of a society to regard themselves as morally obligated (but not physically coerced) to obey particular commands and to conform to particular policies that they may regard as contrary to their self-interests. To accommodate this moral demand, a moral justification needs to be provided to justify this sacrifice of perceived self-interest; appealing to the weight of majority interests alone will not create the consensus that will make the resulting agreement sustainable. Number—that is, force—is not a criterion of right (Flathman, 1966).

PARTICIPATION AND INCLUSION

There are many kinds and intensities of participation, ranging from Gutmann and Thompson's deliberative democracy ideal to routine voting, from open and advisory public hearings to visioning workshops. Each has its benefits and limitations. The example cited above, from the North Local Council in Durban, South Africa, was a fairly modest attempt. It would rank no higher than Consultation on the well-established Ladder of Citizen Participation devised many years ago by Sherry Arnstein, well below the more robust levels of Partnership, Delegated Power, or—the apex—Citizen Control.[1] All that the North Local Council officials were offering was to listen to the public; there was no guaranty that the public's expressed priorities would prevail over the Council's wishes.

I argue for a model of *facilitated deliberative participation*, less idealized than Gutmann and Thompson's ideal version, but well above Consultation on the Arnstein ladder. I agree that a truly deliberative, participatory process is important to the achievement of sustainable development, but I have little faith that most gatherings can achieve such a mature standard of participation without guidance and facilitation. A deliberative participatory process either assumes or includes the ideals of human dignity, social justice, human flourishing and well-being, the common good, safety and security, and similar ideals. Deliberative participation also offers a way to specify, weigh, trade-off, and sequence the realization of these ideals. These are complex objectives, involving multiple conflicts between competing moral values and ideals. In my view, it is a rare gathering that can come to a consensus view that entails many sacrifices of perceived self-interest by the various participants—some sacrificing much more than others in most cases—without the benefit of disinterested facilitation by someone expert in this role.

This quest for an effective means—a deliberative participation model—by which some, but not all, stakeholders might be able to improve their chances of achieving agreement on a workable articulation of the common good raises many moral concerns and values. As stakeholders reflect upon and deliberate over the means and ends of development and good governance, they begin to question who ought to decide what *good* development and *good* governance mean, why these concepts are important, and what should be done when they clash with other values. If stakeholders accept rights-based claims, then what should be done when rights-based claims conflict with other popular development goals or good governance standards? How can and should decision makers respond when rights-based claims make demands on scarce resources? How can and should popular participation in governance be balanced with the role of representative democratic institutions of government? How can and should values be weighed one against the other in deciding development priorities, budgetary allocations, or governance standards? How can and should stakeholders be assured that the full range of important development values has been comprehensively addressed within a development planning, budgeting, or governance process? In short, how should stakeholders conceive and make critical decisions regarding the achievement of sustainable, humane, economically viable development; pursue those ends; and find motivation to sustain this effort?

OPPORTUNITIES FOR PARTICIPATION

The questions above require careful attention to moral concerns. When decisions are made in response to these questions, the decision maker's moral legitimacy, credibility, and motivation deserve scrutiny. I argue that this scrutiny should begin by, but not be limited to, assessing the extent to which opportunities for popular participation exist; the degree to which decision makers view themselves as influenced by and accountable to that participatory process; and the fairness, representativeness, and effectiveness of the participatory process itself. Effective participation is an excellent means to morally based decision making, but it is not the only means, and the influence of ethical leadership (discussed in detail in the preceding chapter) is critical to achieving a sustainable consensus.

If all human beings are regarded as equally dignified and valuable, all human beings within a society ought to be empowered to participate in the critical decisions that affect them, decisions that limit or create opportunities and freedoms for each to flourish.[2] Including all people in all aspects of all decision making is not practical, so societies at national and subnational (local) levels have developed various forms of political leadership and representative and delegated decision making. Under this conception, political leaders and elected or appointed representatives act on the presumption of a vested public trust and a clearly articulated leadership vision, to which they are accountable. The delegation of decision-making authority to political leaders is not by necessity absolute; where possible and appropriate, opportunities ought to exist to allow all citizens and residents of any given society or group to be well informed about the issues and to participate in identifying priorities, strategies, and desirable actions.

In actual development programs and projects, genuine participatory processes are still more the exception than the rule. Donors lack the funds and time to support these processes, and political leadership at all levels of governance in developing countries is nearly always top down or even autocratic, neither accountable to nor inclusive of the residents. Some—donors and leaders alike—try to justify top-down leadership as a way to avoid the difficulties and expense in structuring and sustaining a deliberative participatory process sufficiently robust to regularly register, discuss, and reason through the various concerns, aspirations, claims, and demands of residents and stakeholders. These difficulties may be only self-serving excuses, but equitable, inclusive, and—certainly—*deliberative* participation is hard to accomplish and often expensive. The problems begin with the stakeholder identification process, in which usually the elected and/or appointed decision makers in a government invite a range of participants to join in the formulation of specific development priorities, policies, and actions or to advise on good governance standards. It is seldom possible to select a representative body of stakeholders who reflect a reasonable approximation of the diverse interests, power structures, and demographic and social characteristics (age, gender, ethnicity, religion, etc.) of the area under review. If stakeholder selection can be accomplished to the general satisfaction of all, without the exclusion of any one group, further difficulties ensue. The participatory process must be time sensitive but ought not to be rushed. Participants ought to have the opportunity to be informed on the issues, to be heard by all, to engage in a give-and-take of reason giving and reason assessing, and to have conflicts resolved in terms of outcomes to which all can give their consent. Ideally, the participatory agenda will be rich enough so that participants are not simply being polled, but instead have an opportunity to engage in a deliberative process in which all stakeholders are able to put forward their own arguments and ideas, seek common ground, demand reasons, and record disagreement. In some cases, participants may need training to learn necessary public-speaking skills and/or to find assistance from trusted, articulate advocates.

Credibility demands a participatory process that has a procedural rationale, justified in language that the average stakeholder will easily understand. In some cases, such as in more radical models of participation, outsiders and experts are intentionally excluded. In other situations, particularly where participation addresses complex technical or procedural issues, the stakeholders as well as the experts shape the final process. This participation rationale, the rules and objectives of the participatory game, should persuade stakeholders that a framework is in place through which participants (stakeholders) will be respectfully encouraged to reflect upon, evaluate, and express their considered views and reasons for such views on a wide list of development issues—and that includes assurances that these views will influence decision making. It may be necessary in such a process to begin by restating some of the values and principles that the larger society (the nation) has already formally agreed upon or accepted as universal—in constitutions, treaties, laws, or public policies. Moral values and principles that are relative to that particular group of stakeholders may need to be articulated openly, perhaps for the first time in a public forum.

In terms of facilitation, careful structuring of the participatory process should mean ensuring that principles of fairness and a commonly agreed upon agenda are adhered to, while measures must be in place so that the participation is not manipulated toward predetermined outcomes. Participants should be exposed to and consider different views of means and ends within the larger context of a holistic view of human well-being, human development, and good governance. Those participating will first need to agree on *process*—how best to resolve disagreements and accommodate dissent. Facilitators will also need to keep the process responsive to the time allocated to it.

Very few governments in developed countries, and exceptionally few in developing countries, have engaged in a participatory process leading to the outcome of a comprehensive development strategy or the articulation of good governance standards. There have been well-known examples where cities have engaged in participatory budgeting processes, such as in Porto Alegre, Brazil,[3] which ensure that funding aligns with popularly supported development goals. At the level of formulating integrated, multisectoral, dynamic development plans, policies, and strategies, or improving the quality of governance, very few people have experienced this sort of participation at this level of intensity.

From the base of global experience that we do have, we know that robust participatory processes are time consuming and expensive in the short term, although the counterargument is that spending more time now will create sustainable solutions that ultimately save time and money. That's tough to establish with empirical precision, but few who have experienced them would doubt that participatory processes do give rise to conflicts and expose existing social divisions and—unless very well executed—can easily become politically disruptive, even volatile. To be effective, a participatory process must expect to confront some significant roadblocks and be prepared to resolve these. The chief roadblock may be within the government department or authority that is the official host of the process; those in power have a very strong interest in retaining power and have often achieved their power through exploiting tribal, ethnic, gender, or generational differences. To seek unity across such social cleavages may deprive them of one of their most effective means of imposing their will, and they can be expected to resist efforts at identifying common ground. At a less explicit level, those in positions of power or those enjoying advantages of wealth may cling to a belief that they are so favored due to some moral excellence on their part; they are better than the poor and powerless. So when a deliberative participatory process begins by stressing the equal moral worth of all participants, there may well be unspoken resistance or cynicism—the bank president will often not willingly sit down to deliberate with the trash collector. Another important roadblock, alluded to at the beginning of the chapter, is that some participants are polished performers in a public forum, with excellent access to data and sophisticated advocacy experience. They have advanced education, impressive oratorical skills, and enormous self-confidence. Many others—most often the poor—do not have these capabilities. In many cases, they may never have spoken in a public forum before, and their access to essential information may be highly constrained. In such circumstances, unless the participatory process allocates funds to train such participants in effective deliberative and advocacy skills, or assists them in finding effective advocates for their priorities, their voice will remain a hushed and faltering one.

For all of these reasons, outside experts are sometimes involved to help facilitate the participatory process, advise on avoiding the roadblocks, or train participants to improve their voice. There are no effective, proven, off-the-shelf models of participation for development strategy formulation that such experts apply—there is no way to *ensure* that the process remains constructive in all situations. Threats to success abound. For example, some special-interest groups may perceive some direct benefit by making sure that the larger participatory process fails, and if they are sufficiently powerful, there will be no way for even the best facilitator to prevent the failure of the process. Facilitators are not leaders; if there is a vacuum of genuine leadership in a participatory process, participants may perceive deliberation as only empty political rhetoric. In such cases of weak or absent leadership, credible assurances will be lacking that the outcomes of the process will actually guide policy and direct implementation.

To counter such threats, those entrusted as leaders with public resources and decision-making authority will need to demonstrate their leadership, accountability, and responsiveness within and through the participatory process. The expertise of trained facilitators may be required, but not in lieu of this leadership.

COMPLICATING AN ALREADY COMPLEX PROCESS?

Given the many procedural and logistical difficulties of participation, won't the introduction of moral concerns—social justice, the common good, human dignity, human rights and freedoms, civic virtue, and caring—only make the entire process more unwieldy and therefore less likely to positively influence public policy, governance, and development planning?

This is a legitimate concern. Many people consider moral issues to be largely arbitrary and subjective in nature, changing in scope and intensity depending on which individuals are participating (or not) in any particular public deliberative forum. The forum itself may be problematic; the choice of agenda, chairperson, and/or social and cultural constraints may greatly constrain the quality, honesty, depth, and subject matter covered. In addition, seeking common ground on moral concerns risks upsetting the status quo. Those in power may never have been called upon to justify the moral source of their authority and may shrink from the moral obligations implicit (but seldom clearly articulated) in public service. Once the moral dimension is introduced to participatory processes, those who are most affluent may also become vulnerable to moral challenges by those less affluent to justify why the gap between rich and poor should exist at all, or why it should widen even further in pursuit of short-term "development" goals. Cities or towns may be morally emboldened to demand greater autonomy from the central government. In short, asking the *ought* and *why* questions may unsettle many people who would otherwise be quite complaisant with their status.

In addition to the challenges to the status quo, the quality of a moral dialogue attempted on substantive issues does depend upon the availability of certain moral attributes: tolerance, reflection, mutual respect, and a deliberative ethos representative of the diversity of stakeholder interests and concerns. These and similar attributes are moral qualities and sensibilities that individual participants ought to bring to the process or be able to acquire through it. Situations may exist, however, where such virtues, attributes, and qualities are in scarce supply, and the quality of the moral dialogue would consequently deteriorate.

In addition to these concerns, many people consider moral values and systems to be largely unreliable in policymaking; many values are discounted because they are seen to be relevant only to a particular culture, time, and context or are mistrusted as imposed by outsiders in the name, for example, of moral universalism,[4] skeptical realism,[5] or cosmopolitanism.[6] On the other hand, some values are questioned as being too focused on the interests, concerns, and perceptions of a particular community or society, rejecting claims of a broader moral obligation or accountability.

Finally, moral values, along with many qualitative factors in development, are extremely difficult to measure, monitor, and evaluate, so the impact of policies intended to respond to such concerns are hard to gauge. For this reason alone, many public-policy makers avoid reliance on hard-to-measure moral justifications for allocation of scarce public resources.

A MORAL RESPONSE

These five objections apply to participatory processes specifically, but also to morally based approaches to development and governance more generally. If I leave them unanswered, they will undercut my fundamental argument of the importance of moral appraisal in the definition, formulation, and implementation of development means and ends, and in the shaping of good governance. I therefore offer the following brief responses to each concern described above.

The first objection is the claim that moral issues are largely arbitrary and subjective in nature, and that attending to moral issues in a participatory process is fraught with procedural difficulties. In practice, this objection has merit. Moral issues, if raised at all in participatory workshops, are seldom addressed explicitly in a rigorous, unrushed manner through deliberations, reasoned justifications (and challenges to these justifications), and dialogue addressed at reducing disagreements or building consensus. Common applications of participatory practice largely ignore moral issues or at best channel moral concerns into narrow outlets such as vision statements. Morality is not, however, arbitrary, as the systematic and critical study of moral beliefs, values, and concerns—*ethics*—makes abundantly clear. In ethics, our values and beliefs are organized into various (and, to some extent, competing) systems, each of which more or less exhibits coherence internally and matches our considered judgments and deeply felt beliefs. In this way, individual moral concerns are given context, so that they can be argued from a systematic, well-reasoned set of relationships based on principles that in turn can be argued and justified. Ultimately, the systems of ethics that we have evolved are able to offer potent insights and guidance in complicated situations.

It isn't practical or appropriate, however, to use the limited time and resources of a participatory workshop on development to formulate and justify a complete ethical theory (much less compare it to other contending theories, from first principles). Instead, various process tools can be derived from several well-established theories within the field of *development ethics*. These so-called tool-based approaches, which is just a practitioner's way of describing the application of various moral theories to diagnose, analyze, and offer guidance, are available to be applied—with the guidance of trained facilitators—in a time-constrained participatory process without preliminary philosophical justifications, using language accessible to the diverse range of stakeholders engaged.

The second objection is the claim that attending to moral concerns risks upsetting the status quo by challenging the existing economic and power relationships within any given society. This claim is accepted and often serves as a sufficient (but not necessarily publicly stated) reason for politically insecure elected or appointed leaders to avoid engaging or funding a participatory approach to development or governance. Yet whether through participatory processes or by recourse to other means such as the courts or the ballot box, challenging the status quo is often an essential component of the moral approach to development and good governance. The existence of widespread poverty, corruption, injustice, the skewed distribution of scarce resources, and the lack of universal respect for human dignity demand a challenge. The moral approach offers some fresh insights into the means and ends of changing the status quo in ways which lead to more just, compassionate, and decent societies, and to the protection of the status quo when it is judged to be reasonably just. The changes demanded by moral assessment need not be immediately radical or revolutionary—for example, progressive positive change toward sustainable development through the assertion of human rights–based claims, fulfilled over time, may be sufficient. The fulfillment of such claims will, however, *ultimately* entail radical changes to the status quo.

The third objection is the concern that moral issues must be addressed and deliberated by participants who exhibit moral virtues, and that such participants may be few in number. If this claim were accepted, it would be difficult to imagine any society's moral progress over time. The leadership of morally virtuous persons may well inspire and motivate others toward being receptive to the deliberation of moral issues, but that leadership is not a necessary condition. The commitment of social, political, or religious institutions (and, by treaty provisions, even nations) to moral principles goes some distance in bringing the moral approach to the participatory process. If the participants are able to accept the credibility of an ethical framework, such as a human-rights approach, and a way can be found to apply this (such as through a derived set of participatory process tools, applied with the help of expert facilitators) to the development and good governance agenda under discussion, then the requirement for a wise and virtuous person to preside over the proceedings no longer pertains.

The fourth objection is that asserting values in public policy, whether within a participatory forum or through other operations of governance, is inappropriate because values vary in their moral justifications, from the universal to the relative. This dichotomy between the universal and the relative is a venerable old chestnut of philosophical debate, and a great deal is written and argued in the literature on this subject. I favor an approach that accepts certain values as universal and fundamental to human nature, while also accepting that the local culture, tradition, and context ought significantly to influence and shape the implementation of development initiatives responsive to these universal values. As will be seen in chapter 9, however, I do have some deep concerns about relativistic, communitarian moral values when these are used to justify intolerance and the exclusion, marginalization, or persecution of minorities.

Finally, the fifth objection to morally based approaches to development is that the qualitative dimensions of moral values makes them impractical in the public-policy context. This is a superficial argument. Measuring moral performance may be more difficult than monitoring amoral criteria, the latter being accomplished through gathering empirical data and identifying trends. But empirical data can say a great deal about the changes in achieving morally desirable goals, and the presentation of such data in participatory workshops can be informative. For example, trends in the birth weight of babies is a good proxy for measuring the changes and shortcomings in the quality of life of people, and the need for better nutrition and health care. An extensive amount of work is being done around the world to identify appropriate empirical indicators that measure quality of life. The degree to which national laws reflect internationally recognized human-rights principles is also measurable. Qualitative factors in the experience of poverty, the enjoyment of basic freedoms and opportunities, and the prevalence of respect for human dignity are all subject to meaningful evaluation through a variety of techniques, from focus groups to surveys. The claim that moral issues should not influence public policy or be raised in participatory workshops because they are troublesome to monitor and evaluate speaks more of a failure of political will or methodology than of a basic fault inherent in ethics. I pursue this issue in more detail in chapter 9, which focuses on the concept and measurement of ethical performance.

WHY BOTHER?

Given the complexity, expense, length, and many hazards of public participation, why would this process be adopted in any instance? Elected officials of governments, particularly in representative democracies, can make the case that they are the legitimate, elected representatives of their constituents. They may feel sidelined or intimidated by a parallel process of registering the will and priorities of the citizenry, and such officials will probably have many competing demands on the significant funding needed for a thorough participatory process.

In many cases, elected officials—in both developing and more developed countries—will resist public participation. In societies where elites exist as a distinct class, which generally includes elected officials, the poor may see very little responsiveness from their elected representatives. Many of the poor, such as the residents of sprawling slums in cities in developing countries, will have no vote and hence no elected representative to advocate for them. When the gap between the poor and the elites is wide, or where large numbers of poor are disenfranchised, it becomes the mission of civil-society organizations to advocate for political and social change. Civil society typically will drive any process to institutionalize public participatory processes for certain functions of governance, such as integrated development plans for municipalities or budgeting processes for local governments. To the extent that civil society is powerful and vocal, the elected representatives may feel inexorable pressure to allow the poor to have their say.

The motivations of civil-society activists are generally virtuous, in the civic sense. Many nongovernmental organizations (NGOs) and community-based organizations (CBOs) exist with a strong sense of mission, a desire to make a positive difference, and a vision that is guided by care and concern for the plight of the poor or the marginalized. Some are motivated by human-rights thinking, challenging the elites to satisfy claims for basic human rights. Others may be motivated by religious values or social-justice concepts.

Not all civil-society organizations are champions of the poor, however. Some exist as a platform to promote the personal agenda of a charismatic (and occasionally egotistical) founder or to pursue a narrow or arcane agenda with little popular support. Others claim a seat at the policy table on the basis of representing a constituency that in fact doesn't exist. Others may be special-interest groups linked to fringe political movements, or tied to specific ethnic group or gender interests, and so have little interest in broader issues of good governance or development. The legitimacy of civil-society organizations is rightly subject to scrutiny when organizing participatory processes. Yet even with its flaws, civil society in many developing countries is a powerful force, and elected officials ignore it at their peril. In some cases, elected officials will embrace participatory processes, seeing this process as an effective way to connect with their constituents, establish a public presence as an effective agent of change, and improve chances for reelection.

Ultimately, the best reason for engaging in participatory processes is the moral argument of agency. All human beings are to be regarded as equally dignified and valuable, and therefore all human beings within a society ought to be empowered to exercise their agency—their ability to help shape the decisions that most affect them and that limit or create opportunities and freedoms for each to flourish.

CHAPTER 5

Corruption and Integrity

There's "a lot of rot" in government in Uganda.

So declared the Hon. Geoffrey Ekanya, chairman of Parliament's Local Government Accounts Committee and a Member for Tororo of Uganda's Parliament. Transparency International's esteemed Corruption Perceptions Index (CPI) supports Hon. Ekanya's assessment. The CPI ranks 180 countries according to a composite of indicators, using a range of 0 (highly corrupt) to 10 (without corruption). Any ranking lower than 5 is indicative of a serious corruption problem, and Uganda—with a worrying CPI of 2.8—is among seven countries sharing 111th place in Transparency International's listing of best to worst cases.[1]

ENTRENCHED AND PERVASIVE CORRUPTION

It's no secret that corruption is pervasive and entrenched in Uganda, where even the key institutions of government lack integrity. The newspapers regularly expose the rot, but knowing that corruption exists and doing something to curb it are two very different things. In Uganda, I quickly learned from my Ugandan colleagues that the public institution charged with enforcing integrity standards and bringing the corrupt to book—the Directorate of Public Prosecutions (DPP)—is itself corrupt. Everyone knows this. Even the Ugandan government officially acknowledges this to be the case, with the startling revelation that the DPP claims the number one spot on the list of the Inspector General of Government's (IGG) top-six blacklisted government institutions or agencies. The DPP is in distinguished shameful company, being followed closely by the Office of the Prime Minister and the Electoral Commission.

Even the Attorney General's Chambers, the chief government legal adviser, shares the dubious distinction of being among Uganda's most corrupt institutions. Corruption has become so much part of the daily reality that most bidders for public works in Uganda offer about 10 percent of total contract value as inducements to win bids. Corruption doesn't stop at the grave; in Uganda even ghosts are paid, with monthly salaries of 1.7 billion shillings a month going out as active duty pay to retired, fired, or dead civil servants.[2]

Why isn't something done? After all, the economic impact is anything but insignificant. In a recent study encompassing just 13 central government institutions or agencies, 26 districts, and 7 municipalities, the losses to the government (and hence to the citizens) of Uganda in various flawed procurements were calculated at nearly US$90 million in the 2004/2005 financial year.[3] Alas, even the IGG has been found to be corrupt in a Transparency International report.

Uganda isn't unique among the corrupt notables. The United Nations estimates that across the continent, African leaders pilfer a whopping US$148 billion each year, fully one-quarter of Africa's entire gross domestic product.[4]

PUBLIC-SECTOR PROCUREMENT

Corruption is an enormously complex phenomenon, with a large and growing literature by social scientists, criminologists and lawyers, economists and public-policy specialists, and ethicists. In this chapter, I limit my scope to public-sector procurement, which is a central piece of the corruption problem in developing countries. Can governments in developing countries manage the public procurement process so that opportunities for corrupt behavior are constrained or even eliminated?

Interest in constraining corruption in public procurement isn't limited to Uganda. There are international conferences throughout the world on this subject, and specialized consulting firms offer services to help governments constrain corruption in procurement processes, both through technology-based applications and rewriting procurement procedures and reforming laws. New monitoring and accountability practices are being tested, and where results look promising, they are being replicated widely. Yet despite these many well-intentioned actors, and many sophisticated and often well-funded initiatives, the public perception is that Uganda and many developing countries are losing the battle against corruption in public procurement.

It is not my purpose to disprove that perception. In fact, it may very well be an accurate assessment. It is an accepted fact of economic life that eager private-sector vendors actively pursue substantial government contracts in any extremely competitive environment. In the course of their normal activities, such vendors engage in a high level of interaction with public officials. The result is that the opportunities and incentives for corrupt behavior are plentiful, and corruption frequently occurs. It would seem to be an inevitable part of the human condition.

A QUESTION OF HUMAN NATURE

I boast no glowing record of governments that I have cleaned up, but I do count myself among the many development practitioners around the globe who have been toiling away over the past two decades in the donor-funded confrontation against corruption. I differ from the majority of these experts, however, in that their anticorruption prescriptions are derived from a certain set of perceptions about human nature—perceptions that underpin neoclassical economics. First, they accept as given that it is human nature to be self-serving and greedy. Second, they are convinced that the desire to acquire more and more wealth and power is the primary driver leading all persons to behave as badly as they do in a social context.

While the sobering picture above of the entrenchment of corruption in Uganda would seem to support their assessment, to my mind this is a profoundly cynical view of human nature. While not without a significant and intuitively self-evident component of truth, it is hardly an adequate measure of all human character or behavior. Yes, any society would fail to recognize the influence of greed and selfishness at its great peril. Yet any society also risks significant social erosion and dysfunction by not expecting people occasionally to behave well—or even not expecting many people (particularly those civil servants and elected officials holding positions in the public trust) *consistently* to behave well, as persons of integrity.

A pervasively negative view of human nature as wholly venal and self-interested clouds our vision and limits our possibilities in structuring our response to corruption. To the extent that each society defines itself by its CPI index and fails to recognize, honor, and support the persons of integrity that exist in every society, the struggle becomes hopeless. Any approach to addressing the corruption problem that only looks at the deficiencies in human nature within the phenomenon of corruption leaves the problem of corruption—and the potential solutions—only half addressed. The other side of the corruption coin is integrity; it is the side of the coin that has lain face-down for too long.

Before pursuing that line of thought, however, it is appropriate to review the current international thinking about corruption in public procurement and its many established practical formulas.

CONVENTIONAL WISDOM

All experts agree that *completely* preventing corruption is a utopian notion; some persons will always be motivated to pursue immoral, illicit, and wholly self-serving agendas at the expense of others. We won't be able to stop all of them, so our proper aim should be to minimize the occurrence of corruption to the greatest extent possible. There are many ways to pursue such an agenda. Government purchasing agents *ought to be* encouraged to develop professionalism in how they describe the requirements of a purchase (specifications), how they evaluate and compare competing bids (assessment criteria), and how they qualify bidders to join in the competition (qualification requirements). The lessons from international practice go further, describing the procedures that *ought to be* followed to deter corruption and improve the quality of procurements. These include reviewing the adequacy of existing procurement laws and regulations, identifying conflicts of interests and other actions that could distort a public procurement, and insisting on strict adherence to well-publicized procedures and rules at each step of an open bidding process. Government officials *ought to be* taught how to recognize corruption schemes and indicators, and how best to identify corruption risk factors.

This list includes a great many *how tos* but also a great many *oughts*. For some reason, most experts in public procurement place less emphasis on the *oughts* and concentrate instead on the *how tos*. Not surprisingly, as an ethicist, I'll try to redress this imbalance—for a fundamental precept of ethics is that *ought* implies *can*. There are things that we *ought* to do, which we *can* indeed accomplish. International anticorruption practice doesn't ignore normative—or moral—factors, however. The approaches most commonly applied to curb and limit corruption involve establishing rules and procedures that are intended to promote the moral principles of transparency, accountability, competition, fairness, and honesty (Meyer, 2000).

This is a sensible list. Public procurement that is accountable to the public, that is based on open competition between qualified vendors, using a process that demonstrates fairness and honesty, would seem to be a recipe for deterring corruption. But even if this approach is grounded in moral values, how do we apply it? Is the identification of rules and procedures—which is common practice—the best way to be consistently moral and ethical, much less to be effective in constraining corruption?

No. Any anticorruption initiative based primarily on rules, procedures, sanctions, and punishments—even if grounded in universal moral values—is unlikely to succeed on its own.

Why? Is there something wrong with, or incomplete about, this short list of principles or an approach based on rules? Before I answer that important question, consider the meaning of each principle.

ANTICORRUPTION PRINCIPLES

Transparency refers to an obligation that procurement rules and proceedings ought to be accessible, open, and clear. Ideally, improving the standards of transparency will encourage bidders to trust the public procurement system and will build the public's confidence in government and the way that government spends public funds. Transparency also has a link to deterrence, as rules and procedures that promote transparency mean that openness increases the risk of getting caught for those who engage in corrupt behavior.

Accountability is the obligation that public officials ought to be held responsible for their decisions and actions. In practice, this takes the form of laws, regulations, and procedures that are intended to direct the behavior and decisions of public officials. The expectation is that government will hold implementers responsible for their conduct and the decisions they make, by means of appropriate disciplinary action when and if needed.

Competition is a contest. It is not on its own a moral principle, although the commitment by a government to embrace competition entails moral values of diligently optimizing value (best quality at lowest cost) and responsible stewardship of scarce public resources. In the case of public procurement, it describes a contest among bidders to win the government's procurement contract for goods or services. The qualified bidder offering the best terms ought to win the contract. In the concept of a market economy, it is believed that the buyer (government, in this case) will benefit when there is competition among bidders for its business. Similarly, the government should stand to benefit if there are many bidders interested in, and bidding for, the procurement. Therefore, procurement procedures ought to be designed to encourage open competition and discourage limiting opportunities to participate in procurements.

Fairness refers to the manner in which the competition is pursued. An obligation to pursue fairness means simply that all bidders ought to receive the same treatment—everyone ought to get the same opportunity to win the procurement contract. Favoritism is the enemy of fairness—it distorts the process, undermines public trust, and discourages the participation of honest bidders. The rules ought to be the same for all bidders, and they ought to be applied in the same manner. No bidder should be given an unfair competitive advantage, and none should be discriminated against.

Honesty is the ideal, but practitioners and public officials are more generally concerned about *dishonesty*. The procurement system ought to protect the public funds from corruption by dishonest persons—persons who lie, cheat, manipulate, bribe, coerce, or steal. Less often stressed, but equally important, the procurement system ought to recognize and reward honesty.

PRINCIPLES IN PRACTICE

These are the leading principles—the ideals—that ought to guide how procurement works. Clearly, there are some persons who are ignorant of or fail to follow these principles and the many rules that have been developed to assist individuals in applying these guiding principles to concrete situations. Ignoring for a moment the few arguably truly evil persons who are aware of the implications of their immoral choices, why are these principles and rules—these so-called decision procedures—not more effective?

Decision procedures are tools; they are not substitutes for moral wisdom. It is not sufficient to simply hand people a decision procedure and a list of justified principles and rules if they have not been taught how to integrate rules, principles, and theories in the decision procedure. (Cooper 2004, p. 295)

David Cooper, a leading expert in professional ethics, makes a persuasive argument for the cultivation of moral wisdom so that people know what to do when they confront moral dilemmas (or even to be aware of the moral dilemma in the first instance). Who ought to be responsible for such moral development, and how, are questions I will return to shortly. First, while I support Cooper's argument as far as he takes it, I would suggest that Cooper leaves out an important dimension by failing to adequately explain how one develops both moral wisdom and integrity. Cooper concentrates on how we act and the decisions we make that guide our actions, but there is more to achieving integrity than behavior modification enforced by rules and sanctions. We must be motivated to become persons of integrity. Where does that motivation come from?

The political philosopher Robert Goodin offers one answer when he argues that our motivations are a product of reason: "We want to get people to do the right thing *regularly* and *systematically;* and the surest way to do that simply has to be to get them to do the right thing for the right reason" (Goodin, 1992, p. 9).

While not disputing the important role of reason—in particular the role of *right reason*—I am more persuaded by the influence of character in shaping our motivations. We have to want to be persons of integrity, to be *virtuous.* A virtuous person is a person who makes choices out of a deep-seated way of looking at the world, a way sensitive to the moral dimensions and consequences of his or her actions. We call such individuals *persons of character.* Persons of integrity are always persons of character—good and virtuous character—and we judge them by their character as displayed in their priorities, values, and in the pattern of the choices they make over time. A person of integrity can also make bad choices, but this is much less likely to happen when the motivation driving those choices is virtuous. As the virtue ethicist Christine McKinnon wrote:

If we can see what it is about bad choices that makes them bad, and what it is about persons' characters and the kinds of reasons they appeal to that encourages them to make these bad choices, then we can begin to understand better what kinds of choices person ought to want to make and what kinds of lives persons ought to want to lead, and why. (McKinnon, 1999, p. 2)

McKinnon's choice of words is important. She writes not about the *actions* of persons as expressed through their choices, but instead about the kinds of choices persons *ought to want* to make; not about the lives that people lead as demonstrated through their *actions,* but instead the kinds of lives persons *ought to want* to lead.

Unlike much of moral theory, McKinnon's thinking does not evaluate human behavior as seen through human actions, but instead focuses evaluation on the *motivation* that drives people to act in the ways that they do. Perhaps virtue ethics has something to contribute to the fight against corruption in procurement by teaching us something about the struggle for integrity and the value we should place on society's intentional cultivation—and recognition of—persons of character.

INTEGRITY

While many would argue that *virtue* is an inappropriate, or at least antiquated, notion in public policy, few would suggest that a person's character is unimportant. In governance terms, we all worry about the questionable character of some of our politicians and bureaucrats, and what that lack of integrity might mean as they make decisions that affect our lives. Most of the public focus on integrity is in fact on the lack of it. We complain about the erosion of public integrity (and private integrity, for that matter). We speak of a decline in public morals, about a lack of civic virtue. We don't often talk about integrity itself—what it is, how we get it, or how we live it.

The dictionary offers three definitions of integrity: (1) steadfast adherence to a strict moral or ethical code; (2) the state of being unimpaired, soundness; and (3) the quality or condition of being whole or undivided, completeness.[5] This clarifies matters a little. After all, we generally think of a person of integrity as someone whose actions are consistently moral and ethical. Is that the same as steadfast adherence? Are we back to the question of expecting people to adhere to—to obey—rules and codes, whether or not they have the requisite moral wisdom? Is the listing of rules—and the enforcement of rule-based behavior—the way ordinary persons become persons of integrity? I'll return to that issue shortly.

The definition also describes a sense of soundness, or wholeness. This may be more helpful, thinking in terms of having a unified set of standards to live one's life by. The corrupt vendor usually is selectively corrupt. He or she feels that lying to government is somehow acceptable or justifiable, but it is doubtful that such a person could base all of his or her interactions with all other persons and institutions on a consistent pattern of lies and deceptions. That corrupt person lacks wholeness—he or she has two or more moral standards for interacting with the world. A person who lives out of multiple moral standards and questionable (or unexamined) motivations inevitably makes bad choices. When that person is entrusted and empowered to act on behalf of the public, or in an interaction that directly affects the public interest, bad choices can produce very bad consequences that affect us all. We see that evidence all around us, in the lost opportunities and the waste of scarce public resources that are the products of corruption.

Our moral orientation—our moral standards as captured in our ethics—are inextricably interwoven with our character, and our character both shapes and is guided by what motivates us. Why is motivation important to achieving integrity in procurement? Rational human beings enjoy choices.[6] Some choices are constrained or prohibited by law or custom, as society generally determines what is permissible and in the public interest. Yet even with a wide range of available remaining choices, a person must be motivated to act (or in some cases, motivated to refrain from acting) to pursue choices and to identify which choices are *right* and *good*. Being motivated to know and choose the morally preferable choice—particularly when that is the harder choice—is much more a function of good character than of the influence of external rules, ideal principles, or peer pressure.

If motivation springs from our character development, what can government do about motivating integrity? Governments can do quite a lot to guide human actions in ways that are both ethical and legal, and to this end, governments regularly employ laws, rules, regulations, and codes. But *guiding* and *motivating* are not the same; motivation must start with helping people to achieve the *capacity to discern* what is morally correct before one can expect people to be motivated to *do* what is morally correct. Learning basic skills in moral and ethical perception—providing training to empower persons to see a moral dilemma when exposed to one—is a start, yet even that modest measure must begin with a change in the perceived role of government and a change in public expectations of what good governance includes. In short, government must invest in character formation—in the nurturing of civic virtue. Simultaneously, citizens must demand a higher standard of virtuous service from their public institutions, civil servants, and political leaders.

GOVERNMENT'S PROINTEGRITY LEADERSHIP

In 2002 and with United Nations' assistance, Uganda took an important step in this direction. It began initial efforts to identify and implement its *National Strategy for Mainstreaming Ethics and Integrity in Local Governance in Uganda*, leading to the publication of the formal strategy in March 2003.[7] This strategy includes a focus on character building through the reintroduction of ethics training in public education. The national strategy, led by the Government's Directorate of Ethics and Integrity, also prescribes a structured national examination and dialogue about the value of integrity in public life. This initiative goes beyond the normal anticorruption rhetoric of sanctions and disclosure and includes provisions to cultivate a culture of integrity through a variety of measures—such as the provision of positive incentives (public recognition and rewards) to public officers who are champions of ethics and integrity.[8]

This is an excellent beginning. It explicitly demonstrates the Ugandan government's recognition that raising overall moral awareness, and engaging in a dialogue about the public's moral values, provides the essential foundation for bringing ethical deliberations into the processes of government, including public procurement. By placing such an emphasis on a public role in supporting character development, and by suggesting that Ugandans ought to actively celebrate integrity where they find it, this strategy tackles the important question of motivation. This strategy, however, is a long-term endeavor and has yet to attract the political and financial support that it warrants. Surely, the best place to focus any character-development investments is in public education that includes well-designed curricula, embracing moral and ethical components.

ENVIRONMENT OF VALUES

Motivating integrity in public procurement is not only the government's responsibility. All of us affect each other in the way that we lead our lives, the decisions that we make, and the expectations that we share with each other regarding the ethical performance of government. We live in an environment of values; by fostering an ongoing dialogue in public and in the workplace about moral values, we can begin to find and publicly articulate a common ground of shared values and moral expectations. My sense, based on many years of facilitating processes of public deliberations, is that such a dialogue carried out in Uganda or in any developing country will rapidly generate a surprising degree of consensus—namely, that the *moral character* of the persons whom we entrust and empower to manage our public resources is vitally important to us, and that we ought to demand that only persons of consistently demonstrated integrity be deemed qualified to exercise such power on our behalf.

There are practical measures that ought to accompany any long-term strategy of character development. We ought to take Goodin's advice and strengthen our capacity to exercise reason and discernment in our moral choices. This can be done by raising our awareness of ethical and moral issues; training in ethical discernment; and rewriting codes of ethics in such a way that they capture genuine values, provide realistic guidance, and reflect the moral obligations that apply to all parties—the government institution, the individual public servant, and the public.

Finally, there is broad agreement that the quest for integrity in public procurement must draw upon financial, technical, and political resources. I would add to that list that in Uganda and in every developing country there is a vast wealth of moral resources that can and should be drawn upon. Open the dialogue on values, and this will become evident. We should get a grip on what Goodin calls our inherent "moral sense":

We can simply build upon the presumption that people have a certain latent "moral sense" within them. Motivating moral behavior at all presupposes something like that, anyway: if we are to get a motivational grip on people, there must already be something within them for us to grip onto. (Goodin, 1992, p. 137)

Ugandans, like people everywhere, possess this moral sense. It is the most powerful and plentiful resource available in the struggle for integrity in public procurement, if only Ugandan society can get a motivational grip. This, I argue, is Uganda's primary challenge in the quest for integrity in public procurement, and in this endeavor, Uganda is hardly alone. While rules set important boundaries and make the minimal standards of expected behavior explicit, cultivating and rewarding motivation in a practical way that includes real incentives for recognized ethical performance will enable people and ultimately institutions to gradually transcend rules, eschew corruption, and achieve a consistent pattern of integrity.

CHAPTER 6

Hunger

"You only need put that stick in the ground, and it'll soon be spouting and bearing fruit," Frank Howitt, the old *mzungu* (white expatriate) informed me knowingly with his usual wink, pointing to a very dry stick on the ground beside me. Born at least 75 years ago in Tororo, Uganda, and seldom out of eastern Africa since, his assertion carried some authority. It's a familiar fable told of Uganda, and while it isn't to be taken too seriously, most of the country is indeed blessed with ample rains, a mild climate, and fertile soil. Were it not for man-made problems, such as the two-decade insurrection in the north, arguably no Ugandans would go hungry. A peaceful Uganda, and arguably any developing country that experiences a stable peace and enjoys democratic institutions, does not go hungry.

Unfortunately for many, peace has not been Uganda's history. War and insecurity have left hundreds of thousands hungry and destitute, most recently among the people of northern Uganda, where the women (who carry out most of the agricultural duties) feared to go to the fields near the internally displaced persons' (IDP) camps where they lived. They had good reason to stay within the relative safety of these crowded camps, for many women and girls who ventured out to cultivate the fields (or just to fetch firewood or water) have been abducted, raped, mutilated, or killed by rebels of the Lords Resistance Army (LRA). Even now, when most internally displaced people have begun to return to resettle their ancestral homes, the lack of basic infrastructure and resources (water, roads, farming implements, seeds) and the many disputes that have arisen over land unoccupied for 20 years means that few farms are flourishing.

HUNGER—A GLOBAL PROBLEM

The problem of hunger is even more severe among Uganda's neighbors, particularly in Sudan to the north and parts of Kenya's arid northern deserts to the east. Throughout the developing world, hunger threatens the lives and security of growing numbers of persons, exacerbated severely in recent months by the exponential escalation in costs of even the most basic of foodstuffs. The Food and Agriculture Organization (FAO) asserts that the proportion of man-made food emergencies has more than doubled over the past 14 years,[1] and the warnings that hunger is becoming a global crisis are now widespread and authoritative. The price of foodstuffs has gone up by 41 percent since October 2007, pushing people from the category of "impoverished" to the more life-threatening group of the "hungry."[2] Large NGOs such as Oxfam and CARE are gearing up to address the crisis and to advocate for a commensurate global response, and wealthier countries are considering increasing food assistance.

Is this enough? How bad is it, really, and what are our obligations—if any—regarding global hunger?

Despite the fact that there is enough food in the world today to feed the global population twice over, every seven seconds a child dies from hunger or malnutrition-related diseases. (Kent, 2005, p. xv).

That sobering, mounting death tally is already a conservative estimate, given the rapid rise in food costs worldwide linked in part to the rapidly increasing price of oil. While compassion for the fate of these desperate children might itself suffice for a revision in our thinking about the global supply-and-demand logic as it pertains to food, such children ought not to rely only on the mercy and concern of wealthier persons or periodic emergency relief responses. These children and their families place a claim before all of us, not for pity, but for respect for their fundamental humanity. After all, the human right to food and subsistence is, along with the human rights to security and liberty, the most basic, clearly articulated, and broadly supported of all human rights, both in international moral theory and in international law (Orend, 2002).[3] The number of international treaties, covenants, agreements, laws, and institutional arrangements that specifically address the moral and legal obligations that arise from the human right to food are legion.[4] The moral force that has driven these many agreements and laws is also demonstrated by the long list of significant international conferences, meetings, and related events on the topic of the human right to food, beginning in 1963.[5] With moral reasoning so thorough and robust, with such widespread formal unanimity of conviction by so many political leaders, and with legal principles and mechanisms both clear and unambiguous, why are there now more people dying and suffering lives of misery due to inadequate nutrition than ever before? And why is that rate increasing at an alarming pace?

A MORAL QUESTION OF RESPECT

Even without the overarching framework of formal treaties, laws, and conferences, the moral parameters of the hunger dilemma are not difficult to apprehend. The needless existence of starvation and malnutrition attacks our sense of moral identity and challenges us to substantiate through meaningful actions our often-stated convictions about universal respect for human dignity. In a world where food surpluses coexist with famine, and where people of wealthier nations obsess about weight loss, how can so many people be left to starve? While debate rages in some public-policy circles in the more developed countries about how best to reverse the many negative public-health impacts resulting from a growing trend of obesity, and while the potential to produce more than adequate food to feed the world's population is now clearly documented, how can we not find the will to end global malnutrition and hunger? Or, more modestly, how can we not find the motivation to at least end hunger and malnutrition for the world's children? Is there a more damning example than the unmitigated suffering of children to support the cynical view that human rights fail to motivate moral behavior, or—more cynically still—that most humans simply don't care very much about the suffering and need of others? Where can motivation be found, such that human behavior changes in a positive way, responsive to such an evident, massive, urgent, and growing need?

ETHICS APPLIED?

Human rights are just one form of expressing human moral and ethical thought. Such deontological (duty based) moral reasoning is not automatically linked to human action, however, or even to providing the prerequisite motivation to act. Without action, human-rights moral theory or law has no practical impact on alleviating the suffering and deaths due to hunger and malnutrition.

In human-rights theory, clear principles are established and agreed upon (and, in some variations, linked to metaphysical justifications) as to what constitutes specific human rights. Out of this consensus, specific claimants and claims, and correlated duty bearers and duties, are identified. This is an exercise of sophisticated moral reasoning, involving abstract but carefully conceived moral principles, which in turn are reflected in human-rights laws, instruments, and associated institutional arrangements. The belief underpinning this approach is that the persuasive power of widely supported, robust moral reasoning will be sufficient to generate constructive and beneficial— even radical—changes in the way we address such urgent needs as hunger. The results to date, however, do little to support such an optimistic premise.

AN APPEAL TO REASON

For most human-rights moral theorists, morality and ethics appear to be primarily a matter of external principles. The primary appeal is to reason—to external arguments and conscientious deliberations—and not to some ill-defined internal moral compass. The intellectual externalization of morality and the associated reliance on motivation as a by-product of reason is an idea, which, coupled with a growth in religious skepticism in Europe, led Friedrich Nietzsche to write of a growing trend away from traditional Judeo-Christian moral values toward a harsher world consumed by a focus on power and self-interest (Glover, 1999). Nietzsche argued that the alternative view, which postulated an internalization of moral concerns within human character, was eroded by what he perceived to be a decline in religious conviction among humanity. With no God to guide our hearts or prod us into action, Nietzsche contended that we are bereft of an internal moral compass to motivate or stimulate us to feed the hungry.

Those of religious conviction may place the locus of morality in the soul, or at least in a heightened sense of spiritual awareness that seems to be evident within some persons. A more secular view of an inner morality would make reference to values that we have adopted (and reflected upon) since early childhood, consciously or unconsciously, which now form our conscience or our sensibilities.

Deontological ethics in the form of responding to a list of carefully reasoned duties and obligations is even more a product of reason, and less understandable as a component of an inner morality, although being dutiful is certainly an important virtue in one's character. Among nondeontological ethicists, feminist ethics is often misunderstood and seldom taught in the developing countries most subject to hunger, yet this important branch of moral theory has much to offer to the moral challenge of hunger and malnutrition. Feminist ethics makes space in the dialogue of policy and action for the moral weight of care and compassion, as it advocates a view of morality that springs from "the moral attitude or longing for goodness and not with moral reasoning" (Noddings, 1984, p. 2). In arguing for an environment in which caring is encouraged to flourish, feminist ethics turns away from an exclusive reliance on the power of moral reasoning to motivate us to lead ethical lives.

I take no breakfast at home. I get nothing at school. When it is lunch time, teachers go home to eat and tell us to play. Can you imagine spending a whole day without eating anything?[6]

When contemplating the specific and urgent needs of hungry children in northern Uganda such as this schoolboy at a primary school in Kumi District, most persons influenced by feminist ethics would find that tightly reasoned rational arguments based on the enforcement of human-rights obligations and actions are exercises in abstractions. Arguing principles doesn't provide an adequate response to that schoolboy's hunger, and such intellectual appeals are unlikely to modify human behavior significantly, they would claim. Even if a consensus could be reached on a concept such as a human right to food, feminist ethicists argue that the weight of such reasoning will not drive those who control resources to solve the problems of global hunger and malnutrition. Feminist ethics presents us with a gritty challenge—that if we really want to achieve beneficial change, it is essential to focus on the concrete reality of suffering and one's relationship to those who suffer. When so many moral arguments begin with the premise that human beings are somehow unique and special (and, as some would argue, that children are even more special and precious), the failure to exercise care and compassion in response to this special status and in the face of massive suffering is deeply confounding. Or, put more succinctly: "If human beings are special, why do we treat each other so badly?" (Ignatieff, 2001, p. 77).

Virtue ethics joins with feminist ethics in this nondeontological context in suggesting that we must concentrate on developing virtuous character traits first, so that moral actions will naturally follow. As argued by Aristotle, the best human life will require at its center the exercise of virtue (Sherman, 1997). When confronting the reality of hunger and malnutrition in others, a person of virtuous character will be motivated, by definition, to apply whatever resources and actions he or she can to mitigate this situation. Christine McKinnon, a leading virtue ethicist, supports such a view of the locus of motivation in the context of the character of moral agents,[7] and their quest for meaning in their lives.

Successful character-construction will serve agents well in their quest to lead meaningful, fulfilled human lives; it will also provide agents with reasons to act in ways which permit other humans to pursue their quests to lead meaningful, fulfilled human lives. (McKinnon, 1999, p. 3)

MOTIVATING ACTION

Whether conceived as a problem to be solved, urgent suffering to be relieved, or an impermissible indignity to be eliminated, the challenge of motivating humanity to beneficial and caring actions to alleviate or eliminate the existence and rapidly worsening trends of global hunger and malnutrition remains central. Feminist ethics and virtue ethics both argue that their nondeontological theories of ethics provide this motivation or moral hook. Both moral approaches argue similar positions—that through an inner sense of moral leading, a by-product of our own moral identity and not a product of intentional moral reasoning, we will be motivated to do what we can reasonably do to end hunger and malnutrition. Our moral identity is a function of our character, be that conceived as virtuous or as caring; we act out of how our moral identities lead us to perceive our world and ourselves.

While this argument appeals to many as intuitively accurate, global hunger is an urgent moral dilemma of immense scale and intensity; it demands a commensurate and urgent moral response. A limited number of morally motivated individuals responding independently within their limited capacities will not suffice, even to ameliorate the needs of just Uganda's hungry.

Beyond morally motivated individuals, societies also collectively bear moral burdens and exercise moral agency, most generally embraced as a function of governance through the relevant institutions of each country. While countries may be said to have national characteristics that represent the collective, countries are not moral agents in the same manner as individuals. Countries do not *care* and are not in themselves *virtuous*, although they may act on the basis of the perceived or aggregated concerns and priorities of their citizenry, or reflect a range of civic virtues that are expressed by citizens or by leaders. Yet, if we accept the premise that the most effective potential for confronting the problem, indignity, or suffering of hunger and malnutrition rests with the country and not with individuals, how can human-rights moral theory address the problem of motivating effective actions by such countries? Alternatively, can other moral approaches provide additional—or more compelling—motivational force than trusting in the persuasive power of human-rights reasoning?

Contrary to virtue or feminist ethics, human rights–based moral theories (and associated national and international human-rights laws) are immediately at home with the country as moral actor. Indeed, human-rights theory and practice conceive the country as the primary duty bearer to the claims of human rights, and from fulfilling this duty, a country gains its legitimacy: "Most broadly conceived, human rights are a standard of political legitimacy; to the extent that governments protect human rights, they and their practices are legitimate." (Donnelly, 1989, p. 14).

Yet even with the country situated in this foundational relationship of claimant and duty bearer, historically the national and international responses to problems of malnutrition and hunger have been motivated not on the basis of fulfilling such rights-based obligations, but instead on expressions of compassion and on the more self-interested recognition that reducing malnutrition can be of considerable benefit to the society as a whole (Kent, 2005).

If the leaders and citizens of countries are motivated by compassion or by their perceived common interest, what does this say about the persuasive power of moral arguments arising out of human-rights concepts? Before considering whether reasoning based on these human-rights principles has any efficacy in generating the requisite motivation at the level of a country to address and alleviate hunger, it may be helpful first to consider three different moral and amoral approaches outside of human rights, to see whether these approaches might be effective alternatives in motivating a country to respond in a satisfactory way to hunger and malnutrition (occurring both internationally and domestically). These three different perspectives include two moral approaches, feminist ethics and virtue ethics, and one prudential approach, self-interest (egoism).

THE COUNTRY AND CARING ABOUT HUNGER

Watching a parent feed a hungry child is unremarkable, and we simply accept that some people nurture and care for others; people often act out of a deep sense of caring or being cared for. The sharing of food is among the most obvious expressions of such care, and ignoring the hunger of others (particularly children) is a most callous act. People care about the hunger of others, but do countries?

Feminist ethicists will not be comfortable viewing the country as a moral agent with feelings, able to care, nurture, or be cared for and nurtured. Obviously individuals within a country may be motivated by their natural expression of care and concern for the plight of those who are hungry, and each person may adopt the position that "I must do something." As such concerned individuals come together and express their caring through democratic processes, this moral urge is transformed from a sense that each individual is being challenged to make a moral response to a more general notion that "something must be done" by the larger institutions of the state. In the process of aggregating these individuals' responses to become effectively the country's response, something quite essential may be lost. As Nel Noddings writes:

This change is accompanied by a shift from the nonrational and subjective to the rational and objective. What should be done? Who should do it? Why should the persons named do it? This sort of thinking is not in itself a mistake; it is needed. But it has buried within it the seed of major error. The danger is that caring, which is essentially nonrational in that it requires a constitutive engrossment and displacement of motivation, may gradually or abruptly be transformed into abstract problem solving. There is, then, a shift of focus from the cared-for to the "problem." Opportunities arise for self-interest, and persons entrusted with caring may lack the necessary engrossment in those to be cared-for. Rules are formulated and the characteristic variation in response to the needs of the cared-for may fade away. Those entrusted with caring may focus on satisfying the formulated requirements for caretaking and fail to be present in their interactions with the cared-for. This caring disappears and only its illusion remains. (Noddings, 1984, p. 25)

In this view, one could explain a country's initial groundswell response to alleviating the needs of hungry individuals or groups of hungry individuals—such as those in northern Uganda—as a response arising out of a deep moral sense of care. But at best that motivation only starts the country moving in this direction or fortuitously motivates some key leaders within such a country. Once caring becomes institutionalized, its force as a motivating factor diminishes; the institutions within the country responding initially out of the expressed care and concern of citizens become instead institutions performing to a set of formal performance requirements. The various treaties, laws, and principles formulated on the basis of the human right to food constitute just such an institutional framework of rational, formal requirements. While essential to the determination of the most effective ways to solve the problem of hunger, the *original moral force* of caring for the hungry persons is dissipated. The aggregated, sustained caring of moral agents within the country seems to be an inadequate basis upon which to motivate a full and satisfactory response to claims arising out of the human right to food.

Brian Orend, in discussing the differences between *ethics of rights* thinking and views based on an *ethics of care*, makes reference to the leading feminist ethicist Carol Gilligan. While expressing some concern about simplistic generalizations between male and female points of view, Orend still considers Gilligan's perspective worthy of careful consideration. He summarized Gilligan's perspective as follows:

Whereas men are much more likely to view moral issues in terms of universal rules and rights, or of promoting everyone's fundamental interests, women view ethics more through the prism of a particular relationship. Whereas men demand that their rights be realized, or insist that utilities be maximized, women prefer that people develop the character traits displayed by those engaged in a rewarding personal relationship. So men praise traits like impartiality, objectivity, autonomy, reasonableness, and the performance of duties whereas women look more for empathy, sympathy, loyalty, community and a sense of responsibility for nurturing others. (Orend, 2002, p. 172)

Even where individuals within the country persist in advocating (in watchdog mode, perhaps) that the institutions of the country respond in ways that align more authentically with such caring, the continual strain of shouldering such a moral burden can overwhelm individual moral agents—including a caring leader. Once overwhelmed, such persons will either be unable to continue to care for the other or to act out of such caring in a direct manner. Caring, while a powerful initial motivator, seems an inadequate basis upon which to sustain and continue to motivate the country's response to alleviating the other's hunger and need.

THE VIRTUOUS COUNTRY'S RESPONSE TO HUNGER

If caring individuals—even leaders—are unable to sustain a caring institutional response by the country to the moral challenge of hunger, particularly as this response moves from nonrational moral feelings to rational problem-solving abstractions, what about reliance on virtuous institutional leadership within the country? Is it possible for the country itself, or its constituent institutions, to be virtuous moral agents?

As with feminist ethicists, the virtue ethicist will not expect a country to be a virtuous moral agent. Virtue ethics, with its roots in Aristotelian moral philosophy, directs its attention at the lifelong process of personal character formation, out of which moral (and amoral) virtues are attained. The development of personal character is a matter of discipline, reflection, and growth. While we often talk about group characteristics—even group virtues—common or typical to the citizens of a particular country, we don't view the characteristics of these national traits in the same manner as we evaluate personal character. Yet if virtue ethics concentrates on the individual in his or her quest to develop and sustain a virtuous character, virtue ethics also sees an important—even essential—role for virtuous leadership within the country. Starting from Aristotle and extending to the various framers of constitutions ranging from the United States to Uganda, it has been persuasively argued that government institutions need to be guided and motivated by those of recognized civic virtue, while pragmatically accepting the need for effective constitutional safeguards to be in place for times where such leadership is lacking.

What about President Bush's call in March 2008 for increasing the fiscal 2008 global food budget from $1.2 billion by a further $350 million, or his offer in May 2008 of $770 million in international food aid?[8] Or French president Sarkozy's leadership in doubling his country's food aid to a new level of 60 million euros? Assuming that the institutions and governance of countries such as the United States or France are so situated as to be responsive to the leadership of key individuals, and these individuals are motivated by their own virtues to attend to the needs of the hungry, is this motivation sufficient to move the United States or France to act in ways that would satisfy the human right of Ugandans to food?

While I will avoid the temptation to assess the extent to which virtue defines the leadership and decisions of heads of state such as George W. Bush or Nicolas Sarkozy, the question remains. Can the virtues of institutional leaders (e.g., USAID Administrator Henrietta Fore) or even national leaders (e.g., Presidents Bush or Sarkozy) provide the necessary motivation to propel and sustain the institution or the country to achieve a moral response that fulfils the moral obligations that are associated with the human right to food? Once again, the issue becomes one of sustainability (or perhaps stamina). It is arguable that a highly disciplined, truly virtuous leader might be better able than the leader motivated primarily by caring or by rational moral calculation to sustain virtuous leadership and motivate a country to respond to hunger and malnutrition with the urgency and intensity required, over the period required, to achieve meaningful results. Theoretically, this has intuitive merit, and certainly some institutions have performed in this manner. Whether the relevant institutions of an entire country would be able to respond in a virtuous manner, through the efforts of well-placed virtuous leadership, is more questionable. At best, such a response would be based on the good fortune of having virtuous leaders in positions of authority and influence, at the time of need.

THE SELF-INTERESTED COUNTRY'S RESPONSE TO HUNGER

In many instances, it clearly can be argued that feeding the hungry is in the self-interest of a country that possesses the resources to do so. When the hunger exists within its own citizenry, a country risks political and social instability, loss of productivity, even political collapse by not fulfilling its obligations to ensure that access for food—and the equitable and sustainable distribution of such resources—is achieved for its own people. The security of the status quo, and the protection of the interests of those who wield power (and who reap the benefits of such power), are powerful motivating factors in stimulating a response to hunger within the borders of a country. Despite this logic, some countries will still fail to respond or at least to respond adequately; Uganda is representative of many countries that lack sufficient resources, that suffer under inefficient governance and administration, or whose elites display a lack of concern for the plight of powerless minorities. None of these excuses absolves the country of the moral duty to address the needs of the hungry; indeed some of these excuses merely mask the existence of more fundamental moral problems of authoritarianism, embedded and pervasive corruption, ethnic hatred, or extreme economic stratification.

Will President Museveni solve the problems of hunger in Uganda, where 1.6 million Ugandans are being fed by the World Food Program? After all, he won the Hunger Project's 1998 Africa Prize for Leadership for the Sustainable End of Hunger based on his commitment to decentralization and stability.[9] Reliance on Museveni or on the self-interest of anyone in power in a developing country to resolve the problem of hunger within their own borders is problematic, however, for the reasons stated above. In order to solidify his power base and secure his longevity as president, Museveni has been intentionally undercutting much of the impressive decentralization that he came to be respected for, leaving local governments without essential resources or tax revenues to be effective in responding to hunger in their areas. Even his grasp of global economics leaves serious room for doubt, as he recently expressed the view that the explosive growth in food prices will generate increased revenues for Uganda's farmers.[10] For a country that imports more food than it exports, the so-called benefit of increasing global food prices is difficult to support. In short, Ugandans may well need to look abroad to other countries to come to their aid in solving their own problems of hunger.

Why should other countries rush to Uganda's aid? Expecting that other countries will determine that it is in their own self-interest to intervene in the problems of hunger outside their borders (and often thousands of kilometers away) is even more tenuous. Certainly, there may be some situations where a country may perceive a geopolitical advantage in such offers of assistance, or it may calculate that the potential problems of refugees and economic migrants arising from areas of famine will threaten its own economy and security. The topical issues of terrorism breeding in areas of deprivation, hunger, and hardship may also provide a source of self-interested motivation for a country to seek to assist the hungry and malnourished beyond its borders. History, however replete with such examples of strategic humanitarianism and targeted foreign aid, has no obvious examples where a foreign country does more than relieve some of the severity of the hunger and need, and then only for a limited time. Geopolitical calculations constantly change, and what may be perceived as constituting strategic aid one day may be viewed as money down a black hole the next. Self-interest, therefore, seems at best a fickle source of motivating a country to respond comprehensively and urgently to the needs of hunger and malnutrition.

THE DUTIFUL COUNTRY MEETING
ITS MORAL OBLIGATIONS

In seeking a moral response by a country to the problem, and the moral challenge, of hunger and malnutrition, the initial hurdle would appear to be to frame the problem as a moral dilemma. As stated by Goodin, "Sometimes getting people to *do* what is morally correct involves the more familiar task of getting them to *see* what is morally correct, in the first place" (Goodin, 1992, p. 4).

Moving the dialogue regarding the appropriate response to severe hunger (and the associated problems of poverty, poor governance, and the energy/environmental crises) is an exercise in moral persuasion, using a vocabulary that has eroded through lack of use within the political sphere in most countries. History has shown us that reliance on the presence of virtuous, well-placed leaders to stimulate such a dialogue, and to lead an urgent moral response, is simply unsupportable. Even when there is an outpouring of care and concern by citizens that is directed and supported by political leadership, the momentum seems impossible to sustain—often not even long enough to comprehensively meet the most urgent needs of the hungry.

Is the language of human rights our best remaining option to stimulate, motivate, and sustain the appropriate, comprehensive moral response by the country? Michael Ignatieff makes such a case when he says: "Human rights language is also there to remind us that there are some abuses that are genuinely intolerable, and some excuses for these abuses that are insupportable" (Ignatieff, 2001, p. 22). Ignatieff continues, arguing for the need to use open-eyed realism in our expectations:

So we cannot build a foundation for human rights on natural human pity or solidarity. For the idea that these propensities are natural implies that they are innate and universally distributed among individuals. The reality—as the Holocaust and countless other examples of atrocity make clear—is otherwise. We must work out a belief in human rights on the basis of human beings as they are, working on assumptions about the worst we can do, instead of hopeful expectations of the best
... We build on the testimony of fear, rather than on the expectations of hope. (Ignatieff, 2001, p. 80)

The fact of continued severe hunger and malnutrition in northern Uganda, Sudan, and throughout much of the developing word, coexisting in a world of food surpluses, is without doubt a morally intolerable abuse of human rights and human dignity. While Ignatieff's reliance on human rights appears to be a product of a deeply cynical view of human nature, the "testimony of fear" is emphatically supported by a continuing testimony of suffering among all those who are hungry. Using the language of human rights to draw a clear threshold of what constitutes genuinely intolerable abuse—moral impermissibility—is perhaps the best start to cultivating an international and deep consensus on the need for urgent, sustained action to end hunger and malnutrition. In such a process of consensus formation, there is ample need for the support, energy, and commitment of caring and virtuous individuals and leaders; but at the end of the day, human-rights language may offer the most precise and instructive demarcation of our moral boundaries. Only when the hungry are viewed as members of our own moral community will we begin to treat them as our moral equals, but to get to that point requires a very loud moral alarm, alerting us to the fact that many persons are falling below the moral threshold we have agreed upon.

The task now before us is to build upon the existing moral dialogue of human rights, and the legal framework of human-rights law, to work for commitment to that moral threshold that has already been articulated in the human right to food, and to build a moral alarm capacity that brings the testimony of suffering into the moral consciousness of individuals, leaders, and countries. That moral alarm should be sounding very loudly now, as the global food crisis accelerates.

CHAPTER 7

Conflict

Kevin Doris Ejon is one very remarkable Ugandan woman. At only 25 years of age, she's already established a reputation as an intrepid investigative journalist with a mission. She's from the north of Uganda, and the many problems that have afflicted that region she knows only too well. Born in Atapara, in Oyam District not far from Lira, the two-decade-long conflict caused by the brutal cult known as the Lords Resistance Army (LRA) has affected her, her family, and her community, creating deep insecurities and stagnating development.

Ejon secured her first formal job when she was just 16, working at the newly opened Radio Lira. In time, she came to host her own talk-radio show, dealing mostly with issues affecting women and development, social justice, and family concerns. The war with the LRA was always in the background, however, and one day she was surprised to find her caller was none other than Vincent Otti. The call came via satellite telephone from somewhere in the bush.

At that time, Vincent Otti was the deputy commander in chief of the LRA, an intelligent yet ruthless man under indictment by the International Criminal Court (ICC) on 11 counts of crimes against humanity and 21 counts of war crimes. Otti had been the brains behind a two-decade-long series of horrific atrocities against the people of northern Uganda and the Ugandan army, under the guise of being a war against the Ugandan president, Yoweri Museveni. According to leading human-rights groups, the LRA rebels are responsible for murdering, raping, maiming, torturing, and displacing vast numbers of innocent civilians. They are also accused of abducting, indoctrinating, and physically and sexually abusing over 20,000 young children. Children abductees make up 85 to 90 percent of LRA fighters, and the majority of those who are kidnapped are between the ages of 11 and 15 at the time of their abduction.

Their choices are not complicated: become an LRA bush fighter or die a brutally painful death.

Otti's reputation was well known to Ejon, but she was surprised when he demanded to talk only with her. Despite her deep misgivings, she engaged him on the talk show, and he used that opportunity to make a political statement claiming that the Ugandan government mistreated the people of the North, and other usual LRA claims. On that telephone call, Otti threatened Ejon with abduction if she were to "tell lies" about him or the LRA, and Otti took advantage of his free time on the airwaves to urge the Langi people not to report LRA troop movements to the Ugandan authorities. The entire conversation lasted around 30 minutes. Among the many listeners to that broadcast were the Ugandan military police, who took Ejon into custody after the broadcast and grilled her for four hours in an effort to establish why Otti would ask for her and what link she had with such a wanted terrorist. Finally, they concluded quite correctly that Otti simply liked her style!

For Ejon, however, the call with Otti was a revelation. From that point onward, she committed herself to find the stories of the people behind the conflict—its victims, perpetrators, and beneficiaries. In August of 2006, at considerable risk to herself, she negotiated her way onto a bus that was taking a group of diplomats deep into the bush in southern Sudan to meet with the LRA rebels. Ejon and her diplomatic colleagues' trip was successful. While the diplomats talked with the senior LRA leadership, Ejon managed to meet young LRA noncombatant people. These young people had never seen cars or buses and had never slept in houses; their entire lives, as far back as they could remember, had been spent running from fighting and possible capture. Some of the women Ejon spoke with did not even know their own age and asked Ejon to estimate their ages by reference to the number of children that each had. When Ejon asked them about their views on the LRA and on reconciliation and forgiveness for the many injustices and harms they had experienced, two women admitted that they would not hesitate to kill their abductors if given the chance. They said that forgiving the LRA men who had forced them into sexual slavery was simply not possible. One abducted woman, however, said she would forgive her captors because of her faith as a Christian, and because she knew that Jesus forgives. Another woman explained that if they did not forgive the men who captured and raped them, they would effectively be punishing their own children. Still others considered that forgiveness and reconciliation were essential steps in being allowed to finally end the war and return to their original home villages. When asked about forgiving the LRA leader, Joseph Kony, one woman argued that only if Kony were forgiven would the war ever end and the suffering finally stop.

Ejon's goal had been to travel to this base camp of the LRA to talk with and record—on video and tape—the LRA leader, Joseph Kony. It was not to be, but in a second journey into LRA territory, Ejon was successful; she stayed with Kony and Otti for four days.[1] This was followed by a third trip to the LRA's new base in Rikwamba, in the Garamba National Park in the

Democratic Republic of the Congo (DRC) for a stay of three days. On this last journey, she had the rare opportunity to speak with Kony alone for four hours. She filmed much of this interview, which was unprecedented. Ejon told me later that she found Kony to be a complex individual: handsome, even (in her view) cute, yet clearly dangerous. Kony claimed that he was only following the commands of the spirits that lead him, yet at that time, Ejon felt that here was a man who genuinely regretted his past atrocities. In short, he looked more a man than a monster—not like somebody with such a brutal, bloody history.

She also interviewed some more of the abducted men and women, and their children. The desire of these abductees and so-called "recruits was both uniform and passionate—they wanted to return to Uganda and begin a new and normal life. The emotions are complex; many of the abducted child soldiers have been deeply traumatized and have committed vicious crimes. To begin their lives anew, they feel the need to be forgiven; yet they fear that such forgiveness may be too much to ask given the severity of their transgressions. Yet they can do nothing more than hope for mercy and understanding, and a peace settlement that will allow them to leave the many deprivations and hardships of the bush life. Although these abductees have expressed regret, rage, and helplessness, they all look forward to the day when the LRA rebels say: "We are coming home—the fighting is over."

The children of these young abductees spoke to Ejon with such profound sadness that she was deeply moved, yet she entertained few hopes about their prospects. These children live a life of fear and unquestioning submission, unable to imagine any life that does not entail armed conflict and extreme hardship. Even were there to be a sustained peace, which still has yet to be formalized, many of the young combatants would almost certainly seek a career in the Ugandan army. All that they know is the life of a warrior.

Ejon's journeys to the LRA open up many of the most pressing and vexing moral issues of conflict. She was spared viewing the carrion of the battlefield, yet she walked among the living dead—children and young people so traumatized and fearful that their tender lives have been irretrievably violated, their once innocent, secure, and joyful childhood forever lost to them. Despite their sacrifices, and the disproportionate degree to which they are affected by conflict, children in this and any recent conflict are largely ignored when it comes to building the peace. Alison Watson made exactly this point when she wrote:

The plight of children, however, is little discussed when it comes to agreeing on the minutiae of a peace proposal, despite the fact that children are widely recognized—even from within the institutions of the liberal peace itself—as significant to the sustainability of the peace . . . those attempting to secure peace tend to assume that a program of postconflict recovery requires only the redressing of general systemic wrongs that will eventually "trickle down" to benefit youth along with the rest of the population. (Watson, 2008, p. 37)

Ethical concerns such as the plight of the child victims of the LRA permeate violent conflict, from the evolving but generally well-recognized conditions that lead up to violence erupting to the brutality and carnage of the fighting, and well into the peace negotiations and subsequent peace building. Arguably the most fundamental of all human rights, security is the first victim of violent conflict, as people lose their freedoms to lead their lives in peace, in a productive and meaningful way. Their quality of life, and basic welfare, erode rapidly as security is swept away. Even when peace again becomes a real prospect, what kind of a peace is it likely to be, and who are its beneficiaries? Victor's peace, under which the winning side sets the terms, nearly always leaves unanswered a trail of moral transgressions of startling proportions, while certain other violations are strategically focused on to make a political point. Even the manner in which the peace comes about—imposed by foreign peacemakers who sometimes adopt neocolonial ways—leaves important ethical concerns of representational governance and local autonomy unresolved. Foreign peacemakers may establish and impose governance institutions that local people make use of but feel little ownership of, and when the armed peacemakers leave, these institutions usually fall apart.

Development is of course another victim of violent conflict. It is widely said among development practitioners that a brief period of conflict will destroy the hard won progress of decades of development efforts. The late philosopher Denis Goulet, in almost an aside in his famous 1995 book *Development Ethics,* wondered whether "the explosive release of ancient ethnic, racial and linguistic passions" would "destroy all possibilities of genuine development founded on universal solidarity" (Goulet, 1995, p. 142). Indeed, the realities of recent violent conflicts in Africa have led many people to question whether development is ever to be achieved. Such violence undercuts the premise of universal solidarity, which Goulet envisioned as a moral driver of global development. The assault on that ideal has been comprehensive, captured well in the biographical story *Emma's War* by Deborah Scroggins:

But whereas in 1988 a million dead Africans was a figure that could still shock, today the two million southern Sudanese corpses have been submerged by a tidal wave of death that has washed over Africa in the aftermath of the cold war and the dissolution of the post-colonial states. A million dead in Somalia; another million slaughtered in Rwanda; up to three million killed in Congo; hundreds of thousands killed in smaller wars in Sierra Leone, Liberia, Angola, Eritrea and Ethiopia; not to mention 17 million dead of AIDS and untold millions felled even in relatively safe countries like Kenya by the everyday scourges of crime and disease. All of this has taken place in the last fifteen years. Even for Africans, it has become a blur. As for the West, we have shut our eyes. (Scroggins, 2004, p. 351)

The violent conflicts of Africa involve death, suffering, trauma, and desperation at a scale and intensity that statistics fail to convey. Even the data is flawed. We will never know the precise number and exact fate of the multitude of victims of such conflicts; we will never be able to measure their loss or weigh their trauma. The exposure that we in the West—or, in the language of development, "the North"—receive leaves us astounded, uncomprehending. Many of us shut our eyes or sadly conclude that nothing can be done commensurate to the awful need. The innocent, the infants, the elderly, the pregnant, the child soldiers, the many extremely vulnerable victims of such conflicts will not be reached or, if reached, will be assisted too late, with too little, to too little effect. Others take a more detached, self-interested view: "If Africa couldn't be saved in a very short time and at very little cost, then to hell with it—anyone who went there must be a saint" (Scroggins, 2004, p. 344). Are we morally justified to shut our eyes, arguing that for most of us, Africa is very far away and the primary moral responsibility of others? Are Africa's conflicts arising out of value systems fundamentally different than those of the North, rendering us morally remote and in that sense disqualified to intervene? After all, even in our own histories, many acclaimed freedom fighters would have been remembered as terrorists had their side not prevailed.

Joseph Kony will tell you, as he told Ejon, that he is not a terrorist. He'll even say, as he said to her, that he is a human being just like you or me; he, too, wants peace. His message becomes rather more complicated when he argues that he is "fighting for peace." Yet as Goulet noted wisely: "One's ethical stance on ends is dramatically revealed in the means one adopts to pursue them" (Goulet, 1995, p. 12). By whatever universal standards of sanity and civility, the means that Joseph Kony employs to pursue his unclear goals are either evil or the product of a madman. The activities of this messianic figure and his now diminished but still powerful self-styled insurgency—the LRA—have been truly gruesome:

LRA rebels mutilate, abduct children, and commit rape and other acts of sexual violence against women and girls. The LRA routinely cuts off lips, ears, and breasts; gouges eyes, and amputates limbs. Many of these mutilations are carried out to prevent "betrayals." Killings of civilians are widespread. Women are forced to lie on their backs, and their throats are cut. (Phuong, Vinck, Wierda, Stover, & di Giovanni, 2005, p. 14)

What do the routine brutalities and excesses of a madman and his followers in the far north of Uganda have to do with the universal solidarity—particularly the ethical obligations of those of us in the North—who are far more familiar with framing these obligations in the context of international development or international relief? Who bears the moral burdens of preventing, relieving, stopping, and cleaning up after such conflicts, and meeting the urgent needs that arise because of them?

DEVELOPMENT VERSUS RELIEF

Before contemplating the moral implications of conflict as a separate phenomenon, it is helpful to consider the extensive moral reflections in the literature and practice of development ethics directed at both relief and development. To those in the international development community, different ethical factors define the conceptual (and often institutional) line between *development* and *relief* (or humanitarian assistance). Moral presumptions and available options differ significantly depending on which side of the development–relief line one is situated. Interventions intended to prevent violent conflict may come close to crossing that line, but when significant levels of violence erupt, there is very little or no room for more traditional development.

From an ethics perspective, how does our thinking about international development change when governance crumbles and all social order is gone? Important moral ideals lose their foundation during times of violent conflict; any semblance of public morality is lost, and many people's actions demonstrate that life is of little value. Any notion of human dignity becomes an absurdity. In such morally turbulent times, relief workers move in, with very different assumptions than development specialists as to what constitutes effectiveness. Does the shift away from development to relief, and the dissolution of the various means that were being used to pursue development goals, render those earlier development goals simply inoperative or irrelevant? Do we wipe the slate clean?

A practical division of labor has long existed between the international development community and the international relief community. In times of extreme crisis, such as when widespread and poorly controlled fighting erupts, development work ceases. The risks are much too high, and the prospects of achieving or even sustaining any development goals are negligible under such circumstances. In their place comes a quiet (and always too small) contingent of emergency relief personnel. The enormous sacrifices of these relief workers demonstrate high moral ideals and intense commitment. Yet how different are the central moral concepts between relief and development?

The ethical mandate of relief work is less expansive than that of development work. Emergency relief workers, their institutions, and those who support them operate from a very basic human moral response—to offer urgent care and assistance to all in need, to respect the value of each life, and to treat all persons as moral equals. Relief workers struggle to keep as many people as possible both alive and safe, to help the victims of conflict take the tentative first steps in reconstructing their family and community structures, and to regain some viable form of livelihood. They show solidarity with those who suffer by coming to these dangerous environments, living simply, and working exceptionally long hours under extreme conditions. By this example, they create—at least for some brief time—a microcosm of a global community. Their universal solidarity is tangible, yet relief workers also unintentionally and unavoidably come to represent two troubling moral messages. The first is that the outside world cares, but only so much. The second is that we are here living *our* moral values, and we have no time or capacity to ascertain and respond to *your* moral values. You are the victims, we are here to help, so for now you must trust us and our values.

The first assertion—that there is a paucity in the caring and concern of the North—is demonstrated in every crisis, from natural disasters to violent conflicts. There are never enough relief workers and supplies available to satisfy the needs, they come too late, and they leave too early. The second assertion is that there is an inequitable power relationship that is inescapable, as with any victim and caregiver. The victim is a victim because he or she is no longer able to manage. Victims must trust in the generosity, care, and competence of the caregiver. This relationship between disempowered victim and external caregiver directly raises the more complex moral questions common to relief work: who ought to set the relief initiative's goals and the means to achieve them, who ought to provide these means (relief workers, emergency supplies, food, logistical support), and how much is enough? Is it right to rush relief in to a conflict zone if it enables the warring parties to prolong the conflict?

Even more fundamental than these moral questions surrounding the means applied to relief efforts is the critical *who ought* question: who is morally obliged to shoulder the relief and reconstruction burden, and to establish the essential conditions for justice? When an outsider comes in and takes up the relief burden, does this relieve whatever government remains (or emerges) from moral responsibility to perform basic governance functions? And what about when relief stretches into years or decades, as is the case in northern Uganda, ultimately taking the form of compulsory resettlement of the affected civilian population into underserviced internally displaced persons (IDP) camps? In Uganda, the living conditions in such camps are appalling, yet whole generations have grown up with no other experience. Making life in the camps more humane is impossible under present levels of aid; the quantity of relief available from outsiders is small relative to the need, and the ability or commitment of the Ugandan government to care for these victims of the war is wholly inadequate. Who is obliged to respond?

In the moral division of labor advocated by Robert Goodin, the burden to assist victims of such crises falls to those who are most capable of helping, as he argues that those "who are closest at hand are usually the best situated to *know* what is needed, and they are usually the best situated to *act efficaciously* to do what is needed" (Goodin, 2003, p. 75). When violent conflict first emerges, and the relief operations begin, what becomes of that other important moral resource: the many actors (domestic and international) of earlier development programs? What happens to the energy, ideals, and commitments that propelled these development efforts? Some development specialists, and the programs and institutions they represent, continue to keep hope alive by applying their extensive knowledge of the country to become advocates both to ensure that relief efforts receive the level and quality of support needed, and to chart a path for the fastest possible return to a sustainable, genuine peace. Such peace building has traditionally been deemed the responsibility of diplomats, soldiers, and politicians, who view peace much more narrowly than does the development community. Is the peace that development specialists articulate in their thinking and their work missing from the more common notions of postconflict peace building?

Besides involving relief and development workers, the cultivation of peace takes yet a third group, who specialize in political matters and have the ability and mandate to apply coercive force to achieve public goods, such as basic security. Diplomatic, military, and political experts play a necessary and valuable role in ending conflicts, but they often equate the end of fighting with the securing of peace. Both development and relief specialists know that the absence of violent conflict is far from genuine peace. Peace is won across many fronts: through offering urgent care and providing essential needs, forging a new and viable social contract, holding to account all those who violated human rights during the conflict period, according appropriate respect and validation to those who suffered severe loss, remembering those who lost their lives, addressing important ethical issues of fair and equitable governance, and selecting new leaders of proven moral character who are committed to the welfare of the public and the pursuit of the public good. Even in the best postconflict conditions, these peace-building measures take time, particularly when there is no larger regional or global consensus on what is the *right* thing to do.

Given how difficult it is to build peace, does not the community of development specialists most recently active in the affected country have a role to play in ending conflict and setting the stage for a return to peace? If so, why do so few development institutions have the mandate and resources needed to enable these specialists to be identified, brought together, and supported to carry out such a role? The new UN Peacebuilding Commission established in October 2006 may offer the first coordinated institutional response to the challenges of peace building in the immediate postconflict recovery period, but the Commission works largely with actors at a different level: the regional organizations, regional banks, and international financial institutions. Marshalling that other level of actors—the army of individual specialists who know that country best but who have been scattered by the chaos—is not on the Commission's agenda.

Searching for an ethical response to the barbarity and chaos of a country already beset by violent conflict and conceptualizing the characteristics of any future peace there may seem like a curious and futile undertaking for development specialists, given the global inadequacy of development assistance. While the fighting ensues in country X, many international development specialists typically move on to other countries and other needs, perhaps taking with them a lesson learned in the form of a strengthened conviction that more and better intellectual and financial resources are needed to find some way—through moral persuasion and political pressure—to motivate the requisite political will and resources to help prevent future conflicts of this kind in country Y. Who can fault them for abandoning country X? While the bullets continue to fly in country X, and shortly thereafter, what development can occur, and what ethics are there to talk about? Conventional wisdom dictates that we first allow the diplomats, the military, and the politicians to find a method to impose a workable cessation of hostilities; any talk of justice or a new and genuine peace will just have to wait.

In these kinds of calculations, the development needs and aspirations of country X are seldom considered, as development attentions turn instead to the more fruitful prospects in peaceful country Y. That universal solidarity that Goulet aspired to is a fiction for country X; there are painfully too few resources to support even basic development programs worldwide.

At the institutional level in the United States, the challenges of finding a common ethics agenda to augment any strategic collaboration—itself quite weak—between the Department of Defense, the Department of State, the U.S. Agency for International Development (USAID), and other leading development institutions appear insurmountable. Important considerations of values in the context of relief, development, and redevelopment are largely ignored. Yet what might such a common ethics agenda consist of?

Ethics is the way that people identify and explore moral values to find sufficient common ground to generate order, so that human society becomes possible at a scale and with sufficient collaboration to allow development to occur and be sustained. Conflict environments are nearly always chaotic. During and immediately after severe conflicts, as in Rwanda or Somalia, the entire moral infrastructure of culture, society, religion, civility, and even basic human kindness are swept away. In such situations, individuals commit atrocities against even friends and neighbors, while inexplicably other individuals demonstrate astounding acts of selfless heroism to save the lives of strangers. Building peace in such a context is an ethical minefield; good may be thrust into an uneasy relationship with evil as people make painful compromises to survive. Sitting face-to-face in peace negotiations with perpetrators of the most extreme brutality—what the former UN peacekeeping commander in Rwanda, General Romeo Dallaire, described as "shaking hands with the devil"—is a deeply perplexing moral experience (Dallaire, 2004, p. xviii). When the evil that drives such violent conflicts is brazen and unrepentant, when the ethical institutions and standards of a society have shattered, what voice does a development worker's morality have? As Goulet observed: "Ethics cannot exorcise evil from the realms of political power simply by preaching noble ideas: development ethics wields no prescriptive power unless it takes us beyond moralism" (Goulet, 1995, p. 25). Goulet was advocating for thinking guided by morality (as distinct from thinking muddied by preachy moralism) as an integral component of the many constituent processes and interventions of development—the so-called means of the means. This advocacy should also be applied to crafting a common peace-building ethics agenda, involving relief, development, and political actors. Goulet saw the challenges and opportunities of development through the moral lens, without losing sight of the fact that others have seldom examined much of what we call development (or relief) from such a perspective. While Goulet's focus was more on development than on the undevelopment of conflict, his message applied to both contexts when he said: "Precisely because we are human, we are 'responsible' for creating conditions that optimize the humanization of life" (Goulet, 1995, p. 59).

This responsibility is a moral one and alone suffices to justify an explicitly moral dialogue between relief, development, and political actors. This moral burden needs to be divided in a way that is justifiable and that offers better prospects for timely responses to urgent needs.

MORAL OBLIGATIONS OF THE NORTH

One day of violent conflict will negate decades of strenuous development efforts, along with the lives, hopes, and dreams of many afflicted people. Conflict's terrible dehumanizing forces of death, destruction, and terror ran like strong and unpredictable torrents through African conflicts such as Rwanda, Sierra Leone, Liberia, Angola, and Burundi. As of this writing, it seems that these forces of destruction still hold sway over Darfur, Somalia, northern Uganda, and much of the Democratic Republic of the Congo. Other African nations that perch on a razor edge of peace, able to plummet back into chaos at any moment, include southern Sudan, Ethiopia, and Eritrea.

These wars are not by the rules. The efforts of the last century to create some humane, ethical basis for warfare and to allow space for the possibility of a so-called just war, are nonsensical to the perpetrators and victims of such conflicts in Africa. In Africa, as the evidence of decades of conflict bears grim testimony, life is indeed cheap. No morally significant differentiation is made between combatants and noncombatants, nor is there any special consideration made for women, youths, the elderly, or even pregnant women—all are subject to astounding levels of brutality, violence, trauma, or death.

The advent of modern communications, combined with the remarkable (or, some would argue, foolhardy) fortitude of intrepid journalists, means that the true horrors of such conflicts are no longer hazy, distant, or out of date by the time we are made aware of them. Through news reports and Web pages, we have been exposed to the anguish of Somalia in 1993, Rwanda in 1994, and to the seemingly endless tribulations besetting the peoples of the Darfur region in western Sudan. As the death toll grows, and the accounts become ever more horrific, we grow dispirited, exhausted, and even cynical: conflicts such as those caused by Joseph Kony and his LRA drag on with a relentless inevitability, year after year, through one stalled or ineffectual peace negotiation after another. Yet the grim realities of such a war reach out to us through the Web, as with this account of a 14-year-old boy abducted by the LRA and forced to perform an act of incredible immorality:

A few days later, a commander called me and said he had a special task for me to carry out. He was carrying a newborn baby. He placed the baby in a large wooden mortar, the one we were using for pounding grain. He gave me a heavy wooden pestle and ordered me to start pounding. I was afraid to do it, but I did as I was told. I knew

I would be killed if I didn't. All the boys in the group had been forced to do something similar. I knew the baby's mother. She was one of the captives. She screamed when she saw what I was doing. The commanders beat her up so much, and told her to shut up. But they did not kill her. They told me to continue pounding until they were satisfied the baby was dead.[2]

There was no urgent response to save this baby, the boy, or the baby's mother from this atrocity. In the case of northern Uganda, the sense of urgency is particularly hard to sustain. This conflict is now two decades old, with a tragic legacy of between 20,000 to 30,000 child abductees; 1.7 million displaced persons; and tens of thousands of dead, maimed, mutilated, and traumatized victims. A more graphic assault on every notion of basic human dignity and the innocence of children is hard to imagine, but to extend that assault across 20 years of unrelenting turmoil raises very troubling moral questions—or it should.

Urgency and complexity combine to make conflict situations ethically daunting. As individuals or as nations, we are all under a fundamental moral obligation to do no harm; yet the distribution of positive moral burdens within and between peoples and societies around the world would seem to place the needs of Uganda at a remote distance from most in the North, who have no special relationship with Ugandans. Such special relationships, many will argue, are prioritized to include family, friends, and communities, perhaps stretching out to fellow citizens or close allies, not to the unnamed baby about to be pounded to death in Uganda, and to that baby's many fellow victims.

This view, although commonplace, ignores the fact that a special relationship has been established. There is not a single conflict-affected country that has not been the place of work for many development specialists from the North. Before the conflict, such individuals may have been involved due to personal convictions and moral values, but they nearly always represented a formal aid program of a developed country or NGO. As such, the fact that such development workers are left to scatter at the onset of violent conflict does not diminish the existence of a special relationship between the developed country and the conflict-afflicted country. On this basis, more developed nations that had a relationship of aid with the affected country and who failed to respond promptly and effectively to the widespread harm arising out of the brutality and havoc of such conflict situations bear an unfulfilled, heavy moral obligation.

INTERNATIONAL ASSISTANCE
AND DEVELOPMENT ETHICS

The obligation to provide aid and relief is important, but so too is the need to provide this assistance on an urgent basis. Each passing day of a conflict brings more death, trauma, and destruction—often at a massive scale—yet the wheels of both foreign policy and international relief and development assistance bureaucracies slowly turn at a pace seemingly impervious to urgent appeals from the conflict zone. Nations weigh their strategic options, make their political calculations, and pursue elaborate rituals of diplomatic bargaining with other potential first responders, with trade-offs, institutional turf battles, and political side agreements impeding speedy conclusions. In moral terms, the option of responding to a moral obligation by moving slowly and tentatively in response to the crisis of a violent conflict is impermissible, as to delay is to ensure that further harm will continue, often of unimaginable brutality and against the most vulnerable.

Whether supporting development initiatives across multiple sectors or responding to the urgent needs arising from famines, disease, natural disasters, mass unemployment, financial crisis, or violent conflict, the institutions of international aid are not exempt from confronting ethical dilemmas. Until relatively recently, such dilemmas were poorly perceived and seldom commented upon, and they were certainly not on the agendas of aid decision makers. Gradually, the moral issues of relief and development are attracting the scrutiny and deliberation of increasing numbers of concerned individuals. Much of this rich discourse arises out of the ordinary moral intuitions of average people engaged in development and relief, tempered by their often comprehensive experience in development; but there are also academics, theorists, and policymakers tackling these moral issues in a sophisticated manner, through recourse to international development ethics.

Combining robust philosophical thought, and supported by empirical analysis, the academics, practitioners, and policymakers who are active in international development ethics pose searching, provocative questions regarding the big questions—beginning with continuing efforts to conceptualize, measure, and advocate for development itself. Development ethics considers the human condition; the political, economic, and social processes of development; and the overarching goals of poverty alleviation, leadership, and good governance. Development ethics also generates a remarkable diversity of moral deliberations and helpful guidance on the practical, daily challenges of international development; yet to date, less attention is directed to undevelopment in the form of conflict. With a few notable exceptions, such as the work done by David Crocker, the linkages remain weak between development ethics and the excellent literature and field experience in transitional justice specifically and conflict studies generally (Crocker, 2000).

Much work remains to be done when contemplating a cohesive ethical framework for designing and evaluating appropriate responses to violent conflict, such as how best to deal with urgency, how to access the diaspora of experienced development specialists who flee the conflict, and how to motivate raising the appropriate levels of funding to support a more meaningful response. Where is the appeal to ethical sensibilities and standards to be directed? For those worst afflicted, arguably few such moral resources remain, as conflict often represents the breakdown of morality itself. In development initiatives not associated with conflict conditions, there is some clear moral purchase to be had, some appeal to comprehensible and shared moral standards between the providers and the beneficiaries of aid, some traction with the moral concerns and values that underpin the various social, political, economic, and cultural institutions with whom aid interventions engage. In conditions of violent conflict, however, we are often left only to rely on the moral sensibilities and principles of those few persons assigned to help. Though their moral direction may be clouded by the urgency and the lack of reliable data, many are driven by their various (and often unexamined) moral motivations—their gut response and years of professionalism —to deal with desperate need, to deliver an effective, timely response to an urgent conflict crisis.

The process of engagement between North and South, between aid practitioners and aid recipients, is fundamentally different in conflict settings. In the pursuit of other international development goals during peaceful times, we design, apply, and evaluate interventions in close collaboration and partnership with the stakeholders most affected: the intended beneficiaries. More and more, people in the South have come to lead this process, and we from the North support them by serving as facilitators and resource providers. With them, we delve into issues that vary in intensity—in their urgency for resolution—to seek effective means that result in greater justice, peace, ecological and social harmony, fairness, and human well-being. Throughout these more routine development processes, the overall ethical concerns and principles may or may not be made explicit, but a more ethical standard of international development is made possible when we make the political, social, economic, and perhaps even spiritual space for humanity to become more truly human.

This space for some humanization of development often remains shadowy, superficial, or small as long as the moral dimension of the development processes is only implicit and vague, and not the subject of explicit scrutiny and deliberation. Some would take comfort by pointing out evidence that development is becoming more ethically grounded: we find a more moral vocabulary appearing in the policies, programs, debates, and advocacy that characterizes international foreign assistance, harkening to ideals of global peace, human development, and environmental harmony. This vocabulary, as welcome as it may be, is misleading. None of the major role players in development and aid, with the exception of a now moribund initiative of the Inter-American Development Bank, have made any structured attempt within their institutions to explicitly address development ethics in their thinking, policies, or operations. The World Bank has begun to bring development ethics consultants into a very few specific projects, but for the other multilateral financial institutions and the bilateral donors such as USAID, the rigorous ethical diagnostic, analytical capacities, and moral guidance at the heart of development ethics remains a grossly underutilized resource.[3]

Addressing the ethical content of development is but one dimension of development ethics. Knowing what is right and good is not the same as doing it. When confronted with extreme need, injustice, greed, violence, or exploitation, we react: we express outrage, caring, or other sentiments and thoughts in terms that are clearly moral as well as political. Many of us write letters to our political leaders or send money to NGOs active in international relief and assistance, yet how often do we consciously explore our motivations to act in these ways? Development ethics has the potential to help shape and improve our international development institutions and activities by examining both the content of aid and the motivations that drive aid. Yet despite some progress, these ethical dimensions remain largely unaddressed. Why is this so?

The easy answer, of course, is simply to point to the fact that our nations are governed by those inclined to a realist view of the world (Kapstein, 2006, pp. 38–39), in which moral arguments are said to have relevance only within the boundaries of nation-states, and perhaps only then when convenient: when used instrumentally to support politically or economically derived strategies aimed at defining and maintaining national self-interest. The realist assumption, however, no longer goes unchallenged. Prominent thinkers of the caliber of Nobel Laureate Amartya Sen, building on the compelling arguments of earlier pioneers such as Denis Goulet and others, make a compelling case for the universality of many important moral values associated with what it means to lead truly human lives. Sen, Goulet, and now a long list of prominent thinkers including Sabina Alkire, Luis Camacho, David Crocker, Nigel Dower, Des Gasper, Robert Goodin, Martha Nussbaum, Thomas Pogge, and many others have generated a rich literature and an accessible resource for moral analysis, moral interrogation, and moral guidance in how and why international aid is motivated, conceived, organized, delivered, and evaluated—and how it ought to be.

Many advocate for a more overtly moral approach to international aid, yet the translation of this advocacy into a morally coherent and responsive— meaning *timely*—response to situations of violent conflict (or impending violent conflict) remains unfulfilled. The intensity of human suffering and death, the associated environmental disasters, and the societal upheavals seem overwhelmingly complex, and the urgency too intimidating. If we don't walk away from the situation feeling that there is simply no way to intervene and be effective, we push our various ponderous bureaucracies to respond—*to do something*—and to do it fast, but even those bureaucracies must be propelled by sufficient political will. Some moral precepts apply: we certainly make every effort not to exacerbate a bad situation and create greater harm; but from an ethics perspective, we generally resort to gut reactions and knee-jerk responses, and then try to make sense of it all afterward.

THE CASE OF NORTHERN UGANDA

Consider again the yet unresolved—and still urgent—conflict in northern Uganda. Despite having had 20 years, the world has failed to come to a moral consensus on how best to act to ameliorate this particularly poignant conflict, where children are the primary victims, and savage brutality the most common expression of the LRA's fuzzy message. The LRA has no credible political agenda, and there is no genuine political discussion to be had with Joseph Kony, although several people and institutions have tried.[4] Everywhere there is evidence of profound moral failure—some more preventable than others. It is obvious that Kony has failed the most basic moral obligations of what it means to be a human being, but there are many others less obvious who also bear the moral burdens of failure. Tragically, parents have morally failed in their basic parental duty to protect their young sons and daughters from harm—in this case from the extreme harm of being abducted to become (if they survive at all) deeply traumatized child combatants or sex slaves. Those parents were powerless to prevent this failure, yet they forever bear the burden of that deep loss. The government of Uganda has failed in probably the most basic moral duty of governance—the provision of security to its own citizens, the people of northern Uganda, despite having in its armed forces and police more than 20 times the manpower of the LRA.[5] The people of northern Uganda have been exposed to extremely high levels of violence, yet the Uganda's Peoples' Defense Force has been unable to provide security and, in many cases, has exacerbated the violence (Phuong et al., 2005).[6]

The neighboring country of Sudan (as a country and as individual Sudanese politicians and generals enjoying the fruits of a war economy) has failed to acknowledge or address the moral repercussions of its tacit and sometimes overt support to Kony and his combatants, providing weapons, food, medicines, and money so that the conflict could be sustained.[7] Sudan's moral failure, had it been challenged in moral terms, might have drawn a realist justification that Sudan was legitimately pursuing its larger political interests by keeping the turbulent south of Sudan destabilized (and the Ugandans preoccupied) as a strategy to help dampen the insurrection by the Sudan People's Liberation Army (SPLA).[8] Sudan is not a party to the ICC, yet the ICC's chief prosecutor, Luis Moreno-Ocampo, believed that he had received firm assurances from senior Sudanese leaders that they would cooperate in the arrest of Kony while Kony was based in Sudan, at a location known to the Sudanese.[9] If such a promise was made, the Sudanese conveniently forgot it: yet another example of a simple moral failure with tragic consequences.

The moral failures of Uganda's conflict extend well beyond Africa, however. The international community failed—and arguably continues to fail—to respond in a manner commensurate both with the share of the moral burden that they carry and the immorality of this tragic conflict, having only recently moved the resolution of this conflict onto the agenda of key international and national institutions in the developed world. Even that response is tepid at best, despite the pleadings of Jan Egeland, the Under-Secretary General for Humanitarian Affairs at the United Nations, who recently described the Ugandan conflict as "the worst form of terrorism in the world."

The most significant and potentially long-lasting moral failure, however, may lie in the trajectory of the current peace talks. Sporadic negotiations have stretched over a year between the LRA and the Ugandan government. They restarted most recently on April 26, 2008, in the southern Sudanese town of

Juba, offering a modicum of hope to the prospect of an end to this war, one of the longest and most brutal in Africa. These most recent peace talks showed more structure than previous attempts, perhaps due to greater external involvement, and they made some progress in removing more LRA fighters from northern Uganda. Still, the LRA negotiators were poorly trained, and there were vexing questions as to their legitimacy to speak for and commit the LRA – in the end, Kony disowned these negotiators and the talks failed. If the begin again, the only acceptable outcome, in the view of many people closely concerned with this process, would be one that includes not only a peace agreement but also fair, credible prosecutions for those held primarily responsible for the most serious crimes. This may be the moral sticking point, however.

In this context, the International Crisis Group (ICG) is advocating for a two-pronged approach. First, they argue that the ICC should be provided more assistance from the U.S. and British governments so that it can offer LRA leader Joseph Kony a guarantee of security and livelihood—in other words, offer him an arrangement that does not hold him morally accountable for the outrages that he has instigated and led, and the many lives that he has brutally taken. Second, the ICG advocates for a follow-up national reconciliation forum to be convened to tackle northern Uganda's economic and social alienation, and to present a plan for the region to restore its communities and reintegrate returning rebels. Under the ICG's plan, the controversial issue of impunity from prosecution for Kony and his senior aides is to be swept aside, as the emphasis turns to reconstruction.

While this unreliable peace process staggers ahead, and strategies like the impunity deal proposed by the ICG are considered, the ICC isn't taking any chances. The ICC is crafting contingency plans for a regional security strategy to take action against the LRA, given that the Juba peace talks have again collapsed in failure. The LRA has also made its own contingency plans by continuing to "recruit" new child soldiers and appealing to its former fighters to return to rebuild its strength. Sources in Khartoum also continue to supply the LRA with weapons.[10] The moral outrage continues.

Kony and his colleagues have reason now to expect some degree of immunity from prosecution as a condition of ending the conflict. The situation is further muddied by President Museveni's stated desire to "give Kony a soft landing" through a formal amnesty and the provision of government protection if he would return in peace to Uganda.[11]

Offering legal immunity to Kony is expedient. It also makes possible an alternative form of reconciliation arising out of traditional Acholi tribal culture of northern Uganda, called *mat oput* ("drinking the bitter root"), which requires the perpetrators to admit to their crimes, demonstrate remorse, and seek forgiveness from the Acholi community. The ritual includes drinking a bitter liquid and culminates in the perpetrators being allowed to resume their lives within the community (Phuong et al., 2005). There is no punishment, no retribution, and no compensation to victims.

It is clear from many statements by traditional and religious leaders in the north of Uganda that their first priority is an immediate and final end to the fighting and abductions. These long-suffering people want to get on with their lives, enjoy peace, and leave the squalor and indignity of the IDP camps that so many Ugandans have until recently been required to live in, since the Ugandan military had been unable to secure the countryside (and proved unable even to offer much security within and around the IDP camps). Is there any moral reason not to defer to these local leaders and their values, to allow Kony and his lieutenants back with full legal amnesty and to allow them to rejoin local society after participating in the *mat oput?* Currently the political leadership both in Uganda and among the regional and international nations active in assistance to Uganda seem to be swinging in favor of honoring the wishes and values of these local leaders. The moral implications of such a decision have barely been discussed, however, let alone the implications of what such a decision might mean for Uganda's future.

While the moral weight attached to respecting the expressed wishes and values of the local leaders of the people worst affected by the horrors of the Kony years must be given great weight, I would argue that there are moral concerns that warrant some urgent deliberation. First, what does Museveni's offer of amnesty for Kony and his lieutenants say about the value placed on all of the lives cruelly taken, the brutality inflicted, and the horrible losses endured as a direct result of Kony's actions over the past two decades? What does it say as to the loss of the newborn baby pounded to death? It says that the lives of the baby and all such victims are simply traded away and forgotten, neither valued nor important. No one is held accountable.[12]

Second, Uganda has a troubling history to consider. By offering amnesty for some of the worst crimes imaginable, largely inflicted upon the most innocent Ugandans of all—children—a precedent that began with not holding anyone accountable for the horrors and many human-rights abuses of the Idi Amin Dada years (1971–1979) is being yet again reinforced. First Amin, and now Kony; does this second round of strategically imposed amnesia not make it all the more possible that another turn of the wheel will follow at some future point? What is to stop another person following in Kony's footsteps, inflicting yet more obscene horrors on the citizens of this country, confident of ultimate impunity—that he or she will never be held to account? While everyone wants peace, peace at any price is a profound disservice to the lives lost or shattered by this evil person and his lieutenants, and sets the stage for future atrocities. The political expediency of an amnesty may mean that we sacrifice justice now at the cost of accountability for the past and at the very grave risk to the prospect of a just society in the future. If we follow such a course, we fail in our moral obligations to future generations of Ugandans, and we dismiss the value of innumerable lives lost and sufferings endured.

The offer of amnesty is a very heavy moral price to pay, yet who is to deny the moral right of the traditional leadership in northern Uganda to advocate this course so that peace returns as soon as possible? Try asking the people themselves. While the traditional and religious leaders may be advocating amnesty, and Uganda's senior politicians expressing similar sentiments, credible survey results of ordinary people in Uganda's north tell a different story. Two-thirds of those surveyed believed that there should be accountability by means of formal trials for crimes committed, with those found guilty (in the LRA and on the government side) being sentenced to appropriately severe punishments, while only over one-fifth favored the traditional forms of reconciliation (Phuong et al., 2005). Given these facts, is amnesty really the right choice?

The lessons from transitional justice have not been lost to some of those considering options for northern Uganda. The following draft principles are now in wide circulation among those involved in crafting the response to the Kony dilemma:

First, it is imperative that the wider population views the implementing authorities as both legitimate and impartial. Second, such measures should be selected through a genuine process of consultation with those most affected by the violence. Third, victims must receive formal acknowledgement and recognition of the grave injustices and losses they have suffered. Finally, to work effectively, transitional justice measures must be accompanied by programs that promote security and the rule of law, economic and educational opportunities, access to accurate and unbiased information, freedom of movement and speech, and other comprehensive measures. (Phuong et al., 2005, p. 9)

The balance has yet to be struck between the urgent need for ending the long Kony era's brutal violence and respecting the pressing obligations of justice—to hold those responsible fully accountable. In the interim, there is development work to do, and credit goes to the government of Uganda for setting wheels in motion even before the fighting is truly over. In the recently published *National Peace, Recovery, and Development Plan for Northern Uganda*, the government takes particular note of a comprehensive Amnesty Reintegration Programme, based on the framework of the Amnesty Act (as amended in 2006) as it applies to the reconciliation and reintegration of abducted youth combatants. The tasks are monumental; it estimates that there are more than 17,000 young people eligible for amnesty under the provisions of this act (Cobban, 2006; Government of Uganda, 2006b). Once again the moral questions will arise—who ought to support this level of intervention, which is far in excess of Uganda's financial and institutional capabilities?

HOPE

The many role players in international relief, development, and governance each bear moral obligations to offer resources and assistance to countries in or coming out of violent conflict. These moral obligations arise out of Goulet's sense of universal solidarity and out of a special division of moral labor based on the ability to be effective and on any special relationship that exists. The task now is to recognize the moral dimensions of development, relief, peace-keeping, and peace building; to divide the moral burden; to identify common ethical concerns; and to chart a course for international, regional, and domestic collaboration that is truly responsive to urgent needs. Collaboration of this kind should build upon the comprehensive experience of years of development interventions and should set an unambiguous international standard for transitional justice that no politically expedient settlement can sell short, while remaining sufficiently flexible to allow for practical measures to be adopted to foster a long-lasting and genuine peace. Development ethics has a central role in all of this, but perhaps Goulet best stated its most crucial role: "Most fundamentally . . . the mission of development ethics is to keep hope alive" (Goulet, 1995, p. 27).

CHAPTER 8

Urbanization

Heat and humidity. Those first impressions are unavoidable and constant for visitors arriving at Tanzania's largest city—the coastal metropolis of Dar es Salaam ("port of peace," in Kiswahili). Tanzanians, however, sought to impart different and more flattering first impressions; as in many countries, the airport building and the road from the airport into the capital once received disproportionately more funding and attention than almost any other buildings or roads in the nation. As my Kenya Airways flight from Uganda arrives, however, it is obvious that the formerly gleaming Julius Nyerere International Airport, new in 1984, stands in sore need of rehabilitation if those desired first impressions are to be sustained. A more sober reflection, however, would find many more compelling uses for any available funds; this is after all a big African city, and its investment and renovation needs are many and urgent. The airport may just have to wait; it would be far better for Dar es Salaam to focus on creating a lasting impression among its residents and visitors alike, one characterized by good governance, vitality, and livability.

Dar, as it is commonly referred to, is the rapidly growing Indian Ocean port city of over 2.5 million Tanzanian people. In October 1973, then president Mwalimu Julius Nyerere undercut Dar's prominence when he led the nation in voting that the centrally located small town of Dodoma would henceforth become the capital of the country. For a very long time that decision was largely ignored, although the National Assembly did move there in 1974. Dar, however, remains the administrative and commercial hub of the country, and a very significant proportion of the government offices remain in Dar. Like Kampala and all other burgeoning cities of developing and transitional countries around the world, Dar es Salaam shares many similar development challenges: crushing poverty, weak institutions of local governance, scarce resources, a growing divide between rich and poor, few formal sector jobs, differing universes of formal and informal rules for development and survival, a degraded environment, and so forth.

And so forth? The litany of problems posed by, or constitutive of, urbanization in the developing world makes grim reading—*and so forth* is a very long list indeed. Development practitioners, analysts, and policymakers will capture it in charts and tables, portray it in regression analyses, reflect it in succinct descriptive narratives and empirical calculations, and then move on. If one pauses to look, however, the reality of Dar is so much more that one could surmise from tables, diagrams, numbers, or text. Dar is a community, bustling with resilient, enterprising, hard-working people. Their city is constitutive of their identity, and hearing their urban narrative is important to anyone concerned about urbanization.

I've been a regular visitor to Dar es Salaam ever since the political squabbles between Kenya and Tanzania subsided in 1983 and the border reopened. Given the opportunity of repeated and often extended visits over many years from my home first in Kenya and later in Uganda, I've forged personal relationships and connected in some small way to life in Dar, and to that city's urban narrative. One of my closest friends, Kaisi Kalambo, always welcomes me "home" and guides me through the labyrinth of new developments—political, environmental, and physical. An architect of remarkable integrity and competence, Kalambo nearly always takes me on a tour of his latest buildings, where he strides purposively through the chaos of construction, issuing instructions to the construction contractors, who are usually Chinese in this age of globalization. The contractor speaks no English, and Kalambo not a word of Mandarin or Cantonese, but both communicate well in Kiswahili.

Kalambo's life, even as a successful professional, isn't well insulated from Dar's larger urban narrative of poverty and survival, power and growth. Life in Dar is a struggle, and Kalambo's home is always filled with numerous distant relations from the rural areas, each needing a base in the city as he or she begins a quest to find employment. For many Tanzanians migrating into the city, and even for many longtime Dar residents, their narrative is one of depth and intensity as they struggle to live, love, and raise families in this sprawling city. It is a story that can be heroic or desperate but is usually woven of both strands; losers seem to outnumber winners, and many people simply survive. Few people in Dar flourish, live long and healthy lives, or dare to entertain high aspirations. The struggle is gritty and real, a poignant drama of the human spirit continuously negotiating and renegotiating a grudging, unspoken acceptance of the long list of development burdens—a drama not communicated well by those tables, diagrams, or numbers.

The analytical tools do tell an important part of the story, however. Throughout the developing world, populations are increasingly urban, the amount of urbanized land is expanding with little or no control, and urban poverty is growing. Analysis told us that the year 2006 was a watershed year; for the first time in human history, the majority of the world's population became urban. This majority is predominantly poor, and the developing world's urban areas are filled with many dense but often isolated pockets of intense poverty.

The size and speed of urbanization, the lack of technical capacity to manage growth, the weakness of institutions of local governance, the reluctance if not unwillingness of many national governments to decentralize authority and resources, and the persistence of extreme poverty combine to generate a development challenge of extreme gravity. And while analysts and development practitioners are given to generalize about poverty alleviation and development in countries and regions, generalizations about urban areas quickly run thin; each city and town has its own distinct culture, traditions, resources, and political dynamics, best known to local residents. To some significant extent, therefore, Dar—like each city and town—must find its own answers to the physical and moral challenges of urbanization.

My colleagues in Dar such as my friend Kalambo would undoubtedly agree with me that the technical and governance challenges they confront are complex and daunting. But if I were to ask them what explicitly moral challenges they are confronting, I would expect only confused shrugs. Experts in the built environment—architects, city planners, landscape architects, engineers, environmentalists, city managers, financial, and land experts—do not generally look at Dar and see *moral* challenges. Instead they have framed the urban development challenges in terms of environmental planning and management (EPM), broadening the base of citizen participation in municipal governance, mobilizing increased resources for development, upgrading settlements, providing infrastructure services adequate to meet the city's rapid expansion, improving public transport, collecting and managing the safe disposal of liquid and solid wastes, safeguarding and improving urban parks and open spaces, providing viable and manageable spaces in the city for petty traders, renewing the city center, and resolving the problems of beach erosion.[1] Dar's urban development agenda includes no ethical topics per se, and framing development from an ethical perspective would find little traction in the dialogue, programs, and priorities of the usual urban development actors there. In this respect, we can generalize about most cities and towns in the developing world.

FRAMING THE URBAN CHALLENGE MORALLY

Development actors? Urbanization in Dar es Salaam is about development, and that word alone provides an adequate opening to a rich stream of ethical concerns. Yet these development actors seldom conceptualize their city's development using a moral vocabulary. They take pride in their city's historic buildings, expansive and beautiful beaches, and even in the well-manicured residential areas for its wealthy few. They also feel either distress or even shame, recognizing that coexistent with this historical, attractive Dar is a very different city experienced by the vast majority of its residents. For these less fortunate persons, often unable to meet their basic needs and deprived of opportunities to pursue even modest life ambitions, Dar offers little in the way of quality and little to take pride in.

The existence and impact of such poverty—and the fact that it is getting worse, not better—are gross assaults upon the human dignity of those directly afflicted by poverty. It's a moral challenge. And the urban rich of Dar are not unaware of these dire conditions affecting so many of their less fortunate fellow Tanzanians whom they drive past each day; their passive toleration of this disparity in wealth brings into question the existence of any common baseline of human dignity. That's a moral challenge. The list only begins here. Consider the lack of participation in decision making by the informal settlers in the squatter areas of Dar, the lack of essential security, and the widespread presence of corruption. Consider the lack of basic health and education resources, the limited access to any recreation, and the degradation of sensitive ecological areas in Dar—all moral challenges. Yet the fact remains that the growth and development of Dar is not typically viewed in a moral light. Instead, development actors in Dar will exclaim over advances made through privatizing much of the city's solid waste management, how city traffic has been rationalized by new one-way street schemes, or even how the local governance structures have been improved by the Dar es Salaam City Council, which was reorganized in 2000 into three constitutive municipalities (Ilala, Kinondoni, and Temeke). These are all important *means* to the *end* of development, but by focusing so much on means and so little on the meaning and values of development—the end goal of these various development means—the means become the measure. The larger vision of Dar es Salaam as a livable, humane, safe, economically vibrant, environmentally sustainable, and culturally rich city ought to frame and rationalize the various development investments and projects; but instead the projects become ends in themselves, and the predominant topics of discussion among the development actors. Who has the larger picture in mind, the integrated view, the vision of Dar as an *end*, not just the *means?* Arguably, we should turn to the integrating profession of urban growth and development—the profession of urban planning.

MORAL DIMENSIONS OF URBAN PLANNING

Planners integrate, anticipate, and rationalize. Experts in harmonizing multiple urban development trajectories, it is the urban planner's role to assist administrative and political decision makers to understand the complex dynamics of urbanization in any given urban area, to be the technical interface between the expressed needs and development dreams of average urban residents, as well as the ones who allocate the resources and manage the city. Yet planners only advise the powerful; they do not exercise power themselves. In Dar there are very few persons trained in urban planning, and fewer still are the urban planners in influential positions in urban governance. Yet Dar does have a credible planning heritage. Since 1992, Dar es Salaam has been an active participant in the United Nations' Sustainable Cities Programme (SCP), which has focused on improving some of the technical means applied by planners. This program has included strengthening environmental and planning capacity, and broadening participatory planning techniques. In 1998, the SCP program in Dar was bolstered by new institutional resources, in the form of the Urban Authorities Support Unit (UASU), which was established to provide a source of technical urban development and planning support to local authorities in Dar and throughout Tanzania's other leading cities and towns. With a small staff of planners, engineers, technical officers, information officers, and accountants, UASU made a small effort to improve the means of Dar's development, but UASU seldom addressed the overarching vision of Dar's development and did not allocate any particular effort to articulating the moral and ethical issues that Dar's development entails.

At the national level, Tanzania's Regional Administration and Local Government agency within the Prime Minister's Office released in June 2006 the National Framework for Urban Development and Environmental Management (UDEM). The product of an extensive participatory process, this framework also failed to discuss in any significant way the vision and quality, the values and aspirations, that urban development in Tanzania embraces (or ought to). It is a framework again of *means*, in the form of institutional capacity strengthening and capital development grant funds (largely from Danish donor aid) for municipalities and towns. Moral issues are given no attention in this national framework document.

Tanzania isn't alone in creating institutional capacities to address urbanization. Internationally, the Global Campaign on Urban Governance[2] focuses attention on the needs of the excluded urban poor, and in so doing, they addresses critical moral issues more directly. For example, the campaign promotes the involvement of women in decision making at all levels, recognizing that women are one of the biggest levers for positive change in society. The campaign is intended to make a significant contribution to implementing the Habitat Agenda goal of sustainable human settlements development and to supporting the United Nations' action strategy for halving extreme poverty by 2015 (although I and many others have grave doubts as to the attainability of this goal or even the metrics by which it is being measured).[3]

The campaign theme—inclusiveness—reflects both the campaign's moral vision and its strategy. The vision is to realize the so-called Inclusive City, a place where everyone, regardless of wealth, gender, age, race, or religion, is enabled to participate productively and positively in the opportunities cities have to offer. Inclusive decision-making processes are an essential means to achieve this and are the cornerstone of the campaign. The concept of inclusiveness also links the governance campaign to the United Nations Human Settlements Program's (UN-HABITAT) Global Campaign for Secure Tenure.[4]

As these international efforts make clear, moral issues abound in planning. The techniques of urban planning are not value neutral, since every system of representing desirable future development serves some interests and goals better than others. Also, planners do exercise moral agency, and many *oughts* attach to the planning role. Planners ought to view their work as a form of action embedded in society having a time dimension. They ought to be conscious of being a part of complex and continuing processes of creation, and they ought to see their role as having important moral implications.

In countries that are more developed, urban planners are being challenged by colleagues within their profession to become more reflective in their deliberations, to involve citizens more fully in the planning process, and—most generally—to come to terms with ethical means and ends in their work. As advocated by Norman Krumholz (planner) and John Forester (planner and academic):

> When we speak of ethics in planning, we refer to a capacity to argue about what to do, to a capacity to think about, evaluate, and judge alternative courses of action. We should prize ethical thinking in planning not because it will magically promote consensus or coherence in the field, but because it can help us understand more sensitively just what is at stake in public decision processes and in our own actions. To put it more simply, by enriching our capacities for judgment and questioning, ethical thinking can help us become more insightful evaluators and analysts, better planners, better actors. Ethical thinking concerns ends and means alike. If planners are to pursue something they regard as 'the public interest,' surely they should have some articulate conception of what that involves. (Krumholz & Forester, 1990, p. 253)

Internationally, the planner's role has evolved. Unlike the days when the job of the planner was to craft a master development plan and seek political champions with sufficient power to implement it, most urban planners now see themselves as facilitators and guides in a complex urban growth and planning process—a process that ought to be framed explicitly in the normative context of serving the public interest. Yet largely as a result of the input of the life sciences, anthropology, social sciences, and philosophy, the planning of the city has come to be viewed less as an exercise in serving that public interest—however articulated—and more as a set of technical challenges to be overcome, involving complex social, cultural, economic, political, and physical phenomena, subject to a multitude of interactions and interrelationships. This technology-reliant and putatively value-neutral *technical school* of planning theory still persists from as long ago as the 1960s and remains influential with urban planners in developing countries such as Tanzania.

Sophisticated and powerful high-technology tools of the *technical school* of planning, such as computerized geographic information systems (GIS), are now available in cities such as Dar, and do allow for effective analysis and planning in this problem-solving mode. When the time comes, however, to shift from analysis by planners to decision-making about urban development choices, these decisions are made by government officials, and are less responsive to scientific analysis and more a product of political and social dynamics.

The complexity of human societies and the developmental needs of human well-being within urban environments require more than an exclusively scientific and technical planning approach leading up to a political process of decision-making. I argue that a richer and more integrated approach to urban planning is needed, based upon the ideals of democratic deliberation, a commitment to transparency in the power relationships that most influence allocation of resources within the city, and a new focus on the evolving meanings of *development* for each city. This is a normative as well as a technical urban development process, involving diagnostic, analysis, planning, design, and management functions all anchored in well-articulated secular moral values: social, cultural, and environmental. In the more developed cities of the world, some planners and community groups have begun to see urban development through a moral lens and have together crafted vision statements that capture the moral and aesthetic qualities of development as a guide for all decisions about the means (investments, deliberative processes, projects) to pursue that vision, but in Dar es Salaam—where urban planning has minimal influence in shaping the city's growth and quality—the dynamics of urban planning and governance lack any cohesive moral approach.

CHANGING POWER RELATIONSHIPS

Over nearly 30 years of work as a development practitioner, I have perceived a growing awareness by the public—internationally and within developing countries—of the plight of the powerless poor who live in territorially isolated urban enclaves, deprived of adequate services and opportunities. I attribute this not to a mysterious burgeoning compassion on the part of the powerful elites, whose hearts (and pockets) remain largely closed, but instead to an ever-increasing capacity of the poor to advocate on their own behalf. Through civil-society action, the Internet, and the media generally, more attention gradually is being focused on principles of democracy and participation, mainstreaming gender concerns, and even on reducing corruption. With the affirmation by the poor of their own values, priorities, aspirations, and claims, some urban decision makers are becoming more attentive to such normative ideals as quality of life, empowerment, human rights, deliberative participation, and citizenship. Residents of many cities in the less developed countries now have more opportunities—and sometimes their first opportunity—to identify and articulate some common values and aspirations through visioning exercises, as stakeholders participating in integrated urban development projects. These visioning exercises invite the urban residents as the stakeholders in the urban development process to find consensus on the moral values and qualities that, for their city, characterize the *common good* or the *public interest*.

In its most general sense, the common good may be said to consist of the policies and actions that best serve to promote the essential components of human well-being (or, more ambitiously, human flourishing) for all. Identifying an acceptable consensus on the *common good*, or its equivalent phrase, the *public interest*, is a controversial undertaking because of differing conceptions of human well-being. In utilitarian thinking, the common good is the best net score of individual interests in the community—a concept that obviously sacrifices some people's interests to that of others. Others contend that a consensus on the common good can be articulated only roughly and is often subject to moral disagreements. According to this view, it is through a deliberative democratic process of reasoning together that the common good can be agreed upon and mutually acceptable decisions can be made (Gutmann & Thompson, 1996). Amy Gutmann and Dennis Thompson describe a process in which people in conflict reason reciprocally, recognizing the moral worth of the opposing person, even when they consider his or her position to be morally wrong. Under this concept of deliberative democracy, which is discussed in more detail in chapter 4, there exists a mutual obligation of respect toward opponents and a commitment to the depersonalization of development issues. Through such an approach, a common good acceptable to (almost) all often can be agreed upon.

Serving the common good is more frequently the stuff of rhetoric than reality in cities such as Dar es Salaam, where the powerful are more likely to prevail based not on majority interests but on the pursuit of their own special interests, with very little reference to ideals of city citizenship and common destiny. If we turn to the international context, the rhetoric of serving the common good does have some traction, given that the dialogue regarding the moral dimensions of good urban governance is well advanced and thought provoking. Translating these international intellectual and moral notions to become motivation factors for Dar es Salaam's city councilors or mayor may be a stretch, given the dynamics of power in Dar. The UN-HABITAT, however, continues to make efforts to engage cities, partners, and the international community in a vigorous if somewhat isolated debate on what exactly constitutes good urban governance and has published a normative framework on good urban governance. The campaign to promote this framework began by arguing for the following description of good urban governance:

Urban governance is the sum of the many ways individuals and institutions, public and private, plan and manage the common affairs of the city. It is a continuing process through which conflicting or diverse interests may be accommodated and cooperative action can be taken. It includes formal institutions as well as informal arrangements and the social capital of citizens.

Urban governance is inextricably linked to the welfare of the citizenry. Good urban governance must enable women and men to access the benefits of urban citizenship. Good urban governance, based on the principle of urban citizenship, affirms that no man, woman or child can be denied access to the necessities of urban life, including adequate shelter, security of tenure, safe water, sanitation, a clean environment, health, education and nutrition, employment and public safety and mobility. Through good urban governance, citizens are provided with the platform which will allow them to use their talents to the full to improve their social and economic conditions.[5]

The success of the SCP in Dar has been modest, at best, but commensurate with the relatively modest funding allocated to this initiative. The Dar es Salaam City Council however continues with a variety of initiatives. These efforts are focused on resolving the lack of uniform policy and service delivery standards between the formal and the informal sectors, upgrading basic infrastructure and services in squatter settlements, and improving urban transportation infrastructure and solid-waste management. Unfortunately, and despite the many years of the SCP activities, information and policies are poorly integrated into Dar's urban-planning efforts, and the city's capacity even to monitor its growth is highly constrained. The legal and regulatory framework that currently exists is entirely inadequate to meet the pressing needs of the housing sector—a sector already struggling since the collapse of the Tanzania Housing Bank in the late 1980s. The city also continues to grow organically, with very little control, and very inadequate infrastructure services to accommodate this growth.

At the end of the day, the problem is also a lack of funds. There are simply inadequate national and local government budgetary allocations to enable the city to implement its action plans. At least the planners of Dar are offering good advice, as they actively encourage the political powers in that city to accept the participation of the urban poor in the updating and drafting of all urban policies and programs.

TOWARD NORMS OF GOOD URBAN GOVERNANCE

From the outset, UN-HABITAT's campaign aimed to develop universal norms that could be operationalized, with implementation grounded in the realities of urban planning and development in cities such as Dar. For this reason, the campaign proposed that good urban governance should be characterized by the principles of sustainability, subsidiarity, equity, efficiency, transparency and accountability, civic engagement and citizenship, and security, and that these principles are interdependent and mutually reinforcing. These are largely normative principles and worth closer consideration.

Sustainability applies to all dimensions of urban development. UN-HABITAT argues that cities must balance the social, economic, and environmental needs of present and future generations, and include a clear commitment to urban poverty reduction.[6] This would require leadership at all levels and institutions of urban society to commit to a long-term, strategic vision of sustainable human development and to possess the ability and political will to reconcile divergent interests for the sake of the common good.

Subsidiarity of authority and resources to the closest appropriate level simply means that the responsibility for service provision should be allocated on the basis of the principle of subsidiarity, that is, at the closest appropriate level consistent with efficient and cost-effective delivery of services. Arguably, this will maximize the potential for inclusion of the citizenry in the process of urban governance. Decentralization and local democracy should, it is conjectured, improve the responsiveness of policies and initiatives to the priorities and needs of citizens.

Sharing of power leads to *equity* in the access to and use of resources, in access to decision-making processes and to the basic necessities of urban life. Under this thinking, women and men participate as equals in all urban decision making, priority setting, and resource allocation processes. Cities, to claim the label *inclusive*, must provide everyone—be it the poor; the young; older persons; religious, ethnic, minorities; or the handicapped—with equitable access to nutrition, education, employment and livelihood, health care, shelter, safe drinking water, sanitation, and other basic services.

Efficiency in the delivery of public services and in promoting local economic development means that cities must be financially sound, cost effective, and transparent in their management of revenue sources and expenditures; the administration and delivery of services; and their efforts to engage government, the private sector, and communities to contribute formally or informally to the urban economy. A key element in achieving efficiency is to recognize and enable the specific contribution of women to the urban economy.

Transparency and *accountability* of decision makers and all stakeholders is a fundamental tenet of good governance. There should be no place for corruption in cities, yet ample room for the expression and recognition of integrity in public service. Corruption undermines local government credibility and deepens urban poverty. In fighting corruption, transparency and accountability enable stakeholders to understand their local government and to see clearly who is benefiting from specific decisions and actions. Access to information is fundamental to this understanding and to good governance, and laws and public policies ought to be applied in a transparent and predictable manner. Leadership also must be ethical; elected and appointed officials and other civil-servant leaders need to set an example of high standards of professional and personal integrity. Finally, citizen participation is a key element in promoting transparency and accountability.

In terms of *civic engagement* and *citizenship*, people are the principal wealth of cities; they are both the object and the means of sustainable human development. Civic engagement implies that living together is not a passive exercise: in cities, people have a moral obligation to do no harm and actively to contribute to the common good. Citizens, and especially women given their historical marginalization, must be empowered to participate effectively in decision-making processes, and the civic and social capital of the poor ought to be recognized and supported.

Security of individuals and their living environment means that every individual has the inalienable right to life, liberty, and the security of person. Insecurity has a disproportionate impact in further marginalizing poor communities. Cities, therefore, have a moral obligation to avoid human conflicts and natural disasters by involving all stakeholders in the prevention of crime and conflict, in disaster preparedness, and in strengthening the rule of law (police, courts, and laws). Security also implies freedom from persecution or forced evictions and is commonly expanded to embrace security of tenure. Cities should also make optimal use of social mediation and conflict reduction approaches and encourage cooperation between enforcement agencies and other social service providers (health, education, and housing).

UN-HABITAT's norms of good governance presume that urban governments are democratic, and that they are serving the public interest as expressed through and held accountable by democratic institutions. While the City Council of Dar es Salaam is much improved over its predecessor, it has some distance still to go before it becomes a model of democratic and *good* governance. While residents of Dar await that day, the dialogue of what constitutes a desirable, livable, humane city should be pursued in earnest, so that those placed in positions of power and trust in local government have clear ethical expectations before them.

THE EMERGENCE OF EXPLICIT ETHICAL PRINCIPLES

For the poor in Dar es Salaam, just like the urban and rural poor throughout the developing world, the prospect of receiving large-scale external assistance from the more developed nations anytime soon is unrealistic. Instead, initiatives to eradicate urban poverty and improve urban governance will continue to depend in large measure on incrementally improving the quality and effectiveness of local and national leadership in such cities and towns. Effective local leadership in turn is linked to progress in decentralization—bringing an appropriate level of institutional capacity, resources, and political control from the national to the local level, for urban and rural residents alike.

Moving power and resources closer to local residents by means of decentralization is essential, but it, too, is but part of the solution. Authentic development responsive to the needs and desires of the urban residents demands good governance, which in turn is dependent on ethical political leadership as discussed extensively in chapter 3. Urban development and the planning needed to achieve and sustain it also must be grounded in the recognition of the principal of universal human dignity and the many moral obligations that arise from that recognition. The acceptance of a common human dignity and pervasive moral equality is the starting point for determining what it means for political leadership to be *ethically responsive*, and what ought to characterize the *good* of good urban governance.

The urban development challenge is not just to bring about economic growth, for growth is but a means to something else. Human dignity is fundamental, but urban development is also framed by important and arguably universal values of social justice, human flourishing, the common good, deliberative participation and inclusion, and safety and security. In considering urban development as a moral endeavor, it is worth being clear in our understanding of these various constitutive concepts.

Human dignity perhaps more than any other moral concept justifies the labeling of urban development as a moral endeavor. Urban development, as with development generally, must begin by answering the "development for what" and "development benefiting who" questions. The answers, if pursued in a setting conducive to moral dialogue and articulated by the residents, planners, administrators, politicians, and leaders of each respective city and town, will inescapably embrace ideals of human and social well-being. What might such ideals be?

The concept of human dignity has its roots in the idea of social honor; *dignitas* in Latin means just this—honor. The Israeli philosopher, Avishai Margalit, in his work on portraying the attributes of the *decent society*, claims that the achievement of such a society depends on universal acceptance throughout society that everyone deserves social honor in equal measure, which is best expressed in the concept of human dignity. Dignity, according to Margalit, also constitutes the external aspect of self-respect and the tendency to behave in a dignified manner that attests to one's self-respect (Margalit, 1996, p. 43).

Margalit, as with Rousseau and Kant before him, justifies respecting human nature, a concept closely aligned with human dignity and intrinsic worth. Kant, for instance, listed many attributes of humanity that give it value, including (but not limited to): (1) being a creature who gives things values, (2) having the capacity for self-legislation, (3) having the ability progressively to pursue perfection, (4) having the capacity to be a moral agent, (5) being rational, and (6) being the only creature able to transcend natural causality (Margalit, 1996, p. 63).

Yet Margalit is pragmatic when he states quite flatly that "survival takes priority over dignity" (Margalit, 1996, p. 136). For the poor in Dar es Salaam to achieve the most basic level of human dignity, they must first satisfy their most basic needs and, in so doing, claim the opportunity that they deserve by right of being human to live a truly human life. Without acceptance and satisfaction of the moral right to human survival, discussions of human dignity become merely theoretical.

Social justice is associated with fair, even-handed treatment of all individuals and groups within a society, including within an urban society. An alternative formulation, indebted to John Rawls, is that conceptions of distributive justice[7] clarify and defend how major social institutions should distribute burdens and benefits (however conceived) (Rawls, 1971, pp. 62, 177–180). The important point at this juncture is to indicate that different conceptions of justice offer different conceptions of burdens and benefits as well as different conceptions of the proper principles of distribution.

On social justice, the philosopher Thomas Pogge remarks:

Its current most prominent use is in the moral assessment of social institutions, understood not as organized collective agents (such as the United States government or the World Bank), but rather as a social system's practices or "rules of the game," which govern interactions among individual and collective agents as well as their access to material resources . . . Prominent within our political discourse, then, is the goal of formulating and justifying a criterion of justice, which assesses the degree to which the institutions of a social system are treating the persons and groups they affect in a morally appropriate and, in particular, evenhanded way. (Paul, Miller, & Paul, 1999, p. 337).

Two leading philosophers, Thomas Pogge and Douglas Rasmussen, make reference to the close relationship between social justice and human flourishing. According to Rasmussen, social justice is the prerequisite for the achievement of human flourishing (Paul et al., 1999, p. 27). However, other ways of conceiving the relation are possible.

Manfred Max-Neef, an economist and noted development practitioner, considers that social justice has become, in some instances, conflated with economic growth. He criticized the prevalent thinking that simply by growing the economy there will be more to share, without having to tackle the more thorny issues of distributing or redistributing the proportions of the total. Max-Neef contends that it is ineffectual to focus on the maintenance of static distributive proportions while growth proceeds. The reality is that the poor usually get less and less: "even with growth, the poor's share of the cake diminishes" (Max-Neef, 1992, p. 51).

Some feminist ethicists offer an interesting view on the issue of social justice. Carol Gilligan notes that from a social-justice perspective, the individual as moral agent must judge the conflicting claims of self and others against a standard of equality (e.g., the Golden Rule). As an alternative, she proposes that the interdependent and *caring relationship* becomes the determinate of self and others, under which the self as a moral agent perceives and responds to the perception of need within and around her. The moral question shifts from "what is just" to "how to respond" (Kittay & Meyers, 1987, p. 23).

The notion of *human well-being*, sometimes but not always identified with *human flourishing*, is intuitively understood by each of us, perhaps without consciously attempting to be precise in its definition. For the sake of urban planning and development strategies, this intuitive understanding may suffice. Yet many philosophers have wrestled with this notion, formulating and justifying their varying conceptions, which in turn are challenged by other philosophers. In the short section to follow, I present an overview of the range of these conceptions, not to step into the philosophers' debates by arguing for any one position, but instead to impart something of the conceptual richness and diversity of this important objective of human development.

The concept of flourishing, if not well-being, is to some extent relative to the development agent—the individual person concerned. No one concept of human flourishing is wholly relevant for all, and each person's sense of the good life may differ in many respects. To a considerable extent, the notion depends upon knowledge of the possibilities open to a person and the availability of freedoms and resources essential to pursue those opportunities. Despite agent-relative differences in conceptions of the good, there may still be a defensible cross-cultural conception of *basic* well-being or at least of a human life not going badly.

Nuanced definitions of well-being and flourishing do exist. Philosophers such as Amartya Sen, David Crocker, and James Griffin distinguish between well-being, minimal well-being, and flourishing or the good life (Crocker & Linden, 1998, pp. 366–385; Griffin, 1996, pp. 85–86; Sen, 1999, pp. 70–76). Other philosophers have attempted to characterize the ideal of human flourishing or the less robust notion of human well-being. Rasmussen, for example, proposes a neo-Aristotelian conception of human flourishing, in which he states that human flourishing is a way of living and acting, not something static. It is desirable because of what it is, and while not the only activity of inherent worth, it is the "ultimate end of human conduct" (Paul et al. 1999, p. 3). This is not meant to imply that human flourishing is achieved as some end state of well-being; instead, flourishing is seen in a life that is worthwhile as a whole. Aristotle viewed human flourishing, among other things, as a self-directed activity. The neo-Aristotelian position, according to Rasmussen, dictates that human flourishing is not a direct result of luck or factors beyond one's own control and that it must be achieved through one's own efforts if it is to have value. Moral consideration also is required to determine what form of flourishing is best for each individual (Paul et al., 1999, p. 11). The philosopher Charles Larmore has a more nuanced view; he argues flourishing is more than a self-directed accomplishment. How one responds to factors beyond one's control is also important to the achievement of human flourishing and well-being (Paul et al., 1999, p. 97).

Safety and *security* refer generally to conditions of stability, order, predictability, and freedom from bodily harm (Rosan, Ruble, & Tulchin, 2000, pp. 14, 76). Within the urban context, these concepts can be interpreted in a wide variety of ways. They may be reflected in public health and environmental concerns, such as being able to live within a city without becoming ill or being subject to environmental disasters. These concepts also may extend to economic security, in which access to employment and/or other forms of welfare ensures access to adequate resources for human flourishing, or at least, human survival.

In human-rights terms, security encompasses many negative rights and freedoms. Achieving a sustainable sense of security involves certain critical freedoms, such as the freedom *from* poverty and *from* violence. Positive rights and freedoms are also included—the ability *to* achieve a decent standard of living.

The United Nations Development Programme (UNDP) makes the point that no other aspect of human security is more vital as security from physical violence. It lists several sources of threats of violence, including (1) the state (torture, arbitrary arrest, and detention), (2) other states (war, support for oppressive regimes), (3) other groups of people (ethnic conflicts, street violence, crime), (4) threats directed at women (rape, domestic violence, trafficking), and (5) threats directed at children (child abuse) (UNDP, 2000, p. 35).

While I focus on *participation* and *inclusion* in chapter 4, it is worth noting here that there are many kinds and intensities of participation, ranging from Gutmann and Thompson's deliberative democracy model to simple voting, from open and advisory public hearings to visioning workshops. Each has its benefits and limitations. I argue for a facilitated model of *deliberative participation*, claiming that the notion of a truly deliberative, participatory process is important to the achievement of sustainable urban development, but recognizing that such a pure process is not generally achievable in the absence of expert facilitation. In this respect, a deliberative participatory process either assumes or includes—through a partially structured or facilitated dialogue— the ideals described in this chapter: human dignity, social justice, human flourishing and well-being, the common good, safety and security, and similar ideals. Deliberative participation also offers a way to specify, weigh, trade-off, and sequence (the realization) of these ideals.

URBAN DEVELOPMENT'S MORAL PRIORITIES

Compared to the desolation in 2008 of Cyclone Nargis in Burma, the earthquakes that took the lives of 67,000 persons in 2008 in China, ongoing dictatorial repression in Zimbabwe, or the slaughter of the innocents in Darfur and in the Democratic Republic of Congo, the challenges of urbanization in cities and megacities (roughly defined as cities over 10 million inhabitants) appear far less urgent and garner less media focus. Security and peace come first in the hierarchy of development, as they must.

There is, however, a strong correlation between security and peace, and the increasing pressures of urbanization. These numbers tell an important story of pressure reaching critical and unmanageable proportions, exacerbated recently by severe food shortages and escalating prices for basic foodstuffs. The urbanization subset of numbers in various development reports is not always easy to access, and data analysis techniques and management varies from city to city, but the demographics of poverty and urbanization are readily available and remarkably sobering. Globally, 60 percent of the world's population will be urban by the year 2030,[8] and in just 11 years from now, half of the population on the developing world will be urban residents.[9] Currently, there are an estimated 23 megacities worldwide, and by 2015, this total will rise to 36, the vast majority being in developing countries.[10] Many of the poor are not living *quality* lives, as around the world, 2.4 billion (mostly female) persons already lack access to basic sanitation, and more than 1 billion (mostly female) persons now exist on unsafe water.[11] Stepping down from the billions plateau, nearly 800 million persons are undernourished.[12] Viewed from a daily perspective, 34,000 children younger than five die each day from hunger and preventable disease—that's almost 24 children each and every minute of every month of every year.[13] If awesome numbers start to sound fuzzy, think in fractions. About one-third of all human deaths are linked to poverty, deaths that are in most cases preventable.[14] One-fifth of the world's population lives in cities where the air is unhealthy to breathe.[15]

The empirical dimensions of the development problematic are well described. So, too, are the facts regarding the paucity of resources currently allocated to alleviating the misery and suffering of underdevelopment. Rich countries currently spend about $11 billion annually in development assistance targeted at basic social services. Over 60 percent of this comes from individual people in rich countries through contributions to international NGOs, and the other 40 percent comes from their governments.[16] Estimates place this combined sum at just 3.6 percent of the amount that would actually be needed to eradicate severe poverty,[17] or $300 billion annually—a figure that would lessen significantly over time.[18] This sum may sound like a lot, but raising annual development expenditures at this level would barely make a perceptible impact on the quality of life of those living in the wealthiest countries, who only represent 15 percent of the world's population.[19] Easily affordable,[20] yet current funding levels are $11 billion? Why the discrepancy?

Perhaps the numbers are letting us down. We are unmoved, or at least not sufficiently moved, by the stories that the numbers tell us. As elements in a larger argument, numbers are essential, but without the personal connection to the persons and stories behind the numbers, they only move us a short distance. The numbers even take us to destinations we would rather avoid. Pogge explored this phenomenon, and his observations caused no small degree of consternation. Adopting a largely utilitarian argument, he pointed out the inescapable fact that in a world in which the demand for urgent humanitarian aid and basic development assistance is vastly greater than the supply of resources, decisions about where and how to spend money inevitably leave people out—and in many cases, leave people to die. Even those who contribute to international NGOs (INGOs) share this moral dilemma, as Pogge notes: "Different INGOs prevent different deaths. And by contributing to one rather than another, I am then indirectly deciding who will live and who will die."[21]

Pogge journeys far with these numbers, exploring where money and resources spent on international development assistance ought (and that's an intentionally moral ought) first to be directed. As posed by Pogge, ought the available resources be used to:

a. Protect persons from the most serious harms instead of lesser harms?
b. Protect an extremely poor person from serious harm instead of to protect a merely poor person from serious harm?
c. Protect a larger number of persons from some serious harm rather than to protect a smaller number of equally badly-off persons from equally serious harm?
d. Support a greater number of less expensive development interventions, thereby reaching more people; or to support fewer but more expensive interventions, thereby affecting fewer people?[22]

The answers seem clear enough. We would naturally want to minimize harms, give most aid to those most adversely affected, and distribute our resources so that they achieve maximum benefit for the maximum number of people. Persisting with Pogge's logic, however, the so-called "numbers approach will lead us to some unexpected situations. For example, using empirical analyses of what it costs to take one person permanently out of poverty—which varies by city and country—it seems sensible to use the few resources that we do have to accomplish the most good, in other words, raising the maximum number of people out of poverty. Yet this moral argument, interpreted strictly, would mean that *all* international aid should then flow to those cities and countries where this unit cost is the least, where we could generate the greatest benefit, and to nowhere else. Arguments for distributive fairness of resources across regions, countries, or cities[23] then fail against this utilitarian claim that we ought to maximize the number of people we can help permanently raise from poverty—regardless of whether they happen to reside in just a few countries.

Cities in poor countries have relatively high densities of poor people living in close proximity, and so they fare rather well under this type of analysis. For example, due to high concentrations of poor people, it is more cost effective to provide safe water to an urban location than a rural one. Therefore, by the intentionally provocative philosophical argument that Pogge makes, we ought to maximize the provision of safe water and concentrate our water projects exclusively in cities. After all, for the same cost of providing just one rural person with safe, potable water, many urban residents could have this basic human need met. Is the moral claim of one rural person to safe water more persuasive than the combined claim of many urban persons?

A HEAVY MORAL BURDEN

Where Pogge's argument trails off is where I become even more interested. Pogge's articulation of the dilemma of choices leads us to confront a conundrum central to policymakers and development practitioners who have been entrusted to make decisions regarding the allocation and distribution of resources (money, supplies, services) to poorer people—we bear an untenable moral burden of choice. Our every decision becomes a triage, a tragic decision. If we consult only numbers, the calculation feels less oppressive, but what if we must look the rejected person in the eye, hear her words, connect with her urban narrative? Could we send a father carrying his malnourished toddler, too weak to walk on her own, away to face the suffering of a slow death, because it is not cost effective to distribute food aid in his city?

The numbers and the associated arguments of cost effectiveness only address some of the parameters in deciding where the money goes, because the money will not come close to satisfying all the urgent needs. The political will and national interest of the wealthier nations compel policymakers and development practitioners to walk away from people who—on the basis of political calculations—matter less than others. After all, we (the wealthy) can only do so much. And the numbers have not moved us enough. We read the statistics, but accepting a Pogge-like conclusion, we chose to make the most of what few resources are available and we balk at intervening in complex concentrations of urban suffering—Lagos, Calcutta, Dhaka, Karachi, or even Dar es Salaam. We can agree that it seems wrong to turn our back on whole cities, countries, or conflicts, because our money goes farther somewhere else. Even if the moral cost-benefit argument is that we ought to favor the poor of Africa and Asia over the poor of South America (or North America, for that matter), it seems unfair—even callous—to ignore the poorest people of an entire continent, simply because the poor of a different continent are brought out of poverty at less *unit* expense. Is there no escape from the utilitarian argument claiming that because we can raise more people out of poverty in some locations than in others (e.g., in cities), and that because each person is morally equal to another person, we ought to favor the choice that maximizes results? If it were only a matter of helping people to various stages on the ladder of human flourishing, we could come to some peace with our decisions. Instead, the decisions that development practitioners are left to make keep some people alive and leave others to suffer or die.

CHAPTER 9

Minority Rights

"They are despised."

The Ugandan professor's statement was devoid of emotion, a simple statement of fact. In Uganda, transgender and intersex people are despised, humiliated, rejected, stigmatized, even frequently subjected to violence. Despite Dr. Byaruhanga Rukooko's advanced education and sophisticated intellect, further discussion with my academic friend made it clear to me that he, in common with the vast majority of even well-educated people throughout the world, have very little information about the scientific characteristics and quality of life implications of the transgender and intersex phenomena. Despite the formidable challenges of chauffeuring me safely through the chaotic traffic of Kampala, my friend paused to think and then recalled a boy back in his early school days. This boy believed he was a girl, and according to Rukooko, the boy tried to live as one, with all of the expected tragic consequences. "Well, I must admit," mused my friend, "he showed remarkable courage."

Courage is a virtue that transgender and intersex persons frequently hear attributed to them. It may be as close to a compliment as many will ever receive, particularly in developing countries such as Uganda where most people cling tightly to a communitarian ethical structure in which moral values are defined within the parameters and confines of local culture, only intended to pertain to that society. Among communitarians, individualism does not have pride of place in establishing moral terms of reference, unlike the more liberal and individualistic cultures common to more prosperous societies in Europe, Australia, New Zealand, and North America.

Those Ugandans who come to a realization that their own authentic sense of gender identity (and, in the case of intersex persons, certain characteristics of their body's physical gender manifestations) does not match their socially assigned gender identity confront a very different future than do transgender or intersex persons in more liberal societies. In America, Europe, Australia, New Zealand, and progressively in much of Asia, there is a real prospect through counseling, hormonal therapy, and sexual reassignment surgery that a complete transition to the other gender in the case of a transgender person, or resolution of ambiguous gender traits for intersex persons, is achievable. The majority of those who *transition* in the more developed countries look forward to living the balance of their lives with a gender identity that they believe to be authentic, melting back into society with anonymity as they are accepted in their chosen gender. For nearly all transgender Ugandans, however, the future holds no such cheerful prospect. For them, and for most transgender and intersex persons throughout the developing world, there is no transition—no professional counselors, no hormone therapy managed by endocrinologists, no laser treatments to remove unwanted facial hair, and no surgery to transform the genitals (and, in some cases, certain facial features) from one gender to the other. Instead, most transgender or intersex Ugandans face the prospect of living their lives bereft of fulfillment of their sense of internal authenticity, eternally consciousness of being trapped in the "wrong" body. They cope as well as they can in the face of societal rejection, violence, and shame; but for most of them, it is a life deeply deficient in quality, dignity, respect, fellowship, or hope.

AN INSIGNIFICANT LITTLE PROBLEM

Vast numbers of poor persons throughout the developing world face monumental challenges just to survive, let alone achieve well-being. Compared to this misery, the misfortune of a statistically insignificant number of transgender or intersex persons in a small country like Uganda is at best a curiosity, perhaps worth a moment's sympathy before returning to more commanding priorities. Their condition is rare, and their plight won't attract the attention of the donors, elites, or the policymakers.[1] With the general public lacking specific knowledge about transgender or intersex phenomena, few people will even be aware that such persons exist, or, if people know of them, only a few will move beyond prurient fascination or righteous indignation at such an aberration, to arrive at a point of genuine concern.

Ought we to care? Is there anything distinctive about their situation and our response to it that we should be cognizant of, which may have broader application or be indicative of the moral health and maturity of any given society? Given their small numbers, how compelling is their need, and how ought those who have power over resources distribution, rule of law, and policy to respond?

I must declare a bias. I concern myself with these few complicated Ugandans for a personal reason—in some significant measure, their story is my story. Being of transgender status myself, I was initially drawn to them. Yet beyond our common diagnosis, our future paths diverge fundamentally. The parameters and constraints that I face have some common ground, but also vast differences. By the date this book is published, I will be well advanced along a challenging but well supported and (for the most part) socially tolerated gender transition. For me, transitioning from Stephen to Chloe is tangible. There is a predictable end point to my two-year transition that draws closer each day, while in the interim, the influence of the hormone therapy subtly reshapes my body—I know and can see in the mirror that I am making visible progress. To a very large extent, I already am able to claim my authentic gender convincingly in public. At some near-future point, nearly all the world around me will never know that my gender identity had once not been female. As a transsexual woman in America, there is the growing prospect of being respected not in spite of this condition, but to be respected *as a transsexual woman*. For my Ugandan transgender colleagues, acculturated to being reviled and rejected, such a prospect must be beyond comprehension.

Beyond indulging my bias and my personal resonance with the transgender people of Uganda, their plight does raise important ethical issues that apply to minority groups anywhere. This chapter explores these issues. First, I will consider the ethics of identity, giving due weight to the important work that has been done in this field by the philosopher Kwame Anthony Appiah. Gender identity, like race or sexual orientation, is a fundamental element of autonomy and personal meaning, and the ethics of identity is very relevant. Second, this chapter looks at the ways that communitarian and liberal societies differ in their tolerance of diversity, particularly when diversity takes the form of an audacious transgression of what has been always considered immutable—gender identity. Should there be an automatic deference made to the priority of communitarian values that are supported by an overwhelming majority of persons within a given society, despite the intolerance of such values to the basic interests and welfare of such minority groups as homosexuals, bisexuals, transgendered, or intersex persons? Or should more tolerant universal values such as those contained within the Universal Declaration of Human Rights trump less tolerant communitarian values? Finally, where do international development practitioners place themselves when confronted by ethical systems that differ fundamentally from their own? Do such practitioners have their own moral obligation to use their influence to advocate for certain universalist principles, such as toleration, understanding, compassion, and respect for the universal dignity and human rights of minorities of any kind?

AN ETHICS OF IDENTITY

What's age-old is that when we are asked—and ask ourselves—*who* we are, we are being asked *what* we are as well. (Appiah, 2007, p. xiv)

In Appiah's work, the *who* and *what* questions of personal identity are explored in depth. Every person exists within a set of societal norms and expectations, and in very traditional societies, the society provides the answers on your behalf. Each society has conventions and norms for what it means to be, and to behave as, a man or as a woman, and no one growing up in any society can achieve a sense of self without being deeply influenced by the prevailing social parameters. Appiah however distinguishes *parameters* from *limits*; it may be possible to redefine certain parameters, but overcoming strictly imposed social limits is quite a different matter. When those limits stand in the way of achieving personal autonomy—the ability to rationally decide who and what you are, and what your life plans will be—then the potential for a life of meaning and well-being is threatened. Societies that impose such limits, that reject personal autonomy individually defined outside of the traditional norms, are quick to place a strong burden of obligation on all members of that society to conform to society's expectations. Such societies say little or nothing about what each person morally owes to him or herself in pursuing a life of meaning and dignity, or about the potential harms imposed by these limits to personal choice on those who seek to exercise their autonomy unconventionally. In short, many minorities in such societies are left with nothing but unacceptable choices.

The ethics of identity places emphasis on two competing explanations of how a person shapes his or her identity. First, there is the well-established notion of *finding oneself*, or as described by Appiah:

[Finding oneself involves] discovering, by means of reflection or a careful attention to the world, a meaning for one's life that is already there, waiting to be found. This is a vision we can call *authenticity*: it is a matter of being true to who you already really are, or would be if it weren't for distorting influences. (Appiah, 2007, p. 17)

There is, however, another *existentialist* explanation, in which each person is the creator, and in and through the act of shaping an identity, that person achieves a life worth living. Appiah however feels neither explanation is wholly satisfactory. The authenticity view leaves out the creative elements in shaping a life, while the existentialist view assumes that there is nothing there to respond to. Appiah argues that a middle view exists in which the construction of an identity makes sense to the extent that such identity is constructed in response to "facts outside oneself, things that are beyond one's own choices" (Appiah, 2007, p. 18). For transgender and intersex people, these facts "outside" are complicated by the psychological fact of gender identity disorder (GID).[2]

MORAL MODERNITY

Within ethics, a longstanding debate still rages between communitarians and universalists. On the one hand are the communitarians—moral relativists who believe that most important moral values are a product of evolving community consensus shaped by culture, tradition, religion, and authority, within and only applicable to a specific society. Universalists who argue instead that the majority of significant moral values are common to all humanity, transcending societal boundaries, challenge them. Traditional societies, as commonly found in developing countries, formally hold an ambivalent position. Such societies, through their national political institutions, are willing (officially, if not in practice) to commit to some strongly universalist proclamations such as the Universal Declaration of Human Rights and many human rights and environmental treaties. At the same time, countries such as Uganda have laws that run completely counter to these human-rights obligations, such as the criminalization of homosexuality. Such countries seem quite unconcerned about this inconsistency.

This ambivalence took tangible form in an international conference in Kampala that I helped to organize in July 2006, for the International Development Ethics Association (IDEA), supported largely by World Bank and other donor funding. With over 300 participants from across Africa and far beyond, the many conference papers adopted a universalist or cosmopolitan perspective without encountering any significant dispute. This universalism was articulated in their papers through such prominent moral theories as the capabilities approach, human rights, Kantianism, virtue ethics, and utilitarianism. We were hopeful that the conference would be opened by the Ugandan president, with a speech that would speak to the larger Ugandan society as well as to the conference participants. Given this universalist frame, we simply assumed that such an opening speech would accentuate universal moral precepts and obligations; celebrate the distinguished international, pan-African, and Ugandan participation at the conference; and take note that we were all united in the common pursuit of ethical human development.

My colleagues and I at Makerere University formally approached the Office of the President to see if President Yoweri Museveni would be willing to open the Seventh International Conference on the Ethics of International Development, which was to be the largest international conference at Makerere University for many years. They responded positively in principle but asked us to draft an appropriate opening speech for their review. For reasons that still elude and bemuse me, my Ugandan colleagues assigned this task to me, and I set about drafting my first presidential speech! In this speech, which was closely reviewed and edited by my Ugandan colleagues, I struck a strongly cosmopolitan view, when I wrote words that I hoped would draw strength from becoming a part of President Museveni's oration:

There is no place in Uganda's development for intolerance and attitudes of moral superiority, for the demonization of others, or for simplistic thinking about what is good and bad, right and wrong. We must learn to think morally, and to avoid moral simplification. Reducing complex situations to a few attention-grabbing moral issues solves nothing, even if it does sell newspapers. And we must avoid forcing our own values on others; instead we must all work together to share and shape our common values.

The speech went on to address national development goals from a moral perspective, to excoriate the immoral behavior of Joseph Kony's brutal Lords Resistance Army, whose insurrection in Uganda's north has targeted children more than anyone else; to remember the moral outrages of the Idi Amin era; and to recognize that Uganda possesses many persons of outstanding integrity who ought to be recognized, celebrated, and emulated. All in all, it was an upbeat but serious speech, calling on the conference participants to reflect on to what was needed in order to achieve development leading to lives that are dignified and truly human. We duly submitted the speech to the Office of the President and awaited a response.

With only days before the conference opening, the Office of the President finally advised us that President Museveni would in fact not open the conference; he had instead delegated that task to the Minister of State for Ethics, Hon. James Nsaba Buturo. No mention was made of which speech would be used, but when Hon. Buturo rose to deliver the opening address, not a word of my draft remained. Instead, the Minister of Ethics gave a talk that was short, stilted, and full of the usual formal welcoming pleasantries. Only one strong message was memorable from his speech: Western moral values that tolerated homosexuality have no place in Uganda and were not welcome at the conference. Indeed, this speech was little more than a vitriolic homophobic diatribe, which this Minister has frequently restated in various public addresses since.

Uganda is not alone among developing countries officially to claim universalist values—human rights being the most prominent example—yet in practice and with no sense of the irony involved, go on to create and enforce laws and cultural norms that deny basic human rights to anyone whom the state chooses to isolate as either a threat to security or a moral scourge. Church leaders and even many leaders in civil society join in the demonization of homosexuals; for example, the prominent pastor Martin Ssempa heads up the burgeoning Inter-Faith Rainbow Coalition against Homosexuality. Any conflict between Uganda's human-rights commitments and their antihomosexuality values remains officially unrecognized. Uganda's minority groups, including but by no means limited to transgender and intersex persons, can expect no justice in Uganda on the basis of universal human rights.

Despite the predicament for sexual minorities in Uganda, internationally a major step has been taken in articulating a rights basis for transgender and intersex persons, as well as gay, lesbian, and bisexual persons. The Yogyakarta Principles, published in March 2007 by the International Commission of Jurists and the International Service for Human Rights on behalf of a coalition of human-rights organizations, consist of 29 principles for the application of international human-rights law in relation to sexual orientation and gender identity. All 29 principles were drafted on the premise that sexual orientation and gender identity are integral components of the dignity and humanity of all persons, and that sexual orientation and gender identity ought not to be a basis for abuse or discrimination.

Some countries have gone further still to champion the rights of sexual minorities. The Human Rights Commission of New Zealand in January 2008 published a comprehensive and lengthy report, *To Be Who I Am*, which is an inquiry into discrimination experienced by transgender people (referred to in the report as "trans people"). In its summary statement, the authors state:

Trans people said what they held in common was the struggle to come to terms with who they are, to have others accept them and to be able to live fulfilled lives in the sex they know themselves to be. Human rights are about dignity, equality and security for every person. This report documents for the first time the obstacles to dignity, equality and security for trans people in New Zealand. It shows how discrimination impacts on all aspects of their lives; how from a very young age it can threaten their personal safety, deny a secure family life, undermine health, opportunities to learn, to join a sports team, to get a job, to commit to a career. Equally, it records and acknowledges stories of achievement and of triumph over great adversity . . . The Inquiry's findings show clearly that being trans is not a lifestyle choice; it is simply one dimension of the rich diversity that is humanity. (New Zealand, p. 1)

The examples from New Zealand and the Yogyakarta Principles beg the question of moral and ethical differences between societies, fueling the debate between the communitarian ethics of morally narrow societies like Uganda and the countering arguments for moral universalism—that equal dignity ought to be accorded to all persons by right of their common humanity. Is there a continuum of moral maturity that differentiates societies, with universalism and cosmopolitanism arguing for complete moral equality among all humans at one end, and communitarianism and relativism that denies the dignity and humanity of certain nonconforming humans at the other? Universalism does tend to characterize the ethics of more technologically advanced, economically wealthier, politically more liberal, and—most significantly perhaps—morally more tolerant societies, while developing countries frequently embrace communitarian ethics that explicitly differentiates and rejects those who stray from the norms, promulgating an unrepentant, almost militant intolerance for diversity.

Appiah is unambiguous regarding his view that universalism represents a more mature form of morality:

Our moral modernity consists chiefly of extending the principle of equal respect to those who had previously been outside the compass of sympathy; in that sense, it has consisted in the ability to see similarity where our predecessors saw only difference. The wisdom was hard-won; it should not be lightly set aside. (Appiah, 2007, p. 146)

The compass of sympathy in Uganda does not embrace its transgender or intersex persons in the arc of acceptable diversity. For many communitarian societies, such diversity remains a problem to be shunned or at best solved (a view, Appiah notes, that was once held by Thomas Hobbes and his peers) and not a condition to be promoted (Appiah, 2007, p. 142).

LIFE AS A TRANSGENDER
OR INTERSEX UGANDAN

Intolerance for diversity may protect the illusion of a morally monolithic community and excuse the members of that society from the potentially unsettling task of individually reflecting on and justifying their chosen moral values. In the process, however, great harm ensues to all those who do not fit within the monolith, those whom the majority feels entitled—even obligated—to deny such choices and opportunities as are essential to their human well-being. As Appiah states: "To have autonomy, we must have acceptable choices. We are harmed when deprived of such choices" (Appiah, 2007, p. 30).

What is it like to be outside the monolith? Salongo Mawanda Nikki, 26 and biologically born female, identifies as a man. Thin and youthful, Salongo shared some of his life story over lunch at my Kampala hotel. As a transgender female-to-male of youthful appearance, Salongo's remarkable maturity owes more to experience than years. At that lunch, Salongo wore men's baggy blue jeans, an androgynous shirt, and cream-colored shoes that were discordantly feminine. His hair was styled in short dreadlocks, not uncommon among young men and women alike in Uganda. Yet to most Ugandans, Salongo would be viewed not as a man but as a lesbian (a sexual orientation label that is accurate only to the extent that Salongo is classified as female), and that label alone is sufficient to assure that he is reviled within his society. Very few would take the time to learn that Salongo is transgender, that he tightly binds his/her[3] breasts to not appear female, despite the abrasions, pain, and injuries that long-term binding causes. Even such extreme measures fail to resolve all social issues; Salongo related to me how he was stopped on a crowded public thoroughfare in Kampala and accosted loudly by his aunt, who went into painfully embarrassing hysterics at the apparent disappearance of Salongo's breasts.

Beyond such commonplace humiliations, Salongo's story is full of hardness, exclusion, and tribulation. From a very early age, Salongo knew that she was meant to be a he, and in keeping with a tradition of his Buganda tribe, Salongo would stare toward the sun each day as it transitioned from morning to afternoon in the belief that this would facilitate his own gender transition. Despite a supportive and loving mother, at the tender age of 13, Salongo was disowned by his family because of his declared sexual interest in girls. Since then, Salongo has faced continuing difficulties in holding secure housing or employment. As if his life were not already complicated, Salongo gave birth to a son 9 years previously, who is now being raised by the grandmother.

Like many transgender persons, Salongo's dreams are modest; he just wants a normal life. A fiercely patriotic Ugandan, Salongo nevertheless yearns to join his Norwegian fiancée and marry her, yet Norway has denied him a visa. While searching for some resolution to that quandary, Salongo remains active as a self-styled human-rights defender, particularly in the role of coordinator for a group of transgender Ugandans known as the Transgender, Transsexual, and Intersex Support Group (TTISG). With 28 members, this group meets monthly, although many members struggle even to find the money for transport to and from the meetings. Most of the members of the group are young, poorly educated, unemployed, and with no permanent housing. To a considerable extent, they are all severely persecuted and ostracized for their transgender status; several have turned to prostitution simply to survive. The group is loosely affiliated to another quasi-formal group (quasi in that such NGOs are not legally allowed to register in Uganda) known as Sexual Minorities Uganda (SMUG), but in recent months, SMUG has refocused its advocacy to additionally address the problems of HIV/AIDs. With SMUG's attention and very limited resources being redirected in this way, transgender persons in Uganda are left with no organization to advocate effectively for them or to inform the public about the transgender phenomenon.

Accompanying Salongo was Julius Kaganzi Kaggwa, a handsome and deeply religious man of 38, dressed smartly but casually, who proudly shared with me his photos of his lovely wife and two beautiful children. Until he was able to receive medical attention at the age of 24, Julius was raised as Juliet, a person of uncertain gender with physical attributes of both genders. In different persons, this intersex phenomenon varies from pronounced physical "abnormalities" to subtle genetic traits of two genders. Julius however is a living example that gender identity is not synonymous with genitalia—from a very early age, Juliet knew that she was not a "normal" girl. Still, the societal pressure to live within the gender identity decision that was made by his mother through reference to local witchcraft and an appeal to ancestral spirits while he was but two weeks old kept him in a dress and presenting as a girl until he was a young adult. It was a confusing life; Juliet felt a strong sexual attraction for girls but knew that in Ugandan society this was simply impermissible. Juliet's family was dysfunctional, with a father who was absent for long periods of Juliet's upbringing, leaving his mother nearly destitute. Both parents ultimately succumbed to AIDS, and for an extended period of time, Juliet lived a life on the run, afraid of persecution or discovery that "she" was not the same as other girls. With extended time in Kenya, and later in South Africa, it was either by exceptionally good luck or divine intervention that Juliet met an American woman, Laura, who heard his story and convinced him to come to Sweden for medical treatment. From that intervention, Julius emerged as a biological male, going on to marry and father two children, ultimately to publish in Uganda a small book on his experience.[4] Julius was able to complete his education, and became trained in information technology, communications, and public relations. He remains active in several informal organizations who advocate for the rights of sexual minorities and is pursuing a particular mission to help his fellow Ugandans learn about the intersex phenomenon—hopeful that this outreach will result in a more tolerant attitude toward those who are intersex, particularly children.

From the stories shared by Salongo and Julius, it is clear that Ugandans are not very tolerant of transgender and intersex persons. This hostility, in the view of Julius, is a function of the closed and authoritarian character of

Ugandan society, and its political, religious, and cultural institutions. In his view, there will be little or no progress made in changing this rigid cultural mind-set if any appeal for increased toleration is framed overtly as a moral issue. Julius further argues that if Ugandans are truly to reflect on their values on gender identity, sexual orientation, and sexual rights, a different approach is essential—they must be invited to participate in a story. Storytelling, Julius believes, is a powerful means to help Ugandans connect to the common humanity of all persons: heterosexual, intersex, transgender, and those of bisexual or homosexual orientation.

Ugandans love a story. Storytelling, theater, and film can be used to speak to the common identity of all Ugandans as a nurturing, caring people of a generous spirit. Once this sense of solidarity is established, Julius proposes an incremental and progressive dissemination of information in a way that informs without *moralizing* (defined as the coercive imposition of one set of moral values to trump all other person's moral values), that allows people to see beyond the controversy of their moral values being questioned by diversity that appears to corrupt the integrity of the social moral monolith. Julius clings to the conviction that by grasping their common humanity—the plethora of moral and cultural values that unite Ugandans—instead of focusing on the few prominent values that divide them, Uganda will gradually become a more open social environment, enabling sexual minorities and all other Ugandans to live free and meaningful lives. It is a bold wish.

PROGRESS OF SENTIMENTS?

Salongo and Julius are but two members of a sexual minority, yet their stories are sufficient to call into question the validity—in terms of justice, caring, and fairness—of the current Ugandan society's moral orientation. For Ugandans or anyone brought up by religious and political leaders, and by authority figures in family and society, to believe that nontraditional sexual orientation or questioning gender identity are simply abhorrent, it is a comfortable, clear, and familiar set of values that does not allow for questioning. Should the fact that some small minorities suffer under this majority moral consensus be sufficient reason to scrap these values in favor of more liberal, tolerant ideals?

I share Julius's conviction: the battle for a more tolerant society in Uganda or in any society is not to be won through an intellectual or political assault on moral values that people have grown comfortable with. The recently deceased eminent philosopher Richard Rorty perhaps most convincingly advocated against the belief that fundamental social change would be achievable through intellectual exposure to moral precepts or the persuasiveness of moral theories. For Rorty, society must first achieve a shared moral identity, by "hearing sad and sentimental stories" (Shute & Hurley, 1993, p. 133). Of course, these two modes are not incompatible; moral concepts can reinforce good sentiments (such as "Jews are industrious") as well as help one to resist bad sentiments (such as "Jews are vermin").

Annette Baier (Shute & Hurley, 1993, p. 129) also supports this concept of a "progress of sentiments" as a form of "sentimental education," but Booth (Dunne & Wheeler, 1999, p. 62) and Richard Wilson (Wilson, 1987, p. 8) both reject the notion that sentiment, emotions, or courage alone can adequately and consistently guide a society's actions or rank its development priorities. Chris Brown offers a middle view, describing how a human-rights culture can emerge in reaction to certain perceived injustices—racism, sexism, religious intolerance—and that this, in turn, can become part of a society's shared moral identity. He attributes this process not only to being able to sympathize with the plight of others, but also to the achievement of a level of security in a society in which one is able to assert one's self-respect and worth without having to try to diminish these attributes in others. Brown's views allow only for the limited influence of human-rights deliberations ultimately making the inculcation of human-rights values possible within a given society. Like Rorty, he views human rights as effective only after they have been broadly internalized into the moral identity of a society, but unlike Rorty, he argues that beliefs may have a role to play. Brown contends that without having achieved this moral identity, the external imposition of human-rights concepts onto a society will not immediately or directly result in a shift in attitudes and values by that society. In this light, international efforts to secure universal human rights standards and behavior will only bear fruit—if at all—in the long term, as each society gradually contends with a range of social and developmental issues in which those involved in the deliberations see the value of using human rights as an effective lens to those specific deliberations. Brown sees human rights much more as an end than a means to development, a symptom of civilization instead of a cause, when he argues: "Rights are best seen as a by-product of a functioning ethical community and not as a phenomenon that can be taken out of this context and promoted as a universal solution to the political ills of an oppressive world" (Dunne & Wheeler, 1999, p. 120).

To my mind, the best response to the Rorty-Baier-Brown positions on human rights as an explicit end but not a strategic or effective means may be that of Bhikhu Parekh, who raises two objections. First, he questions whether individuals can—or even should—be persuaded to care for each other on the basis of their similarities. This would lead to intolerance of differences (which can never be eliminated) and demands that others become like us if we are to share solidarity with them. This type of "manipulation of sentiments" to achieve solidarity could be used just as effectively, Parekh claims, to destroy such solidarity (Dunne & Wheeler, 1999, p. 140). Parekh also rejects the notion that solidarity can be achieved through shared experiences and storytelling alone and instead contends that

We need to show why some shared experiences are more significant to, and an integral part of, our humanity, than others, and that requires arguments based on some conception of human being. Although moral reasoning is never wholly in terms of arguments alone and involves appeals to emotions, shared sentiments, imagination and cultural values, as Rorty rightly argues, arguments are necessary to regulate the content of these appeals and to give the resulting sense of solidarity a relatively secure intellectual and moral basis. (Dunne & Wheeler, 1999, p. 141).

Under Parekh's view, there are important opportunities to bring moral reasoning—including moral reasoning responsive to the claims and duties implicit in human rights—to the deliberative processes that shape a society's development, without sacrificing "appeals to emotions, shared sentiments, imagination and cultural values." In this view, which I support, human rights are an important but not exclusive means toward increased toleration of diversity and an end to discrimination against sexual or other minorities. A *moral hook* is an important element in motivating decision makers and stakeholders to engage in and be responsive to moral reasoning. Like Julius's call to engage Ugandans in sharing their stories, people may be drawn to increased tolerance for diversity by a moral hook that itself is the result of emotions, shared sentiments, imagination and cultural values.

On the international stage, human-rights claims by sexual minorities, strengthened by the Yogyakarta Principles and the example of tolerance in more economically developed societies, may in time generate effective if incremental challenges to the complacency of diversity-intolerant societies. The assertion of minority rights by such small populations as transgender and intersex persons, however, even in combination with similar calls by those of homosexual or bisexual orientation, are hardly sufficient on their own to propel a restructuring of the majority's comfortable—and diversity intolerant—moral monolith in any society in the short term.

Where does that leave the development practitioner from abroad, active in a developing country, who is more likely to have come from a society that tolerates sexual minorities or from societies that are moving so far as to offer unqualified moral respect for individual members of sexual minorities? Such development practitioners, through their programmatic interventions and the large components of donor budgets that they may be entrusted to manage, have the potential to influence outcomes affecting human welfare, access to opportunities, and the exercise of political and religious freedoms. When presented with the plight of Salongo or Julius, or any member of a persecuted minority, what is the right thing to do? How ought we (as outsiders) to balance any minority group member's claim to be treated with basic human dignity and to enjoy human-rights protections and opportunities against the competing majority claims of far larger stakeholder groups for undivided attention and priority access to resources, particularly when that majority feels it appropriate, justified, or even its moral or religious duty to deny or exclude the minority?

The overarching moral issue confronting the development practitioner coming to a developing country from a more tolerant society is whether he or she ought to take a position. Ought all societies to adopt a more universal moral stance characterized by values of toleration, understanding, compassion, and respect for minorities of any kind? Or alternatively, is there a persuasive moral justification in adherence to a communitarian values that give primacy to local culture, tradition, and those values that are linked to well-defined roles, authority structures, and intolerance for so-called deviant behavior or any form of individualism that challenges the moral underpinnings of the status quo?

In my case, the question is particularly and personally poignant. When the majority of people in intolerant societies in developing countries where I may happen to be engaged on a program or project intervention exhibit strongly negative positions toward certain minority groups whom I identify with—transgender persons, in my case—am I as an outsider morally obliged to respect the society's majority's communitarian thinking, even at my own expense? As a transsexual woman, am I obliged to remain silent regarding my personal moral sensibilities (shaped by my autonomy and by my own society's values) on such issues, out of respect for their majority cultural values—even if their values place me squarely into one of the rejected and despised categories? And what if I am *read* (recognized as not being female from birth, even if physically female now), can I remain effective—or even safe? Or should I take shelter in my international anonymity or in the simple fact that most persons in developing countries would fail to conceptualize that anyone could successfully breach the gender divide?

Experiencing a gender transition does take remarkable courage. Am I courageous enough to embrace in solidarity the modest and morally legitimate claims by fellow members of sexual minorities when I meet them abroad? Of course, the line between courage and foolhardiness is a thin one.

A WAY FORWARD

Richard Rorty, in his essay "Human Rights, Rationality, and Sentimentality," argues for what he terms *sentimental education* by emphasizing philosopher Annette Baier's position that we ought to think of *trust* rather than *obligation* as the fundamental moral notion effective in moving societies to increasing levels of toleration for diversity.[5] Baier's call for "a progress of sentiments" is characterized by an increasing ability to see the similarities outweighing the differences between ourselves and people very unlike us. According to Rorty, establishing a set of relevant similarities has less to do with finding profound common truths that bond all humanity, but instead the "little, superficial, similarities as cherishing our parents and our children—similarities that do not interestingly distinguish us from many nonhuman animals" (Rorty, 1993). Rorty argues that such sentiment is in fact sufficiently strong, even stronger than reason or the compelling force of power, in changing people's values toward greater tolerance of diversity:

To rely on the suggestions of sentiment rather than on the commands of reason is to think of powerful people gradually ceasing to oppress others, or ceasing to countenance the oppression of others, out of mere niceness, rather than out of obedience to the moral law. But it is revolting to think that our only hope for a decent society consists in softening the self-satisfied hearts of a leisure class. We want moral progress to burst up from below, rather than waiting patiently upon condescension from the top . . . A better sort of answer is the sort of long, sad, sentimental story which begins "Because this is what it is like to be in her situation—to be far from home, among strangers," or "Because she might become your daughter-in-law," or "Because her mother would grieve for her." Such stories, repeated and varied over the centuries, have induced us, the rich, safe, powerful, people, to tolerate, and even to cherish, powerless people—people whose appearance or habits or beliefs at first seemed an insult to our own moral identity, our sense of the limits of permissible human variation. (Rorty, 1993)

Such a slow progress of sentiments isn't likely to offer much comfort to Salongo or Julius, and it offers only scant comfort to me. Yet I know that human beings are far from perfect, and my reasonable expectations of transforming any society's moral values must be pragmatic and realistic. The opinion shapers of any society—those local leaders whose views on morality have the greatest influence on the shaping of their own society's values—cannot be knowledgeable about the many complexities of the human condition. It isn't reasonable, therefore, for me to expect such leaders to be conversant with the scientific and medical factors that describe those very few persons like me who are transgender or intersex, so that they might be objective if not compassionately disposed toward them and me. Many well-informed people would conclude that while it is regrettable for a particular society to reject and despise any minority on the basis of ignorance about the conditions that gave rise to the troublesome but distinguishing differences, it is also not surprising. In short, it's just one of those "it's too bad" situations that most development practitioners and some policy makers express sadness about, before moving on to address and respond to more pressing concerns affecting far larger numbers of the poor, disempowered, and needy. As a member of a sexual minority, the "it's too bad" excuse leaves me very empty.

Gender identity to a very large extent defines the human experience of *identity* and the potential to live a truly human life of dignity, free of shame. For those whose identity is compromised by the psychological or medical condition of being transgender or intersex, achieving the same level of access to rights and freedoms as others in one's society is denied. To a considerable extent, this misfortune is due to ignorance, with society at large viewing transgender or intersex persons as people who choose to exercise an absurd, irrational, or immodestly audacious option, or as persons choosing to live and act with devious, even perverse behavior. In Uganda, the notion that anyone would voluntarily pursue the male-to-female transition such as the one that I have been immersed in is particularly suspect, given the disparity in social rank and privilege between men and women. Yet even when this bias is reversed, there is little sympathy for those Ugandan women who claim that they are in fact men.

Perhaps the idea that a person can exercise a choice on a matter such as gender identity threatens some core values in societies where gender roles are highly defined and differentiated. More likely, most Ugandans reject the very notion that a choice in such matters is an option, leading to the inevitable conclusion that those who demand that their choice of gender be respected are mentally incompetent or morally suspect, or both.

In either case, in the morally confined space within tightly communitarian societies, such persons—Salongo, Julius, and me—are, as my friend Rukooko surmised, to be despised. Yet such persons exist, have relationships, and are a part of other people's lives, and through their lives and stories they weave a larger societal narrative of change toward that toleration that accepts and respects all persons as dignified, valuable, and morally equal human beings.

CHAPTER 10

Ethical Performance

"Do a good job!"

The desire to perform well, achieve valued results, and create a better world for us and for our children is an important element in how most people define a life that is worthwhile. We receive various messages throughout our lives that tell us when others think that we've done a good job, ranging from the proverbial pat on the back to more formal indicators—high examination grades, certificates and diplomas, promotions, and social recognition. We're taught that working hard and "doing good" is the path to reaping the rewards of increasing wealth, power, and prestige.

Of course, there are short cuts. Some people beat the system and—through cleverness, brashness mixed with luck, or bending (and sometimes breaking) the rules—find their way to those rewards without leaving a trail of good deeds and hard work. Our reactions to these people differ; sometimes we accuse them of being cheaters, of betraying a public trust in the system, and of not playing the game fairly. Sometimes we grudgingly admire them, as they seem effortlessly to attract wealth, power, influence, and all the trappings of material success. We wish we could have it all so easily, yet we also know that the satisfaction of having completed the hard work was itself a valuable and meaningful reward. Many of us comfort ourselves with the reflection that, after all, we largely define our character and ourselves through our work.

At the institutional level, private-sector corporations also operate from a variety of motivations. Obviously they need to attend to their shareholders' interests, and to respect the law. Sometimes they reach farther, seeking to also demonstrate corporate social responsibility, and to do good as well as doing well for themselves. When they succeed, their profits often increase, and their public relations almost always flourish.

For the public institution, the challenge of doing good seems, on the surface, to be very straightforward. After all, these institutions are comprised of people who are called *public servants*. In more developed countries, where well-paying employment is not so scarce, people who are attracted to public service are generally not there to achieve fabulous wealth and power, but instead to serve an ideal of public service and the noble pursuit of the public interest that has deep roots in all societies. In developing countries, a public-service job may also attract civic-minded individuals, but given the scarcity of jobs and the opportunities to exploit the public-service position in corrupt ways, we cannot assume that each public servant is deeply committed to serving the public interest.

The reality of doing good in public service, however, also is often quite different. Public institutions have been accused of incompetence, bureaucratic paralysis, and a lack of compassion or care. They have been viewed as a haven for those who would be incapable of attracting a job in the competitive private sector and as places where performance matters less than loyalty to one's patron. All too often, the leaders and senior managers of such public institutions pursue their own personal agendas that have little or nothing to do with ideals of public service.

The manner in which public institutions and their leaders serve the public interest, and provide good governance, is now in the spotlight within international development policy and practice. Donors in particular want their tax monies spent well; they want and need *performance* and *results* to justify international development assistance funding levels. More fundamentally, achieving consistently high standards of quality in public services is essential to everyone's personal health and well-being, and to the health and well-being of each nation.

Within international development dialogue, everyone is talking about *good governance*, but seldom is that concept unpacked in use.[1] If we do try to tie this down, we're generally directed in public-policy documents and public debate to associate good governance with concepts such as social justice, effectiveness, fairness, demonstrating value for public money spent, avoidance of corruption, attainment of high standards of efficiency, and adherence to high standards of ethics. For most of us, placing the ideal of good governance into the dialogue on public service is enough. We're supposed to treat this ideal as a yearning—an aspiration—and we're not asked to define it. It isn't supposed to have a defined end point—a place where *good* becomes *good enough*. In the day-to-day lives of most public servants, *good* remains vague.

The lack of a consensus on the definition of good governance is exacerbated by a similar lack of clarity in delineating just what constitutes high standards of ethics or ethical performance. To the extent that this was undertaken, the efforts were focused on the conduct of the individual public servant, and not on the ethical performance of government institutions. Codes of conduct traditionally stressed a number of "thou shalt not" admonitions, and threats of serious sanctions for misconduct by public servants, but ethical performance has seldom been addressed directly.

ETHICAL RESULTS

There is now a large and growing body of literature in the global effort to translate the ethical sense of the *good* of good governance into specific standards, indicators, and results. This takes many forms, from codes of ethics to sophisticated empirical indicators, and even to the use of narratives.

Kenya is no stranger to the quest for good governance. The January 2000 Strategy for Public Sector Reform had a clearly stated concern for the integrity and efficiency of the public service. A new project, the Demand for Good Governance project is currently under preparation, with expected funding of $12 million for technical assistance to Kenya to assist public-sector institutions to improve their accountability.[2] The emphasis of this intervention will be on capacity—on what measures would best enable public institutions to account for their performance. In neither the 2000 Strategy nor the upcoming Demand for Good Governance project, however, is there any explicit step taken or to be taken to define what constitutes *integrity* and *ethical performance*. Kenya has been and is being told to shine the light of public disclosure more brightly, to make government more transparent, but once the light was directed at the inner workings of government, what was there to be seen?

In August of 2002, the Kenyan government wrestled with this notion of public-sector ethics in a workshop held on the 29th, which was part of a 10-country study by the United Nations Department of Economic and Social Affairs on Public Service Ethics in Africa. From the outset, however, ethics in this discussion was conceived as compliance with regulatory instruments, codes, and laws, and as the institutional infrastructure to monitor such compliance and to sanction offenses. The emphasis was on public servants behaving badly: how to prevent, detect, report, and punish such forms of unethical behavior. The workshop noted the reluctance of the public to report such wrongdoing to the authorities, and bemoaned a pervasive decline in professionalism within the public service. The conclusions of this workshop, as reported, emphasized stronger enforcement, a restoration of professionalism, better management, improved terms of employment for public servants, and better public education in what constitutes public service ethics. The report ended with a very broad conclusion: "The continuing democratization of the political system is likely to be the most effective way of improving public service ethics."[3] This is a singularly important observation, which I will return to later.

While the ethical conduct of public servants is an essential factor in the means by which public institutions achieve ethical performance, it is not sufficient to that end. The measurement of the extent to which an individual public servant does or does not behave badly is a shallow perspective of such an expansive concept as ethical performance; much more is needed to reach such a determination. Yet before the rush to measure, the confusion between ends and means first must be resolved. The goal of public service is to support and sustain—through the provision of important public services—human development within any given country. Ethical performance is one means to that end, and ethical conduct by individual public servants is but one component in the pursuit of the larger means of achieving ethical performance. The discussion must begin and end with development, and what constitutes the best means to achieve that goal.

If we situate ethical performance in the context of human development, we are defining ethical performance quite differently than simply as the degree of compliance with established standards of personal and professional conduct by individual public servants. Taken in this larger context, ethical performance addresses the means and ends of development itself, the degree to which institutions, policies, and programs respect basic human dignity and human rights, and the extent to which such institutions, policies, and programs empower people to lead truly human lives. Ethical performance in this sense is fundamentally about the means and ends of human flourishing.

ETHICAL RESULTS AND HUMAN DEVELOPMENT

As with many countries, the Kenyan government has articulated its priority development goals by means of the Millennium Development Goals (MDGs) framework.[4] This framework establishes empirical targets but does not address the ethical considerations that arise in pursuing any of these targets.

To articulate the ethical performance of an essential public service, I must describe the character of that public service, and of the institution and public servants who are that service's providers. Arguably, the degree to which public officials are committed to ethical standards, and in turn the degree to which they provide such services in an ethical manner, are both important to the effectiveness and value of those services, and to the results that such services will generate. Under this view, ethical service delivery is an important means to achieve development as defined in the MDGs. In evaluating ethical performance, however, many issues arise. First are the evaluation tools themselves; does measuring a values-based concept such as *ethical performance* lend itself to empirical approaches? While we can indeed measure net primary enrollment in universal primary education, the rates of child and infant mortality, the changing prevalence of HIV/AIDS, the percentage of forested areas, or the number of mobile telephones in use, what does this really tell us about the quality of life of Kenyans? What does it tell us about the *goodness* of good governance? Is the complexity of the human experience such that empirical measures only hint—but fail adequately to convey—the quality of life changes being experienced by Kenyans?

Deneulin and Hodgett debunk the sense of authority that empirical measures command by questioning the basis upon which certain indicators are chosen and the quality of the data evaluated. Taking the example of measuring gender equity in a country, which is a very important determinant of overall development, they note that such important issues as domestic violence are seldom measured because of the sensitivity of such data; yet the failure to provide a credible measurement of such occurrences greatly diminishes the ability of the evaluator to determine the equality of women within a given society, or their quality of life. Methods other than formal data collection and analysis may render more enlightening information to policymakers and those in leadership positions.

> Today, empiricism in the social sciences, and especially in poverty analysis, is being increasingly questioned. Qualitative assessments of poverty, such as participatory poverty evaluation or life histories are being collected in order to counteract the significant weaknesses of traditional quantitative assessment. (Deneulin & Hodgett, 2006)

The philosopher Martha Nussbaum also questions whether statistics do justice to the human condition when decision makers consider public-policy options.

> If economic policy-making does not acknowledge the complexities of the inner moral life of each human being, its strivings and perplexities, its complicated emotions, its efforts at understanding and its terror, if it does not distinguish in its descriptions between a human life and a machine, then we should regard with suspicion its claim to govern a nation of human beings. (Nussbaum, 1995, p. 24)

In her critique of the norms of policymaking, Nussbaum leaves herself open to the usual complaint about philosophers—that they are wildly impractical. Being told to understand the "inner moral life of each human being" is not terribly helpful to a beleaguered public servant trying to craft or implement effective policy. Not only is the collection of a meaningful number of such personal narratives a costly and time-consuming task, the reader must exercise discrimination to search for some objective truths in what are essential subjective stories. Yet experiences in Europe, as described by Deneulin and Hodgett, show some promise in combining traditional forms of empirical analyses with some narratives, so as better to portray sensitive ethical issues in public policy and to raise the awareness of policymakers to the many moral concerns that often escape the statistics.

The use of narratives to assess ethical performance is but one of four different approaches to the measurement of ethical performance in support of development that are examined in this chapter; the other three include human rights, the capability approach, and character. In each of these approaches, I consider both the significance of the ethical performance of individual public servants and of the public-sector institutions in which they serve. Finally, I offer some comments on the enabling environment for ethical performance—the ethical and democratic characteristics of the larger Kenyan society in this instance, which arguably is relevant to developing countries anywhere.

TELLING THE STORY

Séverine Deneulin, Susan Hodgett, and other leading development ethics thinkers reject the notion that there exists an effective way to convert normative analysis into an empirical set of indicators. They argue instead for the use of narratives as well as the more traditional empirical approaches to assess development policies and their results (Deneulin & Hodgett, 2006).

Raising important moral concerns about governance through narrative is well established in literature, and in Kenya, the tradition of storytelling through literature and folktale is strong. Just over a decade ago, the author Ngugi wa Thiong'o used a fictional character to raise ethical concerns at the heart of Kenya's governance under former President Daniel arap Moi. In *Matigari*, Thiong'o hero travels the country asking politically incorrect but essentially moral questions about social justice and democratic freedoms, and Thiong'o so enthralled the public imagination that many Kenyans spoke as if Matigari were a real person. Reportedly, the police were even dispatched to arrest Matigari, but when they found he was just a fictional character the authorities had to take what comfort they could in banning the sale of the book (Thiong'o, 1989). More recently, Thiong'o wrote *Wizard of the Crow*, which is a narrative about modern Africa, using a fictional country, an absurd dictator and a "therapeutic" fake wizard to explore moral issues such as corruption, poverty, widening inequalities, and lack of democratic freedoms (Thiong'o, 2006).

Narratives are used throughout Africa, traditionally in the form of folktales and songs, to articulate important moral values and moral lessons. Theatre also thrives in Africa, and many plays focus on moral concerns—domestic, local, national, and sometimes international. While it would be possible to gauge something of the leading moral and ethical concerns within any society in Africa by evaluating the literature, plays, or even the current jokes, this will accomplish little more than raising awareness to what is on people's minds. Through this, areas of ethical focus may become clearer—caring for HIV/AIDS patients despite the stigmatization of this disease, for example—but it is hardly a precise measurement tool for monitoring ethical performance.

Lessons also can be drawn from the exclusion of certain narratives. In February 2005, the Ugandan government, through the Uganda Media Council, banned the production of the *Vagina Monologues*, a play written by American Eve Ensler that explores women's sexuality and abuse. The Ugandan Media Council claimed that the performance promoted and glorified acts such as lesbianism and homosexuality. Local intellectuals and feminists, such as human-rights lawyer Sarah Kihika, offered a different assessment, arguing that simply to use the word *vagina* in public in Uganda was intimidating to local sensibilities, and that the Media Council never considered anything more than the play's title before deciding to ban it as an inappropriate foreign influence. The play's organizer in Uganda, Sarah Mukasa, expressed her views forcefully in response:

I'm extremely outraged at the hypocrisy . . . I'm amazed that this country Uganda gives the impression that it is progressive and supports women's rights and the notions of free speech; yet when women want to share their stories the government uses the apparatus of state to shut us up.[5]

Employing narratives as a measurement of ethical performance allows for such expressions of outrage to be recognized not only as a dissenting commentary, but also as an indicator conveying *intensity*. That intensity, however, may be the very factor that most threatens the status quo, and most easily justifies the official exclusion or dismissal of such narrative expressions as a valid, accepted monitoring approach. Perhaps the less emotive, more objective standards of human rights provide a more effective approach.

RESPECTING HUMAN RIGHTS

Huduma Bora ni Haki Yako! This Swahili slogan—Quality Service Is Your Right—provides bold evidence that the language of rights is not new to Kenya's public sector. In the recent past, the Office of the President established standards to ensure that the right of Kenyans to the timely provision of certain important public services would be respected. By casting the public spotlight on such processes as applying for national identity cards, passports, and birth or death certificates, the public-sector ministries concerned are consciously eliminating one of the more usual justifications for demanding bribes—to hurry up a process. Now, at least in this context, the public can expect that their right to receive prompt service will be satisfied, without an additional—and illicit—fee.

But what is the nature of this *right* that leads Kenyans to believe that they are entitled to get their passport on time, without bribing public officials to make this happen? Is this a human right? A legal right? What is this language of rights, and what does it have to do with ethical performance?

The right of any citizen to receive proper public services in a timely manner without extraneous inducements can certainly be seen as falling under an important human-rights category—entitlement to due process of law. But at a more fundamental level, rights can be characterized provisionally as morally important claims that people make on each other, on social institutions, and on political authorities. Rights depend on two foundational concepts. First, an identifiable subject, who has entitlements, exists. Second, a duty bearer, who is obliged to respond to claims of such entitlements, also exists (Dunne & Wheeler, 1999). Jack Donnelly points out an important related distinction when he differentiates between *possession* of a right, the *respect* a right receives or should receive, and the *enforceability* of that right (Donnelly, 1989). In the context of human rights, for example, many countries are signatories to the Universal Declaration of Human Rights. By signing, these countries formally acknowledge that all persons possess certain human rights, yet in practice a significant number of these human rights are not respected and may not be influential in the establishment of public policy or legislation (see chapter 9 regarding Uganda's failure to honor its human-rights obligations to sexual minorities). Furthermore, where public policy and/or legislation is derived from human-rights principles, there may be a failure of political will or capability, so that the human right remains merely an unenforced right. The failure of a government to legislate or enforce human rights does not necessarily mean that the government concerned actually rejects the existence of that human right.[6] That may seem a diplomatic or rhetorical nicety, but the acceptance of the existence of a human right provides, as will be described later, a potentially strong starting point for political action.

A central claim about human rights is that they are universal—a contention that is grounded in several moral theories. If human rights are to be used as a framework for evaluating ethical performance, this presumption of universality allows for useful cross-cultural comparisons. With the arguable exception of utilitarianism as the presumed (but usually unstated) operative moral approach underpinning neoclassical economics, no other ethical approach besides human rights has come to be more persuasive and recognized in public deliberations on development and social and political organization (Dunne & Wheeler, 1999). No other ethical approach has developed such a substantial legal and diplomatic foundation, nor does any other enjoy such popular support. Human rights–based approaches also benefit from the organized and increasingly networked support of many sectors of civil society and other institutions all around the globe.

The list of human rights is lengthy and begs the question as to which human rights should ethical performance be measured against? Defining the so-called list of human rights is challenging—engaging both political and philosophical minds. Achieving an initial consensus of a list of rights as contained in the Universal Declaration of Human Rights involved an arduous and often contentious process, yet even this document makes no claims to be a definitive list of all human rights. Still, the Universal Declaration of Human Rights, with its 30 articles, provides the most widely accepted international consensus on what ethical performance might be measured against.

In the Preamble to the Universal Declaration, the principal actors are conceived to be nation-states, and the principal actions called for are "progressive measures, national and international."[7] Significant human-rights obligations also are placed upon individuals and social institutions generally:

Every individual and every organ of society, keeping this Declaration constantly in mind, shall strive by teaching and education to promote respect for these rights and freedoms and by progressive measures, national and international, to secure their universal and effective recognition and observance.[8]

Of the variety of human rights articulated in the Universal Declaration, the list traditionally has been divided into two major groupings: civil and political rights, on the one hand, and economic, social, and cultural rights, on the other. The former—civil and political rights, which many still refer to as *traditional* or *first-generation* human rights—include freedom of the press, religion, speech, participation, and assembly; the right to vote and to petition the government; and entitlement to due process of law and other legal protections. The latter grouping—economic, social, and cultural, or *second-*

generation rights—embraces a perspective that is of particular interest to the poor. This perspective concerns rights to basic necessities for a decent standard of living, including education, employment, shelter, nutrition, and health care. Both groupings of human rights can be seen to have direct relevance to good governance and to development through enabling and protecting human well-being or flourishing, although until recently the prevailing international political consensus held that greater priority should be given to civil and political rights.

Building upon the Universal Declaration of Human Rights, the human-rights approach formulated by the United Nations Development Programme (UNDP) embraces both human development and human rights in one theory, contributing to a convergence of the two normative and policy approaches. As such, it offers perhaps a better basis upon which to evaluate progress toward development goals and possibly a more practical framework upon which to measure ethical performance. It is important to distinguish in this practical context that not all moral reasoning is rights based, however, and even when rights based, not all such deliberations involve rights that are internationally recognized as human rights. For example, in the field of environmental ethics, there are wide-ranging debates on various claims of environmental rights and duties, the outcomes of which can or should directly impact development policy and implementation, and governance generally. Only some of these environmental rights are also recognized as human rights, and some environmental rights conflict with human rights.

The language of rights is far ranging, and the specific role of human rights in the measurement of ethical performance of the political and developmental processes remains controversial. For human rights to be effective in measuring positive change, the focus must be strategic. In short, some definitive structure or framework of human rights is needed—such as the UNDP's human-rights approach—derived but separate from the broader and more ambitious agendas of human rights and sustainable development.

The UNDP's *Human Development Report* (HDR) published in 2000, with its theme on human rights and development, has come to be recognized as the UNDP's Human Rights Approach. It is distinctive in its focus on the desirable convergence between human rights and human development. These two ways of thinking and acting, it argues, share a common vision and a common purpose and each of the two ways can and should benefit from the other (UNDP, 2000). Human-rights proponents ask *when* and *by whom* questions and demand specific answers. Effective development and *good* governance depend on having these two questions answered, openly and fully. They are the kinds of questions that policymakers and public servants ought to be concerned about if they are to be effective facilitators of good development and good governance.

This shift in making human development not merely something that *ought* to happen in some undifferentiated sense of *ought*, but also something to which people are *entitled* and something that specific agents have *duties* to bring about, is associated with a significant change in consciousness on the part of all role players concerned. This point also ties back into the earlier human-rights work of Henry Shue, who noted the empowering characteristics of human rights, through which human beings need not grovel for the crumbs off the tables of their (hopefully) benevolent and more affluent leaders, but instead become empowered to assert claims to have their essential dignity respected—and responded to accordingly (Shue, 1996).

Claims impose duties, and the element of accountability places new and rigorous obligations upon government and other social institutions to be responsible to meet the demands of ethical performance in the context of various human rights and to make or facilitate the advances in the associated demands of human development. In an excellent example, HDR 2000 asks who is responsible for a very specific failure in ethical performance—the failure to allow a girl to benefit from free public elementary education. Depending on the particulars, the blame may fall upon the parents, the government, or a combination of factors such as poverty, inadequate school facilities, or a lack of security. Blame is associated with an expectation of blameless behavior, and the human-rights movement has a tradition of holding government officials and those in the public trust accountable for their performance and conduct. This focus on accountability in turn may lead to a process of nuanced institutional analysis, in which the definite specific roles and responsibilities of those associated with determinate failures to satisfy specific human-rights claims are evaluated. The result is that targeted remedies and duty bearers can be identified, and ethical performance improved.

The HDR 2000 argues for a richer view of human development and social progress, in which individuals enjoy—in a secure and stable environment—certain rights and freedoms. The accomplishments of human development become subject to a measured assessment of the extent to which these gains have become protected against potential threats. The gains ought also to be distributed justly; unlike more general community goals for development, human-rights thinking demands that no individuals or groups be excluded from the benefits of development, no matter their minority, economic, ethnic, religious, gender, or social status.

The comparison of human development to human rights and the relations between them in the HDR 2000 leads up to a central argument that many aspects of human-rights performance should be considered as *imperfect duties*: "Imperfect duties leave open both how the duty can be discharged, and how forceful the duty is. Nevertheless, the neglect of the demands of an imperfect duty also involves a serious moral—or political—failure" (UNDP, 2000, pp. 16, 24).

The concept of *imperfect duties* was articulated first by Immanuel Kant (Kant, 1987) and has more recently been championed by Amartya Sen (Sen, 1999). A perfect duty specifies both how the duty is to be performed, to whom it is owed, and that it must be satisfied now. The concept of imperfect duties, by contrast, argues only that the entitlements arising from human-rights claims would be *good* for people to have and *ought* to be provided at some time or other (when conditions are—or can be made to be—appropriate). The *imperfect duties* concept acknowledges the reality that measuring the satisfaction of human rights–based claims may be impossible under current conditions, but it still allows for the assignment of those duties and a measurement of planned incremental progress over time. This assignment places a moral obligation on the associated institutions of society constantly to demonstrate this incremental progress in the discharge of duties imposed by recognized human rights and to maintain this as a priority in policy formulation. Human rights can remain unachieved right now but still impose a moral burden to attend to their progressive fulfillment over time. The identification of certain human rights as imposing only longer-term imperfect duties does not exempt them from the consideration of policymakers and planners now, nor does it make such rights any less forceful or cogent. To the contrary, the concept of imperfect duties can be used by stakeholders to hold governments—at all levels—accountable for making and demonstrating gradual but sustained progress across the entire spectrum of human rights. If the right cannot be respected now, there is an obligation to change the conditions so that it can be.

The articulation, public and institutional acceptance, and fulfillment of human rights generates conflicts, demands for resources, and many challenges to the interests of those in power under the status quo. As such, the evolution of development progress and ethical performance on the basis of fulfilling human rights has properly been called an ongoing political struggle,[9] and the HDR 2000 provides ample empirical evidence of both the progress made to date and the enormity of the challenge that lies ahead. With statistical details of widespread internal conflicts; malnutrition and starvation; huge discrepancies in quality of life; crushing and persistent poverty; the onslaught of HIV/AIDS, malaria, and other health problems, HDR 2000 makes the case compelling—the challenge is indeed daunting.

Central to HDR 2000's approach are its identification of seven essential freedoms and seven key features needed for a broader approach to secure human rights. It can be argued, therefore, that the HDR 2000 "seven freedoms framework" is appropriate to measure progress in development on the terms described above, concentrating the measurement of ethical performance in the realization and securing of seven essential freedoms, both positive (freedom for/of) and negative (freedom from), as follows (UNDP, 2000):

1. Freedom from discrimination—for equality
2. Freedom from want—for a decent standard of living
3. Freedom from being thwarted in self-realization—for the realization of one's human potential
4. Freedom from fear—with no threats to personal security
5. Freedom from injustice
6. Freedom from repression—for participation, expression, and association
7. Freedom from exploitation—for decent work

This is an ambitious and comprehensive agenda for development; measuring a government's ethical performance on the basis of such a framework would be deeply informative.

The HDR 2000 with its seven basic human freedoms is but one framework upon which to structure a human-rights approach to the measurement of ethical performance. Other initiatives are also underway, such as the Human Rights Impact Assessment (HRIA) as developed by the Netherlands Humanist Committee on Human Rights. The emphasis of HRIA is the mainstreaming of human rights, and the integration of human-rights aspects in decision making, policy formulation, implementation activities, and performance monitoring. Other models of human rights–based assessment aim at different goals, such as evaluating the impact of foreign intervention in protecting human rights in a target country, assessing the impact in specific areas of human-rights concern (e.g., women, children, health), or assessing the impact of specific projects in the field of human rights (Radstaake & de Vries, 2004).

Efforts have also been made to try to apply human-rights thinking to measurements made against an MDG framework, so that a distinctly ethics-based perspective on performance could be derived. Given that there is broad support across many nations and international institutions for the MDGs, and taking into consideration that strenuous efforts are being made to develop structural, process, and outcome indicators to measure performance against the MDGs over the time targets stipulated, it appears to make good strategic sense to approach the ethical concerns of performance from the same direction. In practice, however, the results so far have proved disappointing, as in this example with respect to health:

MDG indicators are not necessarily compatible with the right to health, as they can be realized without concentrating specifically on the most vulnerable and poorest groups, do not cover a range of health challenges important to the attainment of the highest level of physical and mental health (e.g. mental and reproductive health) and are not of universal relevance as they focus mainly on poor countries and their corresponding health challenges. (WHO, 2004, p. 148)

The leading multilateral institutions recognize the centrality of respecting human rights to achieving good governance. The World Bank's release in September of 2006 of worldwide governance data and indicators that measure six components of good governance will empower stakeholders to track the ethical and technical performance of institutions, and should help such stakeholders to identify areas in need of capacity strengthening. Of interest, human rights is placed in first place among these six components of good governance:

1. Voice and Accountability—ensuring political, civil, and human rights
2. Political Stability and Absence of Violence—measuring the likelihood of violent threats to, or changes in, government, including terrorism

3. Government Effectiveness—measuring the competence of the bureaucracy and the quality of public service delivery

4. Regulatory Quality—measuring the incidence of market-unfriendly policies

5. Rule of Law—measuring the quality of contract enforcement, the police, and the courts, including judiciary independence, and the incidence of crime

6. Control of Corruption—measuring the abuse of public power for private gain, including petty and grand corruption (and state capture by elites)[10]

It is apparent that the moral theories based on human rights offer considerable scope—as well as considerable challenges—to the goal of measuring ethical performance of public-sector institutions. But does human-rights thinking truly capture an adequate sense of what it is to be human, and of how human beings can become the agents of their own development?

A TRULY HUMAN LIFE

The capability approach is a relatively recent moral theory of human development, originated by Amartya Sen in the early 1980s, who then elaborated it over the next two decades and applied it to a variety of development issues. His book *Development as Freedom* is a popular exposition (Sen, 1999). Other philosophers such as Martha Nussbaum and David Crocker have articulated variations and applied them to particular development challenges such as the status of women (Nussbaum, 2000), consumption practices (Crocker & Linden, 1998), and deliberative democracy (Crocker, 2006).[11] The capability approach has various roots—Adam Smith, Marx, and Kant influence Sen's version, while Nussbaum draws on both Aristotle and Stoicism.

The capability approach poses two questions with respect to development. First, what is important to the good life, to human well-being? And second, how should this good and important thing be distributed? In responding, the emphasis is people focused, recognizing that people can differ greatly in their needs, cultures, and values. There has been considerable attention in the past decade directed toward the capability approach, which is seen as an alternative to utilitarianism but complimentary to human-rights approaches.

The capability approach contends that government and social institutions are obliged to create an environment in which all can realize certain human capabilities—those associated with human dignity. Sen did not itemize those central human capabilities and argues against a fixed list, but Crocker, Nussbaum, and Alkire, among others, have proposed various lists, which in turn may be candidates as sources for parameters for policy analysis and formulation, and for monitoring the impacts of development policies and ethical performance.

In correlation to those human capacities associated with human dignity, the capability approach stresses the importance of valuable human *functionings*. Beyond the basic physical human functionings (digestion, longevity, health, sleep, recreation, procreation) are other activities individuals have reason to value, although each individual may choose to specify and weigh them in different ways. Nussbaum emphasizes freedom in the choice of functionings rather than prescribing that people function in certain ways. She values the exercise of freedom of choice through the application of practical reason as distinctly human, distinguishing human beings from all other animals and emphasizing the freedom to choose: "The person with plenty of food may always choose to fast, but there is a great difference between fasting and starving, and it is this difference that I wish to capture" (Nussbaum, 2000, p. 87).

Although Nussbaum has created several different lists of central human capabilities, the one that she proposed in her book *Women and Human Development* lists 10 separate, irreducible capabilities, summarized as follows (Nussbaum, 2000):

1. Being able to live a normal life span
2. Being able to enjoy bodily and reproductive health and shelter
3. Being able to enjoy freedom of movement and respect for bodily integrity against security threats and violence
4. Being able to use and enjoy the senses, imagination, and thought in a "truly human way"
5. Being able to have emotional attachments to places, things, and people, and to live without emotional abuse
6. Being able to use practical reason to form a conception of one's life plan
7. Being able to affiliate—to live with, for, and "toward" others; to have self-respect; and to exercise compassion
8. Being able to live in a concerned and respectful relationship to other species
9. Being able to play
10. Being able to enjoy freedom to participate in government and in the control over one's environment

According to this moral theory, *each* of these central human capabilities must be satisfied at least to its threshold level before trade-offs, if they can be considered at all, can be made between them.[12] The satisfaction of each human capability does not require direct government intervention but instead demands that government delivers the enabling environment—Nussbaum calls it the "social basis"—for all of these capabilities: "In order to be doing what they should for their citizens, states must be concerned with all the capabilities, even when these seem not so useful for economic growth, or even for political functioning" (Nussbaum, 2000, p. 90).

In the context of measuring ethical performance, the evaluation of the existing social, political, and cultural environment to establish the degree to which it is, in fact, *enabling* under the parameters established by a list such as Nussbaum's 10 categories above is conceptually feasible. It is necessary, however, to first define what *capabilities* mean in this context. Nussbaum distinguishes three types of capabilities. First, *basic capabilities* are the "innate equipment of individuals that is the necessary basis for developing the more advanced capabilities, and a ground of moral concern"(Nussbaum, 2000, p. 84). Second, *internal capabilities* allow a person to exercise the functionings of a mature person. Finally, there are *combined capabilities*, which Nussbaum defines as internal capabilities combined with suitable external conditions to allow the correlative functionings to occur (Nussbaum, 2000).

As mentioned above, Nussbaum regards the achievement of capabilities as having priority over the achievement of functionings, because of the importance of free choice through the exercise of rational thought. But Nussbaum does acknowledge that even the achievement of a basic level of capabilities for all would require some redistribution of material goods (Nussbaum, 2000). One thorny issue in the capability approach is establishing the threshold, the quantity—how much of a human capability is enough, and how should it be measured? Should policies aim at the maximization of human capabilities or aspire to full human flourishing? Alternatively, should the objective be to secure a minimum floor or threshold for all? If so, how should this minimum be conceived and measured? This question emerges as a central debate among development ethicists—should the objective of development be the satisfaction of basic human well-being or, more ambitiously, full human flourishing? Full human flourishing may be an inspirational ideal, but it remains an ideal. For the sake of crafting effective public policy, I take the position that the notion of achieving basic human well-being is more practical, even if it does entail the problems of deciding how much (capability, functioning, freedom) is enough.

The capability approach, with its focus on human dignity, freedoms, and opportunities, shares a close relationship with human-rights approaches, particularly those that include a wide range of rights as human rights. The valuable functions are to be protected and promoted by rights as goals or tools. Nussbaum emphasizes that political liberties have a central importance in establishing the human quality of well-being, and—referring to Sen's writings—in characterizing the mutual respect that people owe each other. Yet Nussbaum's view is that the capability approach does more than complement human-rights approaches, arguing that the best way to think about rights is to see them as combined capabilities:

The right to political participation, the right to religious free exercise, the right of free speech—these and others are all best thought of as capacities to function. In other words, to secure rights to citizens in these areas is to put them in a position of combined capability to function in that area (Nussbaum, 2000, p. 1).

Another very important contribution of the capability approach has to do with who exercises these capabilities and functionings. Instead of the usual *us* evaluating the public sector's impact on *them* through public policies, service delivery, and programs, under the capability approach the *them* is viewed as a very active party interacting with the public sector, not a passive recipient of public-sector largesse. Amartya Sen advocates that citizens must be treated as agents of their own destinies, who can and ought to shape the decisions and the allocation of public resources[13] and public services that affect their own lives (Sen, 1999). To evaluate ethical performance in this view would mean that we must find ways in which to measure the role that ordinary people are empowered to play in their own development—what choices are people empowered to exercise, what information do they receive, to what degree are their choices respected?

At present, the evaluation of ethical performance using the capability approach remains largely experimental. A great effort is underway in many countries, however, to develop evaluation tools and methodologies that employ the most import precepts of this sophisticated moral theory.[14] Given the intellectual rigor of the capability approach, and its remarkable sensitivity to the complex qualitative factors—physical, intellectual, even spiritual—that make ours lives meaningful and valuable, the potential of this moral theory to inform public-sector performance may be unmatched.

TAKING STOCK OF VIRTUE

As noted earlier, the traditional approach to monitoring and evaluating the ethical performance of the public sector consisted of scrutiny of the conduct of individual public servants. Codes of conduct proliferated, egregious behavior was publicly disclosed, and the miscreants shamed in the media. In some cases, even the so-called big fish were fried, in keeping with Robert Klitgaard's advice on building up public confidence in the commitment of the political leadership to constrain corruption and provide good governance (Klitgaard, 1988). More recent thinking expands this premise, to include not just an evaluation of the *corrupt* behavior of individual public servants, but also recognition of the *integrity* of other public servants, as discussed in some detail in chapter 5. It has long been an unspoken truth that every government benefits from a cadre of so-called quiet public servants who are genuinely committed to the principles and ideals of public service, who pursue their duties with diligence and honesty, and who treat the public with both respect and care. These people are models of the ideal of public service, exemplars of integrity, and as such they provide an important moral resource in the shaping of relevant standards of ethical performance. Efforts are now underway to identify and publicly recognize these individuals, and to reward their integrity in some appropriate manner.

Through the combination of compliance and aspirational approaches in shaping ethical behavior standards, and by coupling these codes with serious efforts to train public servants to become better at discernment of ethical dilemmas and resolution of ethical challenges, a powerful appeal is made to both fear of sanctions and to the dutiful commitment of public servants of integrity. This is hardly innovative, however; former American president Thomas Jefferson advocated just such an approach in 1814: "No government can be maintained without the principle of fear as well as duty. Good men will obey the last, but bad ones the former only. If our government ever fails, it will be from this weakness."[15]

Less attention has been paid to date in evaluating the *character* of a public institution. Many would question whether an institution could possess virtue, integrity, or character. If such institutional attributes truly do exist, could they be measured and evaluated?

Institutions are not moral entities, but they do have character, at least in the broadly descriptive sense. We experience, through our interactions with them, that certain ministries are more caring, more polite, more effective, and less corrupt. We can evaluate the policies and practices of institutions to determine how transparent they are, the degree to which they are committed to the welfare of their own employees, the integrity with which they conduct their procurement functions, and the extent to which their employees are recognized in terms of merit. Modern codes of ethics recognize this institutional role and establish ethical standards not just for the individual member of an institution, but also for the institution as a whole. Once so established in terms of specific standards, the ethical performance of institutions in meeting these standards ought to be monitored, measured, and evaluated. In the case of public-sector institutions, this form of evaluation must include the participation of the public to have validity in the eyes of the public.

Ultimately, however, the moral characteristics of the performance of public-sector institutions depend in large measure on the moral quality of the leadership of the institution, as discussed in chapter 3. Not surprising then that so much attention is currently directed at the topic of leadership ethics, transformational leadership, and transactional leadership. Character does matter, and leaders who demonstrate strong moral attributes, vision, charisma, commitment to the welfare of their staff, the ability to intellectually stimulate their staff, and a demonstrated record of personal and professional integrity can and do influence the ethical performance of an institution.

Measuring integrity—personal or institution—to date has largely been limited to measuring the failings of integrity. This approach has become so ingrained that the term *integrity* is now often held to be synonymous only with adherence to regulatory regimes addressed at constraining corruption. For example, the Department of Institutional Integrity at the World Bank (INT) has little to do with integrity and much to do with the failure of integrity. INT does not act directly to strengthen ethical leadership, recognize exemplary ethical performance, or raise public awareness of the importance of integrity as a moral resource in society. Instead, its mission is to investigate allegations of fraud and corruption in Bank-financed projects, and allegations of Bank staff misconduct. It is staffed accordingly, being led by a criminologist overseeing a team of more than 30 investigators, legal specialists, forensic accountants, procurement specialists, and former Bank task managers.[16]

In like fashion, the United States Agency for International Development's August 2005 handbook on assessing integrity in institutions limits its focus to evaluating the institutional incentives, management practices, political and administrative factors, and oversight relationships that either promote or constrain corruption. No positive concept of integrity as something good to be recognized, fostered, celebrated, or strengthened appears in this and similar documents on integrity (Lanya & Azfar, 2005).

Equating integrity to the legal and moral failures associated with the lack of integrity is a strangely perverse way to view a potentially beneficial moral resource, and a potentially strong indicator of ethical performance, but it is indicative of just how cynical our view of basic human nature has become.

ENABLING ETHICAL PERFORMANCE

The public sector does not exist in a vacuum, and expecting a set of moral values and ethical standards within a ministry that are completely separate from the values and standards that exist in the political, cultural, and social environment in which the ministry is based is irrational. Various public-sector institutions often each emphasize certain moral values as being higher in priority or more relevant to the nature of the services that they perform. For example, in three separate workshops that I led with representatives of three Kenyan ministries (Health, Agriculture, and Local Government), each articulated different sets of values as their *core* values, although they shared many individual values.[17] The core values for the Ministry of Health included professionalism, transparency and accountability, integrity, justice and fairness, service and customer care. The core values for the Ministry of Agriculture included justice and fairness, integrity, pursuit of excellence, collective responsibility, acting in the public interest, moral equality, and professionalism. Finally, the core values for the Ministry of Local Government included integrity, accountability and transparency, professionalism, and diligence. In all three cases, these sets of values reflected the values that motivated the individual members (and, in some cases, also the leaders) of these respective ministries. But do they reflect the expectations and aspirations of the Kenyan public in the context of the ethical performance of their public-sector institutions? That data is missing; yet even if it existed, what can be done to strengthen and sustain an appropriate level of demand for ethical performance within the Kenyan public? Do the Kenyan people expect their public-sector institutions to perform ethically? Ought they to expect this standard?

The answer to this dilemma lies in strengthening the democratic culture of Kenya. Specifically, people must be afforded structured opportunities in which to express their values and priorities, make their expectations of ethical governance explicit, deliberate on contentious issues, and participate in the articulation of what constitutes the *public interest*. As argued persuasively by David Crocker, and discussed in chapter 4, it is only by deepening and broadening participation, and making participation more inclusive, that genuine development can be pursued and achieved (Crocker, 2006).

MEASURING THE SPECTRUM

There is a wide variation in the way in which ethical performance of the public sector is conceived. The majority of current thinking views ethical performance narrowly, in the context of seeking regulatory compliance and the crafting of effective oversight mechanisms and other disincentives to compel the public sector to serve the public interest first, not their own individual greed and ambitions.

This chapter argues that a genuine respect of human dignity demands a more positive approach to how ethical performance is conceived and articulated. People and institutions have the potential to perform to exceptionally high moral standards, to provide public services with honor and commitment, and to exemplify the ideals of dedicated public service. Public servants and public institutions often do just this, but such morally commendable performance fails to be recognized. That oversight is itself a powerful incentive to fail in terms of ethical performance.

While taking full note of the potential of self-interested individuals and misguided or poorly led institutions to perform well below ethically acceptable standards, we should devise monitoring and evaluation techniques that measure both ends of the spectrum—the presence of moral achievement as well as moral failings. Ethical performance should be evaluated with the premise that people can and often will be immoral, but that people also have the capacity—and often the propensity—to achieve high moral standards.

The complexity of human behavior, motivations, values, both as individuals and in the context of membership in institutions, is very difficult to capture through empirical measures alone. The use of narratives to complement the empirical view will help to humanize the statistics and will provide important insights that the statistics alone cannot surface. There are also now available a variety of moral theories explored with considerable and persuasive rigor by the field of development ethics. These moral theories offer considerable scope to improving and deepening the basis of measuring ethical performance—evaluating human rights, human capabilities, and human character, along with other factors. Many potential and experimental frameworks already exist, from the United Nations HDR 2000's "seven freedoms" to the Human Rights Impact Assessment (HRIA) approach from the Netherlands. The capability approach offers even more sophisticated methods for measuring ethical performance, particularly by elevating the person from a passive object of study to an active and participatory agent of development. Fostering a public dialogue on the qualities of ethical leadership would go some considerable distance in creating context-specific approaches to measuring ethical leadership, and the leader's (and manager's) role in achieving high standards of public-sector ethical performance.

Clearly there is much work ahead, yet this process is far from just beginning. The demand for public-sector services and behavior that is both effective and ethical is unlikely to diminish, and the public sector has a strong interest in demonstrating a sincere, committed, and respectful response to the public that it serves and whose trust it depends upon.

Notes

CHAPTER 1: INTRODUCTION

1. I define *economism* in the context of this chapter based primarily on neoclassical economics, and excluding economics theories such as Marxism that are strongly normative. I am using *economism* to mean an ideology that places highest priority—in the context of personal, cultural, social, and political life—on viewing human activity and decision making as predominantly a function of economics (or economic growth). On that basis, the success and effectiveness of social, political, and cultural institutions are judged on the nature of the flow of capital, the existence of effective competition, and the maximization of profit. The ultimate unit of measurement is the (self-interested) individual, not the larger community.

2. See, for example, the writings of D. W. Hamlyn, Stephen Toulmin, Bernard Kaplan, John Flavell, Jean Piaget, Lawrence Kohlberg, R. S. Peters, William Kessen, and Theodore Mischel.

3. The literature from these fields is vast, but see, for example, works by Paul Collier, Jeffrey Sachs, Benjamin Friedman, Thomas Carothers, Richard Falk, Hernando DeSoto, Robert Klitgaard, Paul Streeten, Susan Rose-Ackerman, Mahbub Ul Haq, Amartya Sen, and Joseph Stiglitz.

4. Severe poverty is typically defined in economic terms as subsisting on less than US$1 per day, although recent arguments suggest that with the global drop in the value of the dollar, a higher figure would now be appropriate.

5. *Easily affordable* refers to the relative deprivation suffered by those wealthier persons taxed to support this increased level of funding, which would be minimal in its impact on quality of life for these persons—and relative to the impact on the lives of the poor, the gain in quality of life of the poor being lifted out of poverty is incomparable to the incremental decline in the quality of life of the wealthy.

6. The Western tradition of ethics is also often referred to as *moral philosophy*. Moral philosophy is one part of value theory (axiology). The other part is aesthetics,

which in turn is one of the four major branches of philosophy (aesthetics, metaphysics, epistemology, and logic).

7. Sometimes this ordering takes the form of a code of ethics, which is an attempt to crystallize this consensus on principles and values into a set of formal precepts and rules, intended usually to serve as an overarching guide to ethically acceptable behavior.

8. The fundamental principles of liberalism generally are held to include transparency; civil and individual rights, especially the right to life, liberty, and property; government through the informed consent of the governed as expressed through free and fair elections; and equal rights for all citizens under the robust rule of law.

9. From the speech by Andrew Natsios at the Society for International Development in Washington, DC, on December 1, 2004.

10. Among the literature of development ethics, one finds the work of Sabina Alkire, Charles Beitz, Peter Berger, Luis Camacho, David Crocker, Nigel Dower, Des Gasper, Denis Goulet, Godfrey Gunatilleke, Herman Kahn, Onora O'Neill, Martha Nussbaum, Thomas Pogge, Mozaffar Qizilbash, E. Roy Ramírez, Ramon Romero, Jerome Segal, Amartya Sen, Peter Singer, and Paul Streeten, among others.

11. See, for example, the work of Luis Camacho, Jorge Luis Chavez, and E. Roy Ramirez (Costa Rica); Adela Cortina, Jesus Conill, and Emilio Martínez Navarro (Spain); Tarso Genro (Brazil); Godfrey Gunatilleke (Sri Lanka); Kwame Gyekye (Ghana); Bernardo Kliksberg and Oswaldo Guariglia (Argentina); Ingrid Robyns and Des Gasper (the Netherlands); Asunción St. Clair (Norway); Cristián Parker and Manfred Max-Neef (Chile); Peter John Opio (Uganda); Thomas Pogge (Germany); Ramón Romero (Honduras); Wilhelm Verwoerd (South Africa); and Edward Wamala and Byaruhanga Rukooko (Uganda).

12. Two professional organizations have been formed: the International Development Ethics Association (founded in 1987) and the Human Development and Capability Association (founded in 2000). The groups' respective Web sites are (1) the International Development Ethics Association (http://www.development-ethics.org/) and (2) the Human Development and Capability Association (http://www.fas.harvard.edu/~freedoms). Although not explicitly related to development ethics, other associations such as the Society for International Development, the United Nations Association, and the World Development Movement have had serious ethical interests related to development and foreign aid.

13. In Uganda, see the Ethics and Public Management Programme of the Department of Philosophy, Faculty of Arts, Makerere University (http://www.makerere.ac.ug/arts/depts/phil.html).

14. In Uganda, see the Makerere Center for Applied Ethics (MACAE; http://www.macae.or.ug).

CHAPTER 2: EDUCATION

1. This Ugandan initiative has to date focused only on children in primary schools.

2. See the video *Teasing Isn't Pleasing*, produced by the Friends Community School, 5901 Westchester Park Drive, College Park, Maryland 20740.

3. See Bernard M. Bass & Paul Steidlmeier. (1998). "Ethics, Character, and Authentic Transformational Leadership." Center for Leadership Studies, School of Management, Binghamton University, Binghamton, NY. Retrieved April 14, 2008 from http://www.vanguard.edu/uploadedFiles/Faculty/RHeuser/ETHICS,%20MO

RAL%20CHARACTER%20AND%20AUTHENTIC%20TRANSFORMATION
AL%20LEADERSHIP.pdf.

4. For example, as a Quaker, I am a Christian who does not believe in sacraments (not even baptism), believing that these are man-made rituals and not something that is fundamentally spiritual. As a Quaker, I found the type of Christian education and values offered in the sample curricula that was circulated at the Ugandan workshop to be unacceptable, and I would resist having schools in my own country teach such a curriculum to my own two children.

5. *Character Education and Life Skills Lessons*. Retrieved September 11, 2008 from www.character-education.Info/Articles/Motivational-Character-Quotes.htm.

CHAPTER 3: LEADERSHIP

1. One of the leading current applications of virtue ethics is as a component of business ethics. With the renewed emphasis on leadership in both strategic management and business ethics, the ideal of the morally virtuous business leader has assumed prominence and may offer some insights in the context of political leadership.

2. Sunday Monitor Online; see http://www.monitor.co.ug/sunday/news/news 02121.php.

3. Human Rights Watch; see http://www.hrw.org/reports/2001/uganda/.

4. In Uganda, vote buying has become so pervasive that it has now become commonplace for parents of schoolchildren to provide their child with sweets to use as inducements for other children to elect them as class prefect.

5. In 2000, Kenya's parliament had only 4 percent women, compared to 17 percent in Tanzania and 18 percent in Uganda.

6. *Nyayo* means "footsteps" and was intended to indicate that his political beliefs and vision followed in the footsteps of Jomo Kenyatta.

7. President Kibaki's vision for Kenya, delivered in a speech on December 31, 2002, offered little more than a statement of support for the National Rainbow Coalition, reconciliation with political rivals, and attention to various social and economic ills. See http://www.hartford-hwp.com/archives/36/527.html.

8. CBC News. "Shooting death of MP sparks increased Kenyan violence." See http://www.cbc.ca/world/story/2008/01/29/kenya-mp.html.

9. For example, Nyerere—while a university student in Britain—was deeply influenced by Michael Scot of the Fabian Society.

10. For example, the Eighth Global Leadership Forum of June 2006 in Istanbul, Turkey.

11. The African Leadership and Progress Network. "The African Leadership Capacity Development Project." See http://www.africanprogress.net/leadership_capacity.htm for more details on these initiatives.

12. African Leadership Institute. See http://www.alinstitute.org/ for more details.

CHAPTER 4: PARTICIPATION

1. Sherry Arnstein's Ladder of Citizen Participation consists of eight rungs: (1) Citizen Control, such as a neighborhood-run corporation; (2) Delegated Power, where through negotiations citizens achieve a dominant decision-making power over a particular program or plan; (3) Partnership, in which there is a redistribution of power negotiated between power holders and citizens; (4) Placation, usually achieved

by putting a few so-called worthy poor on a committee or two; (5) Consultation, in which decision makers agree to listen to participants, but with no guaranty of any action in response; (6) Informing, which isn't participation at all but only a one way flow of information, officials to citizens; (7) Therapy, in which decision makers only seek to achieve acceptance of their decisions through a process of attitude adjustment; and (8) Manipulation, which consists of a public-relations trick, with entirely staged participation. See Sherry Arnstein, "A Ladder of Citizen Participation," in *The City Reader*.

2. The only exceptions to this general rule are those people not competent to participate in a rational manner, such as children and people with certain mental disabilities, or those people whom society has decided to exclude, such as convicted criminals.

3. For an excellent case study of Porto Alegre's participatory budgeting, see http://info.worldbank.org/etools/docs/library/238102/1.1.2%20sdn71.pdf.

4. Universalism is the view that values or norms, and associated obligations, apply equally to all people and all cultures. Utilitarians and Kantians, for example, argue that the correct or justified ethical principles apply to all societies and all individuals. A variant is *minimum universalism*, which accepts some moral diversity but contends that there is a universally valid body of values that can be accepted by people from different moral and religious communities (agreed on, not discovered) and that can be used to judge public policy (Dower, 1998, pp. 43, 155).

5. Dower defines *skeptical realism* as the calculation of power and national interests, as often used in evaluating relations between states within a competitive framework. These norms of international relations are more maxims of prudence than moral norms—they are abandoned whenever prudence dictates but are often used in moral rhetoric that Dower claims is generally hypocritical (Dower, 1998, p. 18).

6. *Cosmopolitanism* is an ethical approach based on the moral premise that the world is one moral domain, out of which arise certain universal or global moral obligations, values, and responsibilities (Dower, 1998, p. 20).

CHAPTER 5: CORRUPTION AND INTEGRITY

1. For the 2007 Transparency International Corruption Perceptions Index, see http://www.infoplease.com/world/statistics/2007-transparency-international-corruption-perceptions.html.

2. See Geoffrey Ekanya. (2007). "The Parliament: Contributions to and Challenges for Greater Finance Transparency and Accountability to Citizens: A Case Study of Uganda." Paper presented to Organisation for Economic Co-operation and Development Workshop on Ownership in Practice. Paris, September 27–28, 2007. http://www.oecd.org/dataoecd/3/15/39364678.pdf.

3. See Government of Uganda. (2006a). *National Public Procurement Integrity Baseline Survey 2006: Final Report*. Public Procurement and Disposal of Assets Authority & Office of the Inspectorate of Government. Kampala, Uganda. http://www.ppda.go.ug/downloads/Integrity%20survey%20FINAL%20REPORT%202007.pdf.

4. See Agnes Asiimwe & Angelo Izama. "African leaders steal $148 billion a year." *The Monitor*, September 21, 2007. http://exposeugandasgenocide.blogspot.com/2007/10/tour-guide-to-corruption-in-uganda.html.

5. See *American Heritage Dictionary*, http://education.yahoo.com/reference/dictionary/entry/integrity.

6. The range and scope of these choices is dependent on the freedoms and opportunities accessible to each person, and the extent to which any one person is aware of and interested in such freedoms and opportunities. A genuine democracy, particularly one that is relatively free of poverty, typically offers extensive choices to its citizens, enabling each person to make important personal choices about his life and about public policies and actions that affect his life.

7. See National Strategy for Mainstreaming Ethics and Integrity in all Sectors and All Institutions in Local Governance in Uganda, March 27, 2003. http://unpan1. un.org/intradoc/groups/public/documents/UN/UNPAN010806.pdf.

8. See Martin Oiko. (2002). "Report on UNDP Consultancy to Build Consensus on the Strategy for Mainstreaming Ethics and Integrity in all Sectors and All Institutions in Local Governance in Uganda." http://unpan1.un.org/intradoc/groups/public/documents/UN/UNPAN010808.pdf.

CHAPTER 6: HUNGER

1. See the Oxfam International. (2006). *Causing Hunger: An Overview of the Food Crisis in Africa*, Oxfam Briefing Paper 91, July 2006. http://www.oxfam.org/files/Causing%20Hunger.pdf.

2. Washington Post. (2008). "Food Crisis: Food prices are causing hunger around the world." p. A-16, March 14, 2008.

3. The right to food has been endorsed more often and with greater unanimity than most other human rights, while at the same time being violated more comprehensively and systematically than probably any other right. See Philip Alston & Katarina Tomaševski (Eds.). (1984). "The Right to Food, from Soft to Hard Law" (p. 9). Dordrecht, the Netherlands: Martinus Nijhoff.

4. The principal treaties associated with human rights and the year that each went into force are as follows:

1. International Covenant on Civil and Political Rights (1976)
2. International Covenant on Economic, Social, and Cultural Rights (1976)
3. International Convention on the Elimination of All Forms of Racial Discrimination (1969)
4. Convention on the Elimination of All Forms of Discrimination Against Women (1981)
5. Convention Against Torture and Other Cruel, Inhuman, or Degrading Treatment or Punishment (1987)
6. Convention on the Rights of the Child (1990)
7. International Convention on the Protection of the Rights of All Migrant Workers and Members of Their Families (2003)

5. The following are representative of the many conferences and meetings on the topic of the human right to freedom from hunger:

• Special Assembly on Man's Right to Freedom from Hunger, Rome. March 14, 1963: *Manifesto*.
• World Food Conference, 1974: *Declaration on the Eradication of Hunger and Malnutrition*.
• World Food Assembly, Rome. 1984 (comprised mainly of representatives of civil society organizations, questioned the failure of the 1974 World Food Conference to achieve its target relative to ending childhood hunger).
• Conference on Food and Law, Howard University, Washington, D.C., USA. 1986.

- World Summit for Children, United Nations, New York. September 1990: *Plan of Action for Implementing the World Declaration on the Survival, Protection, and Development of Children.*
- International Conference on Nutrition, Food and Agriculture Organization of the United Nations and the World Health Organization, Rome. December 1992: *World Declaration on Nutrition* (endorsed the human right to adequate food).
- World Food Summit, Food and Agriculture Organization of the United Nations, Rome. November 1996: *Rome Declaration on World Food Security* and *World Food Summit Plan of Action.*
- Millennium Summit of the United Nations, 2000: Millennium Development Goals, supported by all 189 nations at the summit, were led by goal 1, to eradicate extreme poverty and hunger.

6. "UPE Goal Could Go Offside," *The Weekly Observer,* Kampala, Uganda, April 20, 2006, http://www.ugandaobserver.com/news/specials/ugecon/econ04201.php.

7. I adopt here the definition of a moral agent as offered by *Webster's Revised Unabridged Dictionary* (1913): "A moral agent is a being capable of those actions that have a moral quality, and which can properly be denominated good or evil in a moral sense." See http://dict.die.net/moral%20agent/.

8. British Broadcast Corporation (BBC). (2008)."Bush offers $770m for food crisis," May 2, 2008, Retrieved on May 3, 2008 from http://news.bbc.co.uk/2/hi/americas/7378807.stm.

9. See the Hunger Project Web site at http://africaprize.org/98/museveni.htm.

10. See Dr. Augustus Nuwagaba, "Uganda: Is Museveni's Claim on Food Prices Logical?" *The Monitor,* May 23, 2008. http://allafrica.com/stories/200805220999.htm.

CHAPTER 7: CONFLICT

1. Vincent Otti disagreed with Kony over tactics, and was later executed by the LRA on October 2, 2007, at Kony's home, on Kony's direct orders. Kony explained the execution by saying that he would not tolerate indiscipline. See BBC. (2007)."Otti 'executed by Uganda rebels,'" December 21, 2007. http://news.bbc.co.uk/2/hi/africa/7156284.stm.

2. See Refugee Law Project. (2004). *Behind the Violence: Causes, Consequences and the Search for Solutions to the War in Northern Uganda.* Refugee Law Project Working Paper No. 11, February 2004. Kampala, Uganda. www.refugeelawproject.org/resources/papers/workingpapers/RLP.WP11.pdf.

3. The Inter-American Development Bank (IDB), with the strong financial backing of Norway and other donors, established the Initiative for Social Capital and the Ethics of Development (ISED) in 2002. It's director resigned in 2007 under a cloud, and the Initiative subsequently foundered for lack of an institutional champion within the IDB.. The World Bank has involved development ethicists in a very limited number of projects focused on leadership, integrity, and procurement.

4. Former Ugandan Minister for the North, Betty Bigombe, has tried repeatedly to negotiate with Kony, first in an official capacity and later as an individual. Jan Egeland of the UN has met with Kony, too, but both Bigombe and Egeland have failed to find any common ground with Kony for a workable peace.

5. See International Crisis Group, *Policy Briefing: A Strategy for Ending Northern Uganda's Crisis* (Kampala, Uganda, and Brussels, Belgium: Author, 2006).

6. The July 2005 report, *Forgotten Voices*, describes the results of extensive surveys carried out with over 2,500 respondents, which showed that 40 percent had been abducted by the LRA, 45 percent had witnessed the killing of a family member, and 23 percent had been physically mutilated at some point during the conflict. See Phuong, Vinck, Wierda, Stover, & di Giovanni. (2005). *Forgotten Voices: A Population-Based Survey on Attitudes about Peace and Justice in Northern Uganda.* International Center for Transitional Justice, Human Rights Center. Berkeley, CA: University of Berkeley Press.

7. See International Crisis Group, *Policy Briefing.*

8. The Sudan People's Liberation Army and related political and military groups led a lengthy insurrection in the south, seeking greater autonomy and a fair cut of Sudan's oil and mineral wealth. In the process, tens of thousands of civilians were slain or injured, and many extreme human rights violations took place.

9. See International Crisis Group, *Policy Briefing.*

10. See Eli Clifton. (2007). "Uganda: Time Is Critical in Peace Talks with LRA Rebels," Inter Press Service (IPS). *The Story Underneath.* (April 27, 2007). http://ipsnews.net/news.asp?idnews=37535.

11. See International Crisis Group, *Policy Briefing.*

12. There is widespread agreement that the child combatants of the LRA are not morally accountable for their crimes, as brutal as they are, since these people have suffered severe trauma, and many were too young to be held to the ethical standards of adulthood.

CHAPTER 8: URBANIZATION

1. See Rutsch, Horst. (2001)."From 'Planning the City' to a 'City that Plans'— The Experience of Dar es Salaam," United Nations Chronicle, Online Edition, vol. 38, no. 1 (2001). New York: United Nations Department of Public Information. http://www.un.org/Pubs/chronicle/2001/issue1/0101p62.html.

2. See United Nations Human Settlements Programme (HABITAT). (2002). *The Global Campaign on Urban Governance Concept Paper*, 2nd Edition. (March 1, 2002). New York: United Nations, at www.unhabitat.org/content.asp?cid=2099&catid=419& typeid=3&subMenuId=0&ContentsByTheme=254.

3. See United Nations Development Programme (UNDP), *Halving Extreme Poverty: An Action Strategy for the United Nations*, Final Draft, November 10, 1999. New York: United Nations.

4. See United Nations. (2001). *The Habitat Agenda in the Urban Millennium.* Urban Millennium newletter. New York: United Nations, retrieved at ww2.unhabitat. org/Istanbul%2B5/booklet8.pdf.

5. See *Good Urban Governance: A Normative Framework* (HS/C/PC.1/CRP.6), February 26, 2000. New York: United Nations. Retrieved May 15, 2007 at http://www.un-habitat.org.

6. See the 27 principles elaborated in the United Nations Environment Programme's *Rio Declaration on Environment and Development*, 1992.

7. Distributive justice is a principle of social justice that requires the distribution— according to some pattern or process—of some good, for instance, resources, wealth, or opportunities (Chadwick 1998, p. 755). This contrasts with retributive and com-

pensatory justice, which are concerned, respectively, with justified punishment for perpetrators of bad deeds and justified reparation to victims of bad deeds.

8. Bloomberg School of Public Health. (2003). *Population Reports: Meeting the Urban Challenge*, Baltimore: Bloomberg School of Public Health, Johns Hopkins University, April 10, 2003. http://www.infoforhealth.org/pr/press/041003.shtml.

9. Ibid.

10. See Consolidation for Social Awareness and Responsibility, at http://www3.simpatico.ca/truegrowth/demographics.htm.

11. United Nations Development Programme (UNDP), *Human Development Report 2003* (New York: Oxford University Press, 2003), pp. 6, 9, 87, http://www.undp.org/hdr2003.

12. United Nations Development Programme (UNDP), *Human Development Report 1998* (New York: Oxford University Press, 1998), p. 49.

13. United States Department of Agriculture. (1999) *U.S. Action Plan on Food Security*, Washington, D.C.: Author (p. iii). http://www.fas.usda.gov/icd/summit/pressdoc.html.

14. Food and Agriculture Organization of the United Nations. (1999). *The State of Food Insecurity in the World 1999*. Rome: FAO Publications. http://www.fao.org/news/1999/img/sofi99-e.pdf.

15. United States Agency for International Development (The Office of Environment and Urban Programs), *Making Cities Work* (Washington, D.C.: 2001), p. 1.

16. UNDP (2003), p. 290

17. Severe poverty is defined as living on less than $1 per day.

18. Thomas W. Pogge, *World Poverty and Human Rights: Cosmopolitan Responsibilities and Reforms* (Cambridge: Polity Press, 2002).

19. World Bank, *World Development Report 2004* (New York: Oxford University Press, 2004), p. 253.

20. *Easily affordable* refers to the relative deprivation suffered by those wealthier persons taxed to support this increased level of funding, which would be minimal in its impact on quality of life for these persons—and relative to the impact on the lives of the poor, the gain in quality of life of the poor being lifted out of poverty is incomparable to the incremental decline in the quality of life of the wealthy.

21. Thomas W. Pogge, *Moral Priorities for International Non-governmental Organizations*, paper presented at University of Maryland seminar, March 14, 2004, p. 3.

22. Ibid., pp. 5–11.

23. The determinants affecting which of these units of distribution to use are themselves worth some consideration, as they are not value free.

CHAPTER 9: MINORITY RIGHTS

1. The incidence of transgender status is statistically relatively rare. Based on the recent available evidence to date on this phenomenon in the Netherlands, less than 1 in 12,000 of those born biologically male and less than 1 in 30,400 of those born biologically female are diagnosed with the symptoms of being transgendered. In the United States, the American Psychological Association has very similar estimates, with a prevalence rate for transgender status at about 1 in 10,000 for biological males and 1 in 30,000 for biological females. Assuming similar incidence rates prevail in Uganda, which has a population of approximately 31 million, there are slightly more than 2,600 transgendered persons in Uganda. The prevalence of intersex status is significantly

higher, but the phenomenon is very broadly defined. In the United States, approximately 1 in 1,500 to 1 in 2,000 infants are born every year with external genitals that are not easily identified as male or female. Based on an assumption of similar levels of occurrence within the Ugandan population, that would mean that around 17,700 infants are born annually with this condition. There is no reliable data available on how many Ugandans are treated for being intersex, but clearly the vast majority of intersex Ugandans go through their lives without medical or psychological support or assistance. At present, the small quasi-formal group of transgendered and intersex persons who meet on a regular basis in Kampala has a membership of just 27 transgendered and 1 intersex, meaning that roughly 99 percent of Uganda's transgender and intersex population remains isolated and unsupported.

2. GID is a formal diagnosis and psychiatric classification used by psychologists and physicians to describe persons who are discontent with the biological sex they were born with. GID is the diagnostic classification most commonly applied to transsexuals and relates to a feeling expressed by such persons—often over a period of many years and with increasing intensity—of being born in the wrong body.

3. The choice of pronouns is a particular challenge when describing transgender persons. Some elect to remain with their pronoun of birth, others with their present gender identity. I refer to Salongo as *he*, except when it makes little sense, as when referring to Salongo's having given birth to a son, or binding her own breasts to appear male.

4. Julius Kaggwa, *From Juliet to Julius: In Search of My True Gender Identity*. (Kampala, Uganda: Fountain, 1997).

5. Richard Rorty. (1993). "Human Rights, Rationality, and Sentimentality," *Belgrade Circle Journal*. Portland, ME: University of Southern Maine. http://www.usm.maine.edu/~bcj/issues/three/rorty.html.

CHAPTER 10: ETHICAL PERFORMANCE

1. See "Good Governance: Definition and Implications" by Palamagamba John Kabudi of the faculty of law at the University of Dar es Salaam, which provides an excellent brief summary of the concept of good governance, accessible at http://tanzania.fes-international.de/doc/good-governance.pdf#search='good%20governance%2C%20definition.

2. See World Bank (2007). *Justice for the Poor: Kenya Concept Note*. Washington, D.C.: Author, retrieved July 19, 2008 at http://www-wds.worldbank.org/external/default/WDSContentServer/WDSP/IB/2007/06/14/000310607_20070614170022/Rendered/PDF/400370KE0Conce1or0Poor01PUBLIC1.pdf.

3. See the report by Dr. Peter Wanyande and Dr. C. Odhiambo Mbai, *Public Service Ethics in Africa: Report on the Dissemination Workshop on Kenya*, August 29, 2002, retrieved at http://unpan1.un.org/intradoc/groups/public/documents/un/unpan006409.pdf.

4. See the time series data table showing the Kenya Country Profile on the Millennium Development Goals indicators, 1995–2006, at http://ddp-ext.worldbank.org/ext/ddpreports/ViewSharedReport?&CF=1&REPORT_ID=1336&REQUEST_TYPE_VIEWADVANCED&HF=N/IDGProfile.asp.

5. See BBC. "Uganda ban on the Vagina Monologues," February 18, 2005, at http://news.bbc.co.uk/2/hi/africa/4277063.stm.

6. I interpret this in practice to mean that the government fails to take appropriate measures to protect or promote the features of a person's life that the specific

human right addresses—access to adequate nutrition, shelter, and clothing (subsistence), for example.

7. See United Nations. (1948). *Universal Declaration of Human Rights*, retrieved October 16, 2004 at http://www.un.org/Overview/rights.html.

8. See the Preamble to the United Nations Universal Declaration of Human Rights at http://www.un.org/Overview/rights.html.

9. Ignatieff refers to human rights as a *fighting creed* and notes: "No authority whose power is directly challenged by human rights advocacy is likely to concede its legitimacy." See Michael Ignatieff, *Human Rights as Politics and Idolatry* (Princeton, NJ: Princeton University Press, 2001), p. 56.

10. See World Bank Press Release, "World Bank Releases Largest Available Governance Data Source," Press Release No. 2009/63/WBI, http://web.worldbank.org/WBSITE/EXTERNAL/NEWS/0,,contentMDK:21050333~pagePK:64257043~piPK:437376~theSitePK:4607,00.html.

11. Nussbaum's focus is on the full person, and her Approach has affinities with virtue ethics. Unlike Sen, she does view happiness as integrated with good activity rather than as a separate mental state. Crocker's Approach employs well-being as the key normative concept and explores its relevance for all sorts and conditions of humans, such as the disabled and elderly, and nonhumans. Crocker, like Nussbaum, has offered an evolving list of components of well-being, but unlike Nussbaum, Crocker argues that clashes among them ought to be resolved through democratic deliberation.

12. Nussbaum claims that her list of essential human capabilities is a list of separate components, and that a person cannot satisfy the need for one component by giving a larger amount to another. The irreducible plurality of the list, she claims, limits the trade-offs that it would be reasonable to make.

13. According to this type of thinking, the evaluation of public resources becomes a central element in the assessment of the quality of the enabling environment for human well-being, using a list such as Nussbaum's 10 categories.

14. Sen continues to write about the capability approach as a tool for measuring development, and he has now been joined by theorists such as Diwakar Khare, V. P. Tripathi, Bernard Delhausse, Stephen Klasen, Andrea Brandolini, Giovanni D'Alessio, Achin Chakraborty, Stephen Jenkins, and Sabina Alkire. Refer also to the Web site of the Human Development and Capability Association at http://www.capabilityapproach.com/Home.php.

15. An excerpt from a letter by Thomas Jefferson to John Wayles Eppes, 1814; see University of Virginia. (1995). "Thomas Jefferson on Politics & Government: Quotations from the Writings of Thomas Jefferson" (53. Duties of Citizens), at http://etext.lib.virginia.edu/jefferson/quotations/jeff1700.htm.

16. See the World Bank's Department of Institutional Integrity (INT) Web site at http://web.worldbank.org/WBSITE/EXTERNAL/EXTABOUTUS/ORGANIZATION/ORGUNITS/EXTDOII/0,,contentMDK:20542001~pagePK:64168427~piPK:64168435~theSitePK:588921,00.html.

17. These three one-day workshops were convened by the Public Sector Reform and Development Secretariat in Nairobi in March 2006 and were facilitated by Dr. Stephen Schwenke. Senior managers from various departments were represented.

Bibliography

Adar, Korwa G., & Isaac M. Munyae. (2001). "Human Rights Abuse in Kenya under Daniel arap Moi, 1978–2001." Retrieved June 6, 2008 from http://web.africa.ufl.edu/asq/v5/v5i1a1.htm.

Alston, Philip, & Katarina Tomaševski (Eds.). (1984). *The Right to Food, from Soft to Hard Law*. Dordrecht, the Netherlands: Martinus Nijhoff.

Appiah, Kwame Anthony. (2007). *The Ethics of Identity*. Princeton, NJ: Princeton University Press.

Arnstein, Sherry. (2003). "A Ladder of Citizen Participation." In Richard T. LeGates & Frederic Stout (Eds.), *The City Reader* (pp. 244–255). London: Routledge.

Aseka, Eric Masinda. (2005). *Transformational Leadership in East Africa. Politics, Ideology and Community*. Kampala, Uganda: Fountain.

Asiimwe, Agnes, & Angelo Izama. "African leaders steal $148 billion a year." *The Monitor*, September 21, 2007. Retrieved October 31, 2007 from http://exposeugandasgenocide.blogspot.com/2007/10/tour-guide-to-corruption-in-uganda.html.

Bass, B., & B. Avolio. (1990). *Manual for the Multifactor Leadership Questionnaire*. Consulting. Palo Alto, CA: Psychologist Press.

Bass, Bernard M., & Paul Steidlmeier. (1998). "Ethics, Character, and Authentic Transformational Leadership." Center for Leadership Studies, School of Management, Binghamton University, Binghamton, NY. Retrieved April 14, 2008 from http://www.vanguard.edu/uploadedFiles/Faculty/RHeuser/ETHICS,%20MORAL%20CHARACTER%20AND%20AUTHENTIC%20TRANSFORMATIONAL%20LEADERSHIP.pdf.

Berkowitz, Peter. (1999). *Virtue and the Making of Modern Liberalism*. New Forum Books. Princeton, NJ: Princeton University Press.

Bettleheim, Bruno. (1991). *The Uses of Enchantment: The Meaning and Importance of Fairy Tales*. London: Thames & Hudson.

Bloomberg School of Public Health. (2003). *Population Reports: Meeting the Urban Challenge*. Baltimore: Bloomberg School of Public Health, Johns Hopkins

University, April 10, 2003. Retrieved May 30, 2004 from http://www.info forhealth.org/pr/press/041003.shtml.

Boje, David M. (2000). *Transform into Super Leaders: Transformational Leadership.* Retrieved April 17, 2008 from http://cbae.nmsu.edu/~dboje/teaching/338/ transformational_leadership.htm.

British Broadcast Corporation (BBC). (2008). "Bush offers $770m for food crisis," May 2, 2008. Retrieved May 3, 2008 from http://news.bbc.co.uk/2/hi/ameri cas/7378807.stm.

British Broadcast Corporation (BBC). (2007). "Otti 'executed by Uganda rebels,'" December 21, 2007. Retrieved January 2, 2008 from http://news.bbc.co.uk/2/ hi/africa/7156284.stm.

Brown, Peter G. (2000). *Ethics, Economics and International Relations: Transparent Sovereignty in the Commonwealth of Life.* Edinburgh: Edinburgh University Press.

Calabresi, Guido, & Philip Bobbitt. (1978). *Tragic Choices.* New York: W.W. Norton.

Chadwick, Ruth (Ed.). (1998). *Encyclopedia of Applied Ethics.* San Diego, CA: Academic Press. S.v. "Development Ethics," by Nigel Dower. 755–766.

Ciulla, Joanne B. (2004). *Ethics, the Heart of Leadership.* Westport, CT: Praeger.

Clifton, Eli. (2007). "Uganda: Time Is Critical in Peace Talks with LRA Rebels," Inter Press Service (IPS). *The Story Underneath.* (April 27, 2007). Retrieved May 5, 2007 from http://ipsnews.net/news.asp?idnews=37535.

Cobban, Helena. (2006). *Uganda's Challenge to the ICC.* Transitional Justice Forum. Retrieved February 21, 2008 from http://tj-forum.org/archives/002087.html.

Cooper, David E. (2004). *Ethics for Professionals in a Multicultural World.* Upper Saddle River, NJ: Pearson-Prentice Hall.

Craig, Edward (Ed.). (1999). *Routledge Encyclopedia of Philosophy*, ed. London: Rout-ledge. S.v. "Development Ethics," by David A. Crocker.

Crocker, D. A. (2000). "Truth Commissions, Transitional Justice, and Civil Society." In R. I. Rotberg & D. Thompson (Eds.), *In Truth v. Justice: The Morality of Truth Commissions.* Princeton, NJ: Princeton University Press.

Crocker, David A. (2001). *Globalization and Human Development Ethical Approaches.* College Park, MD: Institute for Philosophy and Public Policy, Photocopied.

Crocker, David A. (2006). "Ethics of Global Development: Agency, Capability, and Deliberative Democracy—An Introduction." In Verna V. Gehring (Ed.), *Philosophy and Public Policy Quarterly*, 26, 21–27.

Crocker, David A., & Toby Linden. (1998). *Ethics of Consumption: The Good Life, Justice and Global Stewardship.* Lanham, MD: Rowman & Littlefield.

Dallaire, R. (2004). *Shake Hands with the Devil: The Failure of Humanity in Rwanda.* London: Random House.

David, Joe. (1997, Winter). "In the 'Development Vanguard.'" *Moreland Views.* News-letter from Moreland Property Division of the Tongaat-Hulett Group, Dur-ban, South Africa.

Deneulin, Séverine, & Susan Hodgett. (2006). *On the Use of Narratives for Assessing Development Policy.* International Conference of the Human Development and Capability Association, Groningen, the Netherlands.

Donnelly, Jack. (1989). *Universal Human Rights in Theory & Practice.* Ithaca, NY: Cor-nell University Press.

Dower, Nigel. (1998). *World Ethics: The New Agenda.* Edinburgh Studies in World Ethics. Edinburgh: Edinburgh University Press.

Dunne, Tim, & Nicholas J. Wheeler (Eds.). (1999). *Human Rights in Global Politics.* Cambridge: Cambridge University Press.

Efron, Sonni. (2005). "U.S. Grows More Generous Toward World's Poor." *Los Angeles Times,* August 31, 2005. Retrieved October 6, 2008 from http://articles.latimes.com/2005/aug/31/world/fg-aid31.

Ekanya, Geoffrey. (2007). "The Parliament: Contributions to and Challenges for Greater Finance Transparency and Accountability to Citizens: A Case Study of Uganda." Paper presented to Organisation for Economic Co-operation and Development Workshop on Ownership in Practice. Paris, September 27–28 2007. Retrieved March 17, 2008 from http://www.oecd.org/dataoecd/3/15/39364678.pdf.

Flathman, Richard E. (1966). *The Public Interest: An Essay Concerning the Normative Discourse of Politics.* New York: John Wiley & Sons.

Food and Agriculture Organization of the United Nations. (1999). *The State of Food Insecurity in the World 1999.* Rome: FAO Publications. Retrieved December 7, 2007 from http://www.fao.org/news/1999/img/sofi99-e.pdf.

Forester, John. (1989). *Planning in the Face of Power.* Berkeley: University of California Press.

Friends Community School. (2002).Video: *Teasing Isn't Pleasing.* College Park, MD: Author.

Gert, Bernard. (1998). *Morality: Its Nature and Justification.* New York: Oxford University Press.

Glover, Jonathan. (1999). *Humanity: A Moral History of the Twentieth Century.* New Haven: Yale University Press.

Goodin, Robert. (2003). "Globalizing Justice." In David Held & Mathias Koenig-Archibugi (Eds.), *Taming Globalization: Frontiers of Governance* (pp. 68–92). Cambridge: Polity.

Goodin, Robert E. (1992). *Motivating Political Morality.* Cambridge, MA: Blackwell.

Goulet, Denis. (1995). *Development Ethics: A Guide to Theory and Practice.* New York: The Apex Press.

Government of Uganda. (2006a). *National Public Procurement Integrity Baseline Survey 2006: Final Report.* Public Procurement and Disposal of Assets Authority & Office of the Inspectorate of Government. Kampala, Uganda: Author.

Government of Uganda. (2006b). N.U.P.A.R.P., *National Peace, Recovery, and Development Plan for Northern Uganda.* Inter-Ministerial Committee. Kampala, Uganda: Author.

Government of Uganda. (2003). *National Strategy for Mainstreaming Ethics and Integrity in Local Governance in Uganda.* Department of Ethics and Integrity. Kampala, Uganda: Author.

Griffin, James. (1996). *Value Judgement: Improving Our Ethical Beliefs.* Oxford, England: Clarendon Press.

Gruwell, Erin, & Frank McCourt. (2007).*The Gigantic Book of Teacher's Wisdom,* New York: Skyhorse Publications.

Gutmann, Amy, & Dennis Thompson. (1996). *Democracy and Disagreement.* Cambridge, MA: The Belknap Press of Harvard University Press.

Ignatieff, Michael. (2001). *Human Rights as Politics and Idolatry* (Amy Gutmann, Ed.). Princeton, NJ: Princeton University Press.

International Crisis Group. (2006). *Policy Briefing: A Strategy for Ending Northern Uganda's Crisis.* Kampala, Uganda, and Brussels, Belgium: Author.

Kaggwa, Julius. (1997). *From Juliet to Julius: In Search of My True Gender Identity*. Kampala, Uganda: Fountain Press.

Kant, Immanuel. (1987). *Critique of Judgment* (Werner Schrutka Pluhar, Trans.). Indianapolis, IN: Hackett Publishing.

Kapstein, E. B. (2006). *Economic Justice in an Unfair World: Toward a Level Playing Field.* Princeton, NJ: Princeton University Press.

Kent, George. (2005). *Freedom from Want: The Human Right to Adequate Food.* Washington, DC: Georgetown University Press.

Kittay, Eva Feder, & Diana T. Meyers (Eds.). (1987). *Women and Moral Theory.* New York: Rowman & Littlefield.

Klitgaard, Robert. (1988). *Controlling Corruption.* Berkeley, CA: University of California Press.

Kohlberg, Lawrence. (1971). "From Is to Ought: How to Commit the Naturalistic Fallacy and Get Away with It in the Study of Moral Development." In Theodore Mischel (Ed.), *Cognitive Development and Epistemology* (pp. 151–235). New York: Academic Press.

Krumholz, Norman, & John Forester. (1990). *Making Equity Planning Work: Leadership in the Public Sector.* Philadelphia: Temple University Press.

Lanya Anthony, & Omar Azfar. (2005). *Tools for Assessing Corruption & Integrity in Institutions: A Handbook.* Washington, DC: United States Agency for International Development.

MacIntyre, Alasdair C. (1984). *After Virtue: A Study in Moral Theory.* Notre Dame, IN: University of Notre Dame Press.

Margalit, Avishai. (1996). *The Decent Society* (Naomi Goldblum, Trans.). Cambridge, MA: Harvard University Press.

Max-Neef, Manfred A. (1992). *From the Outside Looking In: Experiences in Barefoot Economics.* London: Zed Books.

McKinnon, Christine. (1999). *Character, Virtue Theories, and the Vices.* Peterborough, Ontario, Canada: Broadview Press.

Meyer, JeanMarie Fath. (2000). "Anticorruption Strategies in Public Procurement," *Combating Corruption in the Asian and Pacific Economies*. Manila: Asian Development Bank and Organisation for Economic Co-operation and Development (OECD).

Natsios, Andrew. (2004). "Effective Economic Growth for People," Remarks at the Washington Chapter of the Society for International Development. Washington, DC, December 1, 2004.

New Zealand Human Rights Commission. (2008). *To Be Who I Am*. (January 2008). Auckland: Author. Retrieved July 6, 2008 from http://www.hrc.co.nz/hrc_new/hrc/cms/files/documents/21-Jan-2008_19-03-12_Transgender_Final_2.pdf.

Noddings, Nel. (1984). *Caring: A Feminine Approach to Ethics and Moral Education.* Berkeley: University of California Press.

Nussbaum, Martha Craven. (1995). *Poetic Justice: The Literary Imagination and Public Life.* Boston: Beacon Press.

Nussbaum, Martha Craven. (2000). *Women and Human Development: The Capabilities Approach.* Cambridge: Cambridge University Press.

Nuwagaba Augustus. (2008). "Uganda: Is Museveni's Claim on Food Prices Logical?" *The Monitor*, May 23, 2008. Retrieved May 28, 2008 from http://allafrica.com/stories/200805220999.htm.

Obansanjo, Olusegun. (2000). "Blame Poor Leadership for Africa Decline." Africa News Service, March 6.

Oiko, Martin. (2002). "Report on UNDP Consultancy to Build Consensus on the Strategy for Mainstreaming Ethics and Integrity in all Sectors and All Institutions in Local Governance in Uganda." Retrieved July 12, 2008 from http://unpan1.un.org/intradoc/groups/public/documents/UN/UNPAN010808.pdf.

Orend, Brian. (2002). *Human Rights: Concepts and Context.* Peterborough, Ontario, Canada: Broadview Press.

Oxfam International. (2006). *Causing Hunger: An Overview of the Food Crisis in Africa,* Oxfam Briefing Paper 91, July 2006. Retrieved May 22, 2008 from http://www.oxfam.org/files/Causing%20Hunger.pdf.

Paul, Ellen Frankel, Jr., Fred D. Miller, & Jeffrey Paul (Eds.). (1999). *Human Flourishing.* Cambridge: Cambridge University Press.

Pellegrino, Edmund D. (1989). "Character, Virtue, and Self-Interest in the Ethics of the Professions." Jack W. Provonsha Lectures—February 15, 1989, Center for Christian Bioethics, Loma Linda University, Loma Linda, CA. Retrieved February 4, 2007 from http://www.llu.edu/llu/bioethics/prov89.htm.

Phuong, Pham, Patrick Vinck, Marieke Wierda, Eric Stover, & Adrian di Giovanni. (2005). *Forgotten Voices: A Population-Based Survey on Attitudes about Peace and Justice in Northern Uganda.* International Center for Transitional Justice, Human Rights Center. Berkeley, CA: University of Berkeley Press.

Pogge, Thomas W. (2004). "Moral Priorities for International Non-governmental Organizations." Paper presented at University of Maryland seminar, March 14, 2004.

Pogge, Thomas W. (2002). *World Poverty and Human Rights: Cosmopolitan Responsibilities and Reforms.* Cambridge: Polity.

Porter, Noah (Ed.). (1913). *Webster's Revised Unabridged Dictionary.* Springfield, MA: G&C Merriam Co. Retrieved October 3, 2007 from http://dict.die.net/moral%20agent/.

Radstaake, Marike, & Jan de Vries. (2004). *Reinvigorating Human Rights in the Barcelona Process: Using Human Rights Impact Assessment to Enhance Mainstreaming of Human Rights.* Paper presented at the Fifth Mediterranean Social and Political Research Meeting, Florence, Italy.

Rawls, John. (1971). *A Theory of Justice.* Cambridge, MA: The Belknap Press of Harvard University Press.

Refugee Law Project. (2004). *Behind the Violence: Causes, Consequences and the Search for Solutions to the War in Northern Uganda.* Refugee Law Project Working Paper No. 11, February 2004. Kampala, Uganda. Retrieved February 4, 2007 from http://www.refugeelawproject.org/resources/papers/workingpapers/RLP.WP 11.pdf.

Rorty, Richard. (1993). "Human Rights, Rationality, and Sentimentality," *Belgrade Circle Journal.* Portland, ME: University of Southern Maine. Retrieved May 28, 2008 from http://www.usm.maine.edu/~bcj/issues/three/rorty.html.

Rosan, Christina, Blair A. Ruble, & Joseph S. Tulchin (Eds.). (2000). *Urbanization, Population, Environment, and Security.* Report of the Comparative Urban Studies Project. Washington, DC: Woodrow Wilson International Center for Scholars.

Rost, Joseph C. (1991). *Leadership for the Twenty-first Century.* Westport, CT: Praeger.

Rutsch, Horst. (2001). "From 'Planning the City' to a 'City that Plans'—The Experience of Dar es Salaam," *United Nations Chronicle*, Online Edition, vol. 38, no. 1 (2001). New York: United Nations Department of Public Information. Retrieved April 18, 2004 from http://www.un.org/Pubs/chronicle/2001/issue1/0101p62.html.

Safty, Adel. (2003). "Moral Leadership: Beyond Management and Governance." Harvard International Review. Harvard University. *Leadership*, Volume 25(*3*), Fall 2003. Retrieved September 12, 2007 from http://www.harvardir.org/articles/1165/.

Scroggins, Deborah. (2004). *Emma's War.* New York: Random House.

Sen, Amartya. (1999). *Development as Freedom.* New York: Alfred A. Knopf.

Sherman, Nancy. (1997). *Making a Necessity of Virtue: Aristotle and Kant on Virtue.* Cambridge: Cambridge University Press.

Shue, Henry. (1996). *Basic Rights: Subsistence, Affluence, and U.S. Foreign Policy.* Princeton, NJ: Princeton University Press.

Shute, Stephen, & Susan Hurley (Eds.). (1993). *On Human Rights: The Oxford Amnesty Lectures.* New York: Basic Books.

Thiong'o, Ngugi wa. (1989). *Matigari* (Wangui wa Goro, Trans.). Oxford: Heinemann.

Thiong'o, Ngugi wa. (2006). *Wizard of the Crow.* New York: Random House.

United Nations. (2001). *The Habitat Agenda in the Urban Millennium.* Urban Millennium newsletter. New York: United Nations. Retrieved June 22, 2003 from http://ww2.unhabitat.org/Istanbul%2B5/booklet8.pdf.

United Nations Development Programme (UNDP). (2003). *Human Development Report 2003.* New York: Oxford University Press.

United Nations Development Programme (UNDP). (2000). *Human Development Report 2000.* New York: Oxford University Press.

United Nations Development Programme (UNDP). (1999). *Halving Extreme Poverty: An Action Strategy for the United Nations, Final Draft.* (November 10, 1999). New York: United Nations.

United Nations Development Programme (UNDP). (1998). *Human Development Report 1998.* New York: Oxford University Press.

United Nations Environment Programme. (1992). *Rio Declaration on Environment and Development.* New York: United Nations. Retrieved August 2, 2007 from http://www.unep.org/Documents.Multilingual/Default.asp?DocumentID=78&ArticleID=1163.

United Nations Human Settlements Programme (HABITAT). (2002). The Global Campaign on Urban Governance Concept Paper, 2nd edition. (March 1, 2002). New York: United Nations. Retrieved September 20, 2005 from http://www.unhabitat.org/content.asp?cid=2099&catid=419&typeid=3&subMenuld=0&ContentsByTheme=254.

United Republic of Tanzania. (2006). *Draft National Framework for Urban Development and Environmental Management (UDEM) in Tanzania.* Dar es Salaam, Tanzania: Prime Minister's Office. Retrieved June 6, 2008 from http://www.pmoralg.go.tz/documents_storage/2006-6-15-7-55_volume_ii_udem_framework_design_13_june_2006%5B2%5D.pdf.

United States Agency for International Development (USAID), Office of Environment and Urban Programs. (2001). *Making Cities Work Urban Strategy.* Washington, DC: Author. Retrieved April 3, 2005 from http://www.makingcitieswork.org.

United States Department of Agriculture. (1999). *U.S. Action Plan on Food Security.* Washington, DC: Author. Retrieved on December 3, 2007 from http://www. fas.usda.gov/icd/summit/pressdoc.html.

Washington Post. (2008). "Food Crisis: Food prices are causing hunger around the world." p. A-16, March 14, 2008.

Watson, Alison M. S. (2008). "Can There Be a 'Kindered' Peace?" *Ethics & International Affairs*, Vol 22 Issue 1. Washington, DC: Carnegie Council on Ethics and International Affairs (pp 35–42).

Wilson, Richard A. (Ed.). (1987). Human Rights, Culture and Context: Anthropological Perspectives. London: Pluto.

World Bank. (2004). *World Development Report 2004.* New York: Oxford University Press.

World Health Organization (WHO). (2004). *The World Health Report 2004, Changing History.* Geneva: WHO Publications Retrieved January 19, 2006 from http://www.who.int/whr/2004/en/report04_en.pdf.

Index

About the Author

CHLOE SCHWENKE is a Senior Associate at Creative Associates International in Washington, D.C., and adjunct professor of applied ethics at the School of Advanced International Studies of the Johns Hopkins University, the Public Policy Institute at Georgetown University, and at the School of Public Policy at the University of Maryland at College Park. She has advised the World Bank, Inter-American Development Bank, United Nations Development Program, U.S. Agency for International Development, and leading NGOs on applied ethics, anticorruption, governance and civil society, leadership training, and urban planning. She was Fulbright professor of ethics and public management at Makerere University in Kampala, Uganda. She spent 30 years as a development project manager and ethics advisor in developing countries in Asia, the Middle East, Latin America, and Africa. Until 2008 she worked and published as Stephen Schwenke. She is coauthor with David A. Crocker of *The Relevance of Development Ethics for USAID* (2005).